The general series of the
Miegunyah Volumes
was made possible by the
Miegunyah Fund
established by bequests
under the wills of
Sir Russell and Lady Grimwade.

'Miegunyah' was the home of
Mab and Russell Grimwade
from 1911 to 1955.

FIRST AUSTRALIANS

FIRST AUSTRALIANS

EDITED BY RACHEL PERKINS AND MARCIA LANGTON

with Wayne Atkinson, James Boyce, RG Kimber,
Steve Kinnane, Noel Loos and Bruce Pascoe

THE
MIEGUNYAH
PRESS

THE MIEGUNYAH PRESS
An imprint of Melbourne University Publishing Limited
187 Grattan Street, Carlton, Victoria 3053, Australia
mup-info@unimelb.edu.au
www.mup.com.au

First published 2008
This edition published 2010
Text © individual writers, 2008
Design and typography © Melbourne University Publishing Ltd, 2010

Printed in Australia by Griffin Press, South Australia

A Cataloguing-in-Publication entry is available from the National Library of Australia

CONTENTS

PROLOGUE

Marcia Langton

Historians tell stories about the past and, among other things, about people, ideas, institutions and, importantly, nations. Most of us were first introduced to the idea of history at school. In most Australian schools that my generation attended, Aborigines were represented almost universally as animal-like, cunning and treacherous—as enemies of the nation—in what passed for history lessons, learnt by rote as a set of dates, in the 1950s and 1960s. Teachers would mention a few exceptional Aboriginal people, such as Jackey Jackey, the famous 'native servant' and guide who remained loyal to the explorer Edmund Kennedy. In 1848 Edmund Kennedy's expedition through Cape York Peninsula met with fatal results: Kennedy and most of his team were killed by Aboriginal men in the far north of the peninsula, Jackey Jackey being one of two survivors. Jackey Jackey's account of the incident was transcribed and became a famous pamphlet, and the man himself a strange hero.

As a child growing up in Queensland, I found these stories bizarre. Occasionally, there was something of interest, but the overwhelming tone was one of turgid prose about utterly boring subjects such as the discovery of rivers, flocks of sheep, wheat crops, stump-jump ploughs, railway gauges, Governor This and Governor That, and *Australia Felix*. The occasional Aboriginal characters represented bore no resemblance to the people I knew and had grown up with. Gradually, there was a dawning realisation that I was seen by my teacher and classmates as one of those Aborigines. History was for me a terrible burden because it was in this class that I learnt that people like me were hated, and that the only stories told about us provided a steady stock of evidence about our supposedly shockingly violent tendencies, savagery and, most importantly, our innate tendency to steal and pilfer.

In the past half century, as a new generation of historians has interpreted the records, a dazzling view of Australian life has emerged. Instead of the drudges who peopled the pages of the old books, convicts, women, children, African-American slaves, adventurous European aristocrats, artists, con-men, bushrangers and thousands of Indigenous people have assumed more detailed, nuanced and intriguing personas, and their endeavours have become better understood. The ridiculous and audacious, as well as the common or garden, activities of ordinary and extraordinary people have replaced the monotonous tales of the March of Civilisation.

Only a handful of historians, mostly amateurs, persist in vilifying all the original inhabitants of this continent and their descendants. Despite their less than rigorous skills in the discipline, their few works have an enormous influence, principally because they propose racially slanderous views that most educated people would reject, but that remain attractive to those who prefer to imagine the Australia of the old school books, the Progress of the White Man: courageous white explorers in the colonies, staking out the wilderness for God-fearing farmers amid the demise of the backward natives according to the laws of natural selection. That such views remain enormously popular and attractive is one of the reasons for this book. We have a high regard for the importance of the history of Australia to all of the people who call this place home in the twenty-first century.

Without history, how would we believe in the idea of Australia? The story of the people who have lived here is not a straightforward one, however. Far too many Australian history books have demeaned the Indigenous people and society that the British encountered, so the purpose of the *First Australians* project has been to understand the part played by Indigenous people in the events that caught our imagination. In a modern Australia, the past cannot be exploited simply for triumphalist purposes, to attribute cause and effect to more palatable theories, to elevate the colonial 'pioneers' over the first peoples—the squatters and settlers over the traditional owners of land—without the risk of concocting an incredible and insubstantial mythology. Fortunately, there are both primary and secondary documents that give due weight to the Indigenous part in the story. These have enabled us to depict in great detail some of the Indigenous people who were so often ignored in the making of Australian history.

History is a world of alternatives. Readers of the archives will each follow their own trail through the pages of journals, diaries, past accounts and images, perhaps lured by a special character or intrigued by a particular event.

First Australians begins appropriately with the First Fleet, whose commander, Lieutenant Arthur Phillip, encountered the peoples of the Sydney region. The harbour was named Port Jackson by Lieutenant James Cook, although he did not sail through the heads but went on north after his few days at Botany Bay. Phillip's journal, and those of his officers, surgeon, scientists, artists and visitors, tell a complex story of their relationships with the clans who called the harbour's shores their home. Friendships developed between Phillip's contingent and the local people and, although they were caught up in the imperial mission of conquest, their journals reveal their sense of wonder, practical courage and wit in extraordinary circumstances. We storytellers have been charmed by their sentiments, and sometimes amused and intrigued by their wry turns of phrase.

Bennelong, particularly, captures the imagination, and while our understanding of his life is filtered through the views of very eighteenth-century English men as well as our own, nevertheless his light shines through the texts and images. The tales of sex, violence, hunger and desperation that surround Bennelong and his people are horrifying. Phillip and his companions became involved in this world and left us textual glimpses of a society that collapsed soon after these events transpired. Our story is scored with the troubling implications of hindsight: Bennelong's fate and that of his people were tragic, but for a few years after 1788 the events at Port Jackson and surrounds were extraordinary. We have tried to hold on to the substance of the affairs represented by the historical records; to avoid unnecessarily transposing our present sensitivities into the narrative. Yet it has been impossible to ignore the strangeness of the ambitions, skills, intellect and emotions of the people who wrote the texts. The story is as tangled as any epic might be. Values, morality, the role of the gods, the hand of fate: we thought it best to let them play their role.

First Australians is told through written records and illustrations of the colonial and post-Federation periods of Australian history. We might want to know about what happened before these events. But how could such a story be told? There are no photographs or written records to explain what happened. The Aboriginal and Torres Strait Islander understanding of the past before colonisation—which occurred at different times across the continent and its islands—is expressed in song, performance and art, much of it religious and concerned with the sacred stories of the creative dramas of the ancestral beings. Archaeologists and prehistorians have discovered the hard evidence of human occupation on this continent from at least 60 000 years before the present. But neither oral history nor archaeological evidence reveals the details that the story after 1788 contains. We can dig up neither the names of the people and their everyday routines, nor their conversations and actions in the course of events. The archaeological method usually involves a landscape survey and, on the basis of some knowledge of the prehistory and geology of the area, locations are identified where pits and trenches are excavated. Middens (or mounds of shell, animal remains and charcoal layered among the strata of ancient sand dunes) are rich with evidence, as are the floors of caves and rock shelters. The floors, shores and banks of ancient seas, lakes and waterways have also given up their secrets.

'Aborigines have lived in Tasmania for more than 35 000 years—more than three times as long as the human occupation of the British Isles.' So writes James Boyce in chapter 2 on events in the colony of Van Diemen's Land, or Tasmania, as we know it now. They adapted to extraordinary climate change and were 'the southernmost human beings in the world during the last Ice Age'. The furthest extension of human life in the southern hemisphere, not to mention the earliest human journeys across open seas in small craft across the Sunda-Sahul region, are among the unique accomplishments of the first Australians.

Prehistory has recorded mere fragments of these millennia of human occupation, but nevertheless accumulated enough evidence to explain the contours of the extraordinary story of human society before British settlement. It is the interpretation of layers of sediment, charcoal, clay, sand and loam, studded with perhaps some human skeletal material, animal bones, stone tools and the remains of oysters and other shellfish and crustaceans. How prehistorians interpret such strata and its contents is largely scientific speculation based on humdrum quantification and measurement of materials of these types as they are excavated according to precise grid lines, both horizontal and vertical. The prizes they seek are few indeed; some bones or charcoal might reveal their antiquity through such processes as carbon dating or thermoluminescence.

Boyce tells us that Tasmanians used black silica, or 'Darwin glass', from a deposit near Macquarie Harbour, and red ochre consistently from about 20 000 years ago. While millions of stone tools have been collected and classified, the periodic changes in their style and manufacture are measured in thousands of years. A picture of human activities, and type and density of occupation in particular places and times, is thus construed from dust, rock and debris. We therefore know a great deal, as Boyce explains, about the sweeping changes during the long-ago past of the Palawa people of Trowunna (Tasmania).

Rock painting and engraving, carved objects such as bone fish hooks, carved trees and ancient pathways straddling the continent are more observable evidence of human life here before 1788. They illuminate the lives of the ancient Australians more readily than layers of charcoal and sand, but any attempt to draw out the relationships, emotions and intellectual life of those involved is also speculation, however insightful, well informed and knowledgeable.

The human drama of the colonial period, on the other hand, is thickly described, perhaps not accurately or fairly, but certainly in enough detail to conjure up the past. The records are rich with the details and illustrations of encounters between the British and the Indigenous people, the weather, the flora and fauna, the languages of both societies, and the many subtleties and

coarseness of phrase through which the chroniclers expressed
their sentiments, motivations and responses. We have not entirely
ignored the archaeological story, however. The evidence of the
ancient world intervenes in our story in many ways. The British
explorers and settlers moved out across the continent from
Port Jackson led by Indigenous guides along ancient pathways.
Disputes between the British and Indigenous people were often
caused by competition for particularly important places. The destruction and defacement of rock art by white settlers tells us at
least about the rage and vengefulness that they felt towards the
first people (which some still feel) and their frustrations at the
difficulty of winning supremacy over them and their homelands.
Some rock-art galleries depict white men on horses, wearing hats
and sometimes carrying guns, and their sailing ships, intimating
the watchfulness of Indigenous people and their need not just
to observe but also to record the remarkable changes they were
witnessing in their world. As the settlers became more familiar,
some Indigenous people took up crayons and paint brushes to
document the tumultuous life around them.

An Australian history explained with theories and using
such terms as 'imperialism' or 'colonisation' is a poor substitute
for the real-life action that the people in our history offer us.
However, once we begin to see the larger trend of Australian life
over some 200 years after 1788, the period dealt with in *First
Australians*, it is difficult to explain what happened to so many
Aboriginal societies and their people without resorting to the
ideas that historians and philosophers have used to explain the
fate of the people in the New World following Columbus' discovery of 'America' more than 500 years ago. The term 'imperialism' refers to the rule by empires of other parts of the world,

where peoples and territories were, perhaps at first, spheres of influence, but later annexed as colonies. The European empires eventually subjugated most of the world's population in Africa, Asia, the Americas and, lastly, Oceania. The lives of Indigenous Australians are part of this wider global experience.

The eastern part of Australia became a colony of England and a part of the British Empire in 1770, when Lieutenant James Cook declared it a British possession at Possession Island in Torres Strait. It was Eddie Koiki Mabo from Mer in Torres Strait who, almost 200 years later, challenged the arrogance of this imperialist declaration and the legal fiction on which it was based, and overturned it in the *Mabo* case before the High Court of Australia. The legal fiction called the doctrine of *terra nullius*, or Blackstone's theory of ceded colonies, held sway for those two centuries. After 26 January 1788 the colony of New South Wales was established, and thereafter other parts of Australia were declared colonies, eventually six in all. Aboriginal societies and their territories were overrun by settlers, and in many parts of the continent and its islands, if they survived at all, they did so in much-reduced and horrible circumstances.

In the following seven chapters authors bring their own experiences to the archive, and each has a special connection to the people who lived the history told. Some are descended from the people in these histories while others have made their homes in the places about which they write. They are writers of both Indigenous and immigrant heritage and have a range of experiences as historians, teachers, authors, geographers, revivers of language, activists and environmental researchers. Their varied experiences are reflected in the diversity of these chapters, but they share the ancient gift of storytelling and a dedication to building a more sophisticated and inclusive version of the Australian story.

In Van Diemen's Land, while imperial relations were complicated by economic and political affairs in many parts of the world, much of the story of the early colonial encounters is a litany of horrors. In chapter 2 Boyce tackles the question that struck us during the research for the television series: what happened to the people? In 1803 a British fleet arrived in Van Diemen's Land with 300 convicts, and challenged the Aboriginal population of 6000 to give way to their vicious penal settlement. Until the British came to these islands in the Great Southern Ocean, nine tribes lived on this, the largest of them, and each of these tribes consisted of bands, their members living in neighbouring areas and speaking the same language. They were hunting and fishing people and fire-stick farmers who shaped the ecosystems of the island to supply their needs, opening pathways for their island-wide social life of kinship networks.

Before the convict ships arrived, some first Tasmanians had become acquainted with the sealers who plied their trade in the 'roaring forties', the winds blowing their ships from the Cape of Good Hope at the southern tip of Africa across the Great Southern Ocean to this group of islands. At Furneaux Island, the sealers used Aboriginal women in their gangs because of their hunting skills, and although the evidence is scant, it seems that they had been captured and subjected to great brutality. Between 1800 and 1806 more than 100 000 seal skins were obtained,[1] but sealing continued for another three decades. After the sealing ships had harvested their lot, the individual sealers were able to stay on and exploit the situation provided to them. With the aid of Aboriginal women, a new economy developed. The sealers were now able to settle on the islands and develop their own economic independence away from the authorities on the mainland of Tasmania.

On the largest island, the colonists were at war with the tribes. The 'Black War', conducted from 1824 to 1831, was waged with the explicit intention of exterminating the Aboriginal population. When the fighting stopped in the New Year of 1832, only twenty-six Aboriginal people were left from the Lairmairrener (Big River) people and Paredarerme (Oyster Bay) people. A few remained in Bass Strait and a few other areas. So what happened to the others? Some writers concerned with this aspect of Australia's past have claimed on the basis of flimsy propositions that they died from disease, but Boyce contends that there is no evidence for that contention. His account is a refreshingly humanist view of these terrible events and the fate of the first Tasmanians. Seventy years after the arrival of the British, bloody war came to an end in 1873. On the windswept islands of Bass Strait, where sealers and whalers had preyed on the Tasmanians, capturing women and killing men, a new generation of Tasmanian people, a new Aboriginal society, was born.

Bruce Pascoe relates the story of the heartbreaking results of the invasion of the Kulin nations' homelands in Victoria and the events that followed the 'signing of John Batman's fraudulent treaty'. The changes to the survivors' ways of life were radical. Pascoe has carefully examined the official records and compared them with the letters of the Kulin leaders, and the letters and records of the settlers who fought, violently and surreptitiously, to steal the lands of these once rich and productive societies. The Kulin were starved out of their territories and, as Pascoe writes, 'By war's end the Kulin nations were devastated and resorted to dwelling on the fringes of pastoral stations where they could acquire work and food'. Eventually, some retreated to the mission stations, many of which failed. These Aboriginal people adjusted quickly to their much-reduced circumstances and became successful farmers, so much so that their neighbouring settler landowners, coveting their productive lands, ground down the protectorate system and parliament to prevail.

William Barak, who was present at the signing of the Batman treaty, was a witness to 'the defeat of his people in war and the broken promises of the government'. Accompanied by other Kulin, Barak tirelessly walked to Melbourne several times to negotiate with the government. Giving evidence at an inquiry in 1882, he described the nefarious activities of the Aboriginal Protection Board, which made their lives miserable, and appealed for title to their land and control of their income from farming. After losing his son in tragic circumstances, Barak lived out the end of his days writing and painting to record the life of the Kulin as he remembered it before the invasion. In 1886 the Board amended the Aborigines Act, which removed 'half castes' from the reserves and intended to 'let the old "full bloods" die out'. The resulting destruction of Aboriginal families has resonated through the generations.

Richard Kimber sees the colours and the properties of the ever-changing light refracted on the landscapes of Central Australia, the 'chocolate and purple colours of the gibbers and the ancient sun-bleached yellow-flanked residual hills'. He draws to our attention the coincidental paths from the southern coast to the desert of the spirit ancestors and the railway line, the first ever-present, inducing the mind to focus on the landscape behind the landscape, and the second sturdy and industrial, a sign of the earliest of the postcolonial changes to reshape the world that became the Northern Territory. 'The answer to why all of their travels, formalised routes and variations were so similar, from the time of the Urumbulla youths onwards, is the presence of precious, and rarely permanent, waters,' Kimber writes.

The missionaries, police and cattlemen were at odds, and always caught in the crossfire were the Aborigines, as the notorious Mounted Constable William Willshire demonstrated. Although the evidence of his horrific deeds was strong, he was found not guilty at trial. Kimber has delved into the records and laid out the evidence starkly and compellingly. Aboriginal people found an accommodation in the cattle industry and, although the conditions were often brutal and difficult, they were involved in the evolution of a new polity and society. The conflicts were bloody and the battlegrounds well marked by bones. The central and northern frontiers were as much of Aboriginal making as they were the result of the thrust northwards of speculators, cattlemen and other settlers from the southern states. The drought and the depression in the 1890s hindered the expansion of the cattle industry for a while, but the goldrush at Arltunga brought many more people to the Centre.

Along with them came the scientists, among them Professor Baldwin Spencer, biologist and photographer, whose legacy is 'a remarkable, unmatched record of the era', as Kimber puts it. Kimber has struck a brilliant lode of Central Australian history to share with us in chapter 4; it was Spencer's description of Ayers Rock, now called Uluru, that grabbed the public imagination more than any previously: 'a huge dome-shaped monolith, brilliant venetian red in colour'. Spencer's friendship and collaboration with Frank Gillen, who operated the telegraph station at Alice Springs, was fortuitous; they produced detailed accounts and records of the most significant Aboriginal ceremonies of the region, including the famous *Native Tribes of Central Australia*, published in 1899. Our understanding of the Arrernte people and their neighbours owes much to Spencer and Gillen. They were among the first in the world to use both film and sound recordings, as well as photographs, which, along with their written accounts, are vivid eyewitness accounts of the 'most extensive and elaborate ceremonial cycles ever recorded in Australia'.

In 1895 missionary Carl Strehlow arrived at the then-abandoned Hermannsburg and set about re-establishing it. From these twin themes of violent conquest and missionary endeavours to save souls, the problem of the injustice done to Aboriginal people was defined by a dark history glimpsed through the prism of a gradually awakening consciousness of its burden, the burden that Henry Reynolds has rightly framed as the 'whispering in our hearts'. As policeman and self-proclaimed 'nigger-hunter' Tom Coward put it, 'We have gained his possessions by might, and without some degree of reparation we cannot conscientiously establish our right.'

In Western Australia, as Steve Kinnane explains in chapter 5, the legend of Jandamarra is a powerful link with the not-so-distant frontier. In the latter half of the nineteenth century, expeditions from the Swan River settlement had reached the northern area of the colony, the Kimberley. By 1881 news of their success gave impetus to speculators, and by 1884 their titles and claims covered the entire region.[2] The resistance here too was fought fiercely by men like Jandamarra, and the period from 1889 to 1905, when the colonial government and the settlers sought 'pacification' and absolute control, is still referred to as the 'Killing Times'. By the early 1890s a quarter of the whole Western Australian police force was based in the Kimberley, where only 1 per cent of the European settlement population lived.[3]

Jandamarra, or Pigeon as the white men called him, served as police tracker, a position that offered both 'opportunity and subterfuge', as Kinnane writes: 'no greater dilemma could have faced Jandamarra than to have to arrest his own elders in their own country'. Like Windradyne and Mosquito, Jandamarra rebelled, with the consequence of a wave of bloody violent revenge and retribution. Jandamarra's exploits raise the question so often asked by historians about the Aboriginal leaders who fought back: Were they freedom fighters or murderous outlaws? In Kinnane's version, the complications of Jandamarra's story are revealed: 'It is also the story of relationships struck amid the fray of colonisation that are unable to straddle the divide'.

From 1915 to 1940 the lives of thousands of Aboriginal people of Western Australia were managed in minute detail by AO Neville, Chief Protector of Aborigines, who had ultimate power under the *Aborigines Act 1905* (WA). Kinnane's conclusion is that he 'oversaw the imposition of some of the most racist and damaging legislation ever inflicted on a civilian population'. Kinnane makes it clear that Neville's orchestrated assault on the Aboriginal population was as much a scientific experiment as part of the British ideology of 'improving' the conditions of the 'coloureds' from the native camps—and it was Neville's administration that laid the foundations for the present-day problems of towns such as Fitzroy Crossing in the Kimberley region, where the disastrous outcomes of poverty and alienation are so evident: short life expectancy, high disease burdens, over-crowding in substandard houses, alcohol abuse, and high rates of unemployment, imprisonment and suicide.

Further south in the Central Murray and Goulburn Valley regions, the Yorta Yorta people are the traditional owners of the large and ancient Aboriginal estate—called Dhungulla in their language—of rivers, lakes, lagoons and wetlands on both sides of the Victorian – New South Wales border. As historian Wayne Atkinson explains in chapter 6, it was the education system established at Maloga Mission that enabled men like William Cooper to inspire the Yorta Yorta in their long campaign for justice. William Cooper, son of Granny Kitty, was born in 1862 and lived at old Maloga Mission where he was educated; his aptitude for learning was remarked on by Daniel Matthews, a Christian ship-chandler who befriended the Yorta Yorta. Matthews, keenly aware of how he and other settlers had benefited from the theft of Aboriginal land, had funded Maloga as a private mission and gathered the men together here to talk about reforms to the government's policies. 'On the Murray and Goulburn Rivers there are hundreds of these poor wretches worse than uncared for ... Large tracts of land should be set apart for them,'[4] Matthews wrote in a letter. The administration of Aboriginal affairs in Victoria was as cruel as in the other jurisdictions, but the Yorta Yorta were able for a while to cross the river and enter New South Wales whenever the authorities came to take their children. In the end, the miserable approach of both governments won out, and Victorian Aboriginal people were left virtually landless.

Maloga Mission was closed in 1888, but it had a decisive influence on generations of Aboriginal people. Leaders of the Aboriginal campaigns of the twentieth and twenty-first centuries are the descendants of their pupils. The 1881 petition of the Maloga residents to the Victorian Government exerted an influence more than a century later when it was used in evidence in the Yorta Yorta native title case.

Noel Loos and I, writing in chapter 7, describe the inequity and cruelty of the administration of Aboriginal affairs in

Queensland and the remarkable people who campaigned against its system of racial exclusion. They established the Federal Council for the Advancement of Aborigines and Torres Strait Islanders (FCAATSI). By 1967 they had convinced Australians to vote 'Yes' in a referendum to remove two racist clauses from the Australian Constitution. This resulted in the inclusion of Aboriginal and Islander peoples in the census and the right of the Federal Government to legislate for Aborigines and Torres Strait Islander peoples.[5]

The life story of the late Edward Koiki Mabo is inspirational. He was the man who, with his fellow Meriam litigants, James Rice and Dave Passi, destroyed *terra nullius*, the legal fiction on which Australia was colonised. Born in 1936 on Mer, or Murray Island, one of the smallest and most remote islands in Torres Strait, he withstood racism in North Queensland throughout his life by developing his keen intellect, reading, writing and thinking deeply about the injustice of the Crown's appropriation of his land. In the 1980s, with the support of Noel Loos, Henry Reynolds and a brilliant team of legal counsel, he initiated the most remarkable legal challenge in Australian history. He initiated the case, now known as the *Mabo* case, in which High Court judges, by a slim majority, recognised the native title of his people on Murray Island. 'Since time immemorial' is the apt phrase the judges used to describe their ownership. Mabo died of cancer on 21 January 1992, four months before the High Court decision swept away the concept of *terra nullius*.

The *Mabo* arguments successfully challenged these antediluvian views. It was such ideas and the persistence of formal racial separation, especially in Queensland long after other states and even the Northern Territory had introduced substantial reforms, that led to the upsurge of Aboriginal and Torres Strait Islander aspirations for freedom and land rights.

There were more victories to come, and many defeats as well. Aboriginal and Torres Strait Islanders have continued a proud tradition of asserting their rights and defining the nation by its capacity to meet the standards of decency and fairness. The story goes on, and there is no neat place to end our version of it. The reverberations of the nation's past on its present are clear in the case of Captain James Cook's declaration of possession, but far less so in the case of Governor Arthur Phillip with his attempts to follow his king's orders and befriend the natives. If there had been a commitment on the part of either of these men to another aspect of such orders—to obtain the consent of the natives—we might have a very different outcome and a very different story to tell. With Phillip's inability to sustain his initial enthusiasm for a new colony without slavery and oppression, following the murder of his gamekeeper, and his harsh retribution, the die was cast. A series of conflicts were ignited with each expansion of the colonies westwards and northwards, and there were only a few gentle people who refused to participate in pushing the first Australians to the brink of extinction. Throughout these two centuries, on the Aboriginal side, there were heroes and heroines who would not submit easily. We hope we have done justice to them, on both sides of the frontier.

This book is not intended to be a complete history of the Indigenous experience in Australia. Nor does it claim to be representative of regions, states or peoples. Other books address Indigenous history on national and state bases. Our approach has been to illuminate the story of just a few Indigenous individuals, and the times in which they lived, who, because of their extraordinary and transformative lives, have carved themselves into our historical record. There are thousands more such people, some well known, others remembered only by their descendants and many more forgotten and ignored. We have been unable to present all the stories of resilience, treachery, courage and tragedy that populate our nation's history. But by illuminating a handful of lives, we hope to suggest the richness of the experiences of these people and those they struggled against, loved, defended, were betrayed by and made friends with. We hope that those of you who have picked up this book will be inspired and moved by their lives, and through the experience gain a deeper understanding of the place we now call Australia.

Ngura barbagai
COUNTRY LOST

1

'THEY MADE A SOLITUDE AND CALLED IT PEACE'
Tacitus, Roman historian

Marcia Langton

If it is possible to imagine the scene on a summer's night around the harbour known as Warrang, when the tall sails of the British ship under the command of Captain Arthur Phillip sailed into the harbour that Captain James Cook had sailed past eighteen years earlier, naming it Port Jackson, then we might wonder what the Wangal man Bennelong was doing. Cook had seen people fishing along the coastline and imagined the country to be largely unpopulated. Yet we know from the records of the First Fleet that fires were burning along the coastline, and people were watching the ships tack into the harbour. With their fires, and perhaps messengers flitting between the camps, the response must have been an overwhelming feeling of suspense as they watched this strange apparition on the water. It was larger than anything they had seen, and voices would have been heard coming from it, drifting across the water. Then another and yet another appeared. Perhaps one of the men on shore, awed into silence, might have pushed a finger and thumb of one hand into the wet sand, then pushed one finger in again. That's how many there were, but what were they? One spoke of a story he had heard as a child of people who looked like ghosts coming in giant canoes with wings. It might be them. The ships dropped anchor close to Bennelong's camp.

Of all the characters in the historical records of the colony, this man stands out: Bennelong. He was tall, strong and well built, intelligent and charismatic. Born into the Wangal clan, he lived in his estate, from where he exercised power and influence across a large area. He was an admitted womaniser and a fearless fighter, and he entertained his captors with tales of brutal adventures. What was he doing on that fateful night? If we could imagine how his world fundamentally altered in a few years, and his life and those of his fellow survivors changed beyond all their expectations, the events might have unfolded like this.

The glowing coals of his fire, like fires anywhere, might have emitted a soft snapping sound. Then Bennelong, seated on the sand, might have reached over to the fire and stirred the coals with his long wooden baton. One of his wives, the young and striking Barangaroo, may have been tending her own hearth of hot coals with its small tongues of fire, while Bennelong's young sister, Warreweer, might have hovered in the darkness beyond the glow of the fire. Were other members of the family preparing to sleep, whispering and fidgeting in their bark shelters built on the sand near the rocks? Could they hear flying foxes rustle in the giant fig trees extruding from the stone walls?

29th January 1788. They pointed with their sticks to the boat landing place, and met us in the most cheerful manner, shouting and dancing ... these people mixed with ours and all hands danced together.

William Bradley

This headland pushing its sandstone fingers and beaches out into the waters of the harbour was one of their favourite places: Tubowgulle. Perhaps they heard men paddling quickly in canoes across the waters. Did Bennelong stand up on this night and grab his bundle of spears from the sand? Did he hear a voice rupture the quiet and tell of the shocking news? The announcement would have caused alarm. The white strangers who travel across the seas had come back. They had not been seen since Bennelong was a child. 'Light fires! Strange spirits are coming on the water!' Perhaps, then, he wiped some of the white ochre off the grinding stone with his wet hands and, with a sense of determination and foreboding, smeared a streak across his forehead, then with two fingers, another across his nasal bridge, to appear as he does in the most famous of the paintings of him.

1788: '... TO TAKE POSSESSION OF HIS NEW TERRITORY'

Eight days earlier, Captain Arthur Phillip's fleet, accompanied by dolphins, approached the bay that Cook had first named Stingray Bay, then changed it to Botany Bay out of deference to his wealthy and powerful patron Joseph Banks.

On 18 January 1788, the world of the First Australians changed forever. With the arrival of the First Fleet at Botany Bay, the societies that had inherited the coastal estates where the sailors landed were the first to meet the British before an endless influx of people, arriving in yet more ships, took control of their homelands. The fleet's journey to this place had been planned meticulously in London. Without losing one of the eleven ships under his command, Captain Arthur Phillip brought more than 1300 people—men, women and children, more than half of them convicts—to a strange new land on the other side of the world.

The British searched for a place to settle: the *eora*[1] of the Gweagal, Gadigal, Gameygal, Wangal and Wallumedegal and other clans, and inland the 'woodland' Darug, Gandangarra, Dharawal and Darkingyung language groups, and many others, each owned a territory, bounded by a stream, mountain ridge or headland. One by one, their lands were taken over. Within a few years, the colonists would be pitted against them in a bloody struggle.

At first, friendships developed among Phillip's contingent and the local people, and although the new arrivals were caught up in the imperial mission of conquest, their naval journals and letters reveal their sense of wonderment in these extraordinary circumstances and their encounters with the people of this new land, among them leaders, diplomats, warriors and beautiful women, such as Bennelong, Patyagarang, Pemulwuy and Windradyne.

As the ships arrived, groups of Gweagal men ran down to the white sand beaches, shaking their spears. The young marine Watkin Tench found 'the natives tolerably numerous' and 'had reason to conclude the country more populous than Mr Cook thought it'.[2] Captain Phillip went ashore 'in order to take possession of his new territory, and bring about an intercourse between its old and new masters'. Phillip and his party were followed closely by men in their canoes: 'The boat in which his Excellency was, rowed up the harbour, close to the land, for some distance; the Indians keeping pace with her on the beach.'[3]

The first task of the crew was to obtain fresh water, so they went ashore to negotiate with a group of natives, offering trinkets and friendship. 'The Indians, though timorous, shewed no signs of resentment at the Governor's going on shore; an interview commenced, in which the conduct of both parties pleased each other,' Tench recorded, and noted that the Gweagal 'seemed highly entertained with their new acquaintance, from whom they condescended to accept of a looking glass, some beads, and other toys'.[4]

The conclusion was that the reports from Cook's voyage had grossly misrepresented the natural features of Botany Bay, for there was insufficient water in this 'poor country' for a settlement. Their searches for an appropriate place ended in Port Jackson, 'one of the most spacious and safe harbours in the known world'.[5]

> On my showing them that I [lacked] a front tooth it occasioned a
> general clamor and I thought gave me some little merit in their opinion.
> *Arthur Phillip*

On the night of 25 January 1788, as Phillip sailed in through the heads of Port Jackson, he would have seen the contours of the headlands outlined against the black sky by the glow from the horizon that remains so long after sunset in the antipodean summer. The smoke of hundreds of fires lining the cliffs and shores that drifted across the water to them, and the movements caught in the firelight as their ship sailed on the dark waters, must have heightened the tension they felt. Watkin Tench wrote with his usual elegance of this new turn of events: 'The evening was bright, and the prospect before us such as might justify sanguine expectation. Having passed between the capes which form its entrance, we found ourselves in a port superior, in extent and excellency, to all we had seen before. Indians were frequently seen, till we arrived at a small snug cove on the southern side, on whose banks the plan of our operations was destined to commence.'[6]

If the first night of the arrival of the British was alarming, on the next day the Gadigal and Wangal people would have been shocked by 'the rude sound of the labourer's axe' as convicts and troops chopped down trees and pitched tents on the shores of a large cove near Bennelong's estate. David Collins' description of the events of this day refers to the 'downfall of its ancient inhabitants' and the 'busy hum of its new possessors'.[7] His confident words, written *ex post facto*, give no hint of the complications that entangled them during the next few years in local politics and, eventually, violent conflicts with the neighbours of Bennelong's people, which escalated into open warfare across three frontiers.

What would Bennelong's compatriots have thought when, on Sunday 27 January, artificers and convicts cut down the forest and erected an encampment of tents for the battalion? Or of the display of military discipline maintained by Phillip, now the Governor of the settlement? There must have been some alarm at the scale of harvest and destruction of their resources and the occupation of their home by strangers, who, in a matter of days, outnumbered them. Obtaining fresh food remained a high priority for Phillip and 'The boats ... were sent to haul the seine', with 'great success', it was remarked when they returned with unexpectedly large quantities of fish. Phillip gave 'strict orders', Surgeon Worgan recorded, 'that the natives should not be offended, or molested on any account ... they were to be treated with every mark of friendship' and on 'no account to fire at them with ball or shot'.[8]

TROUBLE IN THE COLONY

The last ship to be unloaded on 6 February, more than a week after landfall at Botany Bay, contained the female convicts, who were immediately set upon by the male convicts and troops in a night of orgy during which a ferocious storm erupted. As described by Arthur Bowes Smyth, ship's surgeon on the *Lady Penrhyn*, 'tempest, though so violent that the thunder [that] shook the ship exceeded anything I ever before had a conception of'.[9] A disgusting scene rarely mentioned by historians celebrating the foundations of the new nation took place amid the frenzy of the rain and lightning, yet it was referred to in somewhat delicate terms by those present. This account was penned by Bowes Smyth:

> At five o'clock this morning, all things were got in order for landing the whole of the women ... The men convicts got to them very soon after they landed, and it is beyond my abilities to give a just description of the scene of debauchery and riot that ensued during the night ... The sailors in our ship requested to have some grog to make merry with upon the women quitting the ship, indeed the Captain himself had no small reason to rejoice upon their being all safely landed and given into the care of the Governor, as he was under the penalty of £40 for every convict that was missing. For which reason he complied with the sailor's request, and about the time they began to be elevated the tempest came on.[10]

The supply ships did not arrive and, with dwindling rations, the colony soon foundered. Convicts and troops were unable to avoid conflict with local *eora*. While they were out fishing, the locals demanded a share of the catch, and uncontrolled tempers turned to violence. Food shortages threatened their survival, and there was little communication with the *eora* that would inform the settlers reliably of their environment and potential enemies. Attention was diverted from these dire circumstances with the capture of Arabanoo, whom, it was hoped, could be used as a liaison with the inscrutable *eora* and perhaps as a source of information. Arabanoo was brought into the colony, quivering with fear. He was, wrote Tench, 'about thirty years old, not tall, robustly made'. But 'his agitation was excessive, and the clamorous crowds who flocked around him did not contribute to lessen it'.[11] Tench was fascinated and closely observed Arabanoo's every reaction, his fear of the strangeness, his initial courtesy, then his anger at being tethered: 'his delight changed to rage and hatred ... he was seated on a chest near a window, out of which, when he had done eating, he would have thrown his plate, had he not been prevented'.[12] Phillip and his men sought to elicit from him words from his language. One they learnt when, amusing him with a trip to the observatory, he saw the sign of his people—*gweeun*, fire—on the opposite shore where he had been free: 'he looked earnestly at it and sighing deeply two or three times uttered the word,' Tench wrote.[13]

This prelude of tense calm ended abruptly in April 1789 when, as Judge Advocate David Collins explained, 'An extraordinary calamity was now observed among the natives'.[14] 'Repeated accounts bought by our boats', of finding 'bodies of the Indians in all the coves and inlets of the harbour', gave some indication of the impact of the epidemic: 'Pustules, similar to those occasioned by smallpox, were thickly spread on the bodies. The Number that it swept off, by their own accounts, was incredible.'[15] Within two months, hundreds of the traditional people of this place were felled by the disease without affecting one of the foreigners, aside from a Native American man they brought with them, who quickly perished. The English had developed immunity during the Black Plagues that had long before swept through the populations of Europe. The local people called it *galgalla*,[16] and their grief and desperation were overwhelming. Collins wrote of Arabanoo's response:

> At that time Arabanoo was living with us and on our taking him
> down the harbour to look for his former companions, those who
> witnessed his expression and agony can never forget either.
> He looked anxiously around him in the different coves he visited;
> not a vestige on the sound was to be found of human foot; the
> excavations in the rocks were filled with putrid bones with those
> who had fallen victim to the disorder; not a living person was
> anywhere to be met with. It seems as if, flying from the contagion,
> they had left the dead to bury the dead. He lifted up his hands and
> eyes in silent agony for some time; at last he exclaimed, 'All dead!
> All dead!' and then hung his head in mournful silence ...[17]

Did the British bring the smallpox with them? There can be only speculation on this matter, but the coincidence of the pandemic so soon after the first anniversary of the colony has caused some to ask whether it was deliberately planted in blankets to cause disease among the locals.[18] Others have argued that it had spread from the far north of the continent, where Macassans arrived annually in their *perahu* from Sulawesi to trade with Aboriginal people and to collect the prized sea creatures, bêche-de-mer, or sea slugs, used as an aphrodisiac by the Chinese. In any case, the pandemic was a fatal assault on the *eora*, resulting in the near-collapse of their population by the 1830s, when a local man called Boatswain Mahroot gave evidence to the British House of Commons Inquiry, telling them that only three people, including himself, of his group remained.

Arabanoo was freed, and within three weeks he, too, was dead from smallpox. Tench reported: 'The Governor who particularly regarded him, caused him to be buried in his own garden and attended the funeral in person.'[19] But the survivors, unable even to continue their own burial practices, fled from the scourge, except for one family, brought into the settlement. Soon, except for a boy, Nanbarry, they died too. 'The father, although barely able to raise his head ... kept looking into his child's cradle ... and with dying eyes seemed to recommend him to our humanity and protection. Nanbarry was adopted by Mr White, surgeon general of the settlement, and became henceforth one of the family.'[20]

It could not have been worse for Governor Phillip. The chance of engaging local Aboriginal people became more remote following the smallpox epidemic. Governor Phillip, Collins, Tench and other officers must have discussed their options with growing concern. The threat of further violent incidents, such as had occurred the previous year, increased with each day, along with the vulnerability of the settlers to starvation, reliant as they were on the friendly attitude of the locals to their fishing. Tench wrote of their situation: 'Intercourse with the natives, for the purpose of knowing whether or not the country possessed any resources, by which life might be prolonged, as well as on other accounts, becoming every day more desirable, the Governor resolved to make prisoners of two more of them.'[21]

BENNELONG, LEADER OF THE *EORA*

'Love and war seemd his favourite pursuits ... in both of which he has suffered severely.' Watkin Tench[22]

On Wednesday 25 November, 'The Governor sent a boat down the harbour to catch one of the natives.' In the event, they captured two 'chiefs', Colbee and Bennelong, and took them in shackles to the Governor's house. Lieutenant William Bradley wrote, as the officer in charge, that he found it 'by far the most unpleasant service I was ever ordered to Execute'.[23] Each of the captives was restrained with an iron shackle on one leg, to which a rope was attached, and two guards were detailed to them.[24] Bradley observed, 'They were very sullen and sulky.'[25] Fowell reported: 'Nanberry [*sic*] called them both by their names & he gave us to understand they were two chiefs.'[26]

Watkin Tench described them as 'two fine young men'. He thought Bennelong to be about 26 years old, 'of good stature, and stoutly made, with a bold intrepid countenance, which bespoke defiance and revenge'. Colbee seemed to Tench to be nearer to 30 years of age, 'of a less sullen aspect than his com-rade, considerably shorter, and not so robustly framed, though better fitted for purposes of activity'. 'They had both evi-dently had the smallpox; indeed Colbee's face was very thickly imprinted with the marks of it.' Colbee escaped a week later, 'with a small iron ring round his leg'.[27]

Tench's attentions focused on Bennelong, who 'threw off all reserve; and pretended, nay, at particular moments, perhaps felt satisfaction in his new state'. 'He was the only native we ever knew who immediately showed a fondness for spirits.' Among the first habits he learnt from them was to raise his glass and drink a toast to 'the King'.[28] Phillip became fond of Bennelong's company and trusted him to the extent that he gave him his own short sword, a typical weapon in the personal armoury of a British officer.[29] Yet, despite all the show of friendship, obtain-ing information from Bennelong about the intentions of his people and the geography of the area was difficult. Nanbarry, who spoke both the local language and 'Pretty good English', had been assigned the task of asking him a list of questions. Bennelong slapped him and refused to speak to him. As an initiated man, Bennelong could not consider Nanbarry, a boy with all his teeth, as an equal.[30]

An unlikely relationship developed between Bennelong and Governor Phillip. However, Bennelong was too intelligent to allow the master-captive bonds to stand and, for a short time, he was celebrated and seduced by wine, cloths and favours to lend local legitimacy to this small, vulnerable colonial society. Later, he was feted as a curiosity by Lady Dundas, Lord Sydney and others in London society. Although the intentions of Phillip and his masters in enticing Bennelong into their midst were nefarious—to garner acquiescence to their possession of the land—it is clear that on both sides fascination went hand in hand with calculated strategy. The relationship that ensued was full of drama, excitement and, in the end, misery. Within a few years, Bennelong's life and those of his fellow survivors became wretched as events overcame them, their courage and ingenuity unable to save them. Bennelong's fate and that of his people was tragic, as we will see, but, for a few years after 1788, the events at Port Jackson and surrounds were moving and repulsive by turn, and the thrill felt by the protagonists, native and colonist alike, palpable in the evidence left by the gentlemen of the British navy. To Phillip's increasing chagrin, Bennelong's wily politicking for advantage with the British, and more particularly to make them allies against his traditional enemies to the north and to the south, did little to assist Phillip's mission to establish a penal colony, which, for some years, was in a precarious state.

The fear of starvation in this strange land where fish and stingrays were the only recognisable food drove the colonists into an adventure with their native hosts. Like the colony's

His powers of mind were certainly far above mediocrity. He acquired knowledge, both of our manners and language. He willingly communicated information, sang, danced and capered, told us all the customs of his country and all the details of his family economy. When they attended a church with us, which was a common practice, they always preserved profound silence and decency as if conscious that some religious ceremony on our side was being performed.

Watkin Tench

other captives, Bennelong must have been suffering from hunger and malnutrition. A few convicts had already died from starvation. The growing sense of resentment at the food demanded by Bennelong, and an even greater fear that he might discover their parlous state and escape to tell his colleagues, is evident in Tench's record:

> Our friend Baneelon, during this season of scarcity, was as well taken care of as our desperate circumstances would allow. We knew not how to keep him, and yet were unwilling to part with him. Had he penetrated our state, perhaps he might have given his countrymen such a description of our diminished numbers, and diminished strength, as would have emboldened them to become more troublesome. Every expedient was used to keep him in ignorance ... the ration of a week was insufficient to have kept him for a day ... want of food has been known to make him furious and often melancholy.[31]

At about two o'clock in the morning, 'he pretended illness', and 'awaking the servant who lay in the room with him, begged to go down stairs ... Baneelon no sooner found himself in a backyard, than he nimbly leaped over a slight paling, and bade us adieu'.[32]

On 7 September, Phillip and a small party went ashore on the northern side of the harbour in Gamaragal territory, where his men had reported a large gathering of local people, including Bennelong, dining on a beached whale. Unarmed, Phillip approached a man standing near Bennelong. As Captain John Hunter wrote, 'the native, stepping back with his right leg, threw the spear with great violence, and it struck against Governor Phillip's collar bone, close to which it entered, and the barb came out close to the third vertebrae of the back'. He was astonished at the 'behaviour of Bannelong [Bennelong] ... He never attempted to interfere when the man took the spear up, or said a single word to prevent him from throwing it.'[33] For six weeks, Phillip was incapacitated by the horrendous injury.

Our native has left us, and that at a time when he appeared to be happy and contented. This too is unlucky as we have all the ceremony to go over again with another, and I think that man's leaving us proves that nothing will make these people amends for the loss of their liberty.
Arthur Phillip

Tench reported that Chaplain Johnson and Lieutenant Dawes had learnt from 'two Indians that Wil-ee-mar-in was the name of the person who wounded the governor'. Dependent on Bennelong for his knowledge of the native societies and territories, and with the colony being so vulnerable to starvation and to attack, Phillip gave explicit orders that no one was to be punished.

He sent his men to search for Bennelong to tell him he would be most welcome in the Governor's home. Bennelong insisted that the Governor must first come to him. Finally, a meeting was arranged, and Phillip in his boat met Bennelong, who arrived in his canoe, on the harbour. Phillip surprised Bennelong by inviting him to dinner at his house. As usual, Tench describes the scene: 'When we reached the Governor's house, Bennelong expressed honest joy to see his old friend, and appeared pleased to find that he had recovered of his wound ... Bennelong seemed to consider himself quite at home, running from room to room with his companions and introducing them to his old friends, the domestics, in the most familiar manner.'[34]

Phillip's diplomacy was driven by the desperate conditions in the colony. He promised Bennelong and his people that they were free to come and go from the settlement as they pleased, and food, blankets and hatchets would be given in return for an end to their resistance. The ever-canny Bennelong negotiated a brick house for himself.

Tench persisted with his task of obtaining information from Bennelong but, he wrote, 'he had lately become a man of so much dignity and consequence that it was not always easy to obtain his company'.[35] Soon Bennelong was playing host at his new house for his friend Governor Phillip. Like the Governor and Bradley, Captain John Hunter observed the 'carribberie' (corroboree) with great attention to detail: 'Their music consisted of two sticks of very hard wood, one of which the musician held upon his breast, in the manner of a violin, and struck it with the other, in good and regular time.'[36]

Phillip observed the new relationship developing with his colonists: 'They were frequently visited by many of the natives, some of whom daily came to the barracks. All of them very fond of bread, and they now found the advantage of coming amongst the settlers.'[37] Elizabeth Macarthur wrote a letter in March

1791 with news of the increasing presence of the *eora* in Sydney
Town: 'A great many have taken up their abode entirely amongst
us, and Bannylong and Coleby, with their wives, come in frequently.'[38] The strategy of treaty and containment was essential
but perilous. David Collins was shrewdly aware of the dangers, as
this passage shows:

> It was also conceived by some among us, that those natives who
> came occasionally into the town did not desire that any of the other
> tribes should participate in the enjoyment of the few trifles they
> procured from us. If this were true, it would for a long time retard
> the general understanding of our friendly intentions toward them;
> and it was not improbable but that they might for the same reason
> represent us in every unfavourable light they could imagine.[39]

With growing familiarity between Bennelong's people
and the colonists, it quickly became clear, as Judge Advocate
David Collins relates, that sexual liaisons were added to the
dangerous social mix: 'Several girls who were protected in
the settlement had not any objection to passing the night on
board of ships ...'[40] For their part, women of consequence like
Daringa and Barangaroo were equally repulsed by the brutality
of the floggings of a convict who stole Daringa's fishing tackle.
Tench relates that 'Daringa shed tears and Barangaroo, kindling
into anger, snatched a stick and menaced the executioner'.[41]
Sexual urges, and their management, are recurring themes in
the annals of the colony. With ultimate responsibility for the
lives he commanded, and with orders to become friendly with the
natives and to seek their consent to establish the colony, Phillip
managed their health and discipline, giving orders as to food
rations to avoid scurvy, and punishments to deter insubordination, theft and the many other activities that threatened good

order. More difficult was the challenge of reining in the carnal cravings of his officers, crew and convicts. There was the problem of the ratio of men to women in the population of the First Fleet, which, at about ten to one, meant that the women were vulnerable to sexual predation, and those women who had worked as 'ladies of the night' in London before their transportation might also have been a force to be contended with in this regard. There was little he could do about this, as we shall see, except to acknowledge that lust suppressed throughout the long journey would demand an outlet. More threatening to the safety of the proposed colony was the risk of his men satiating their physical appetites with local women on these strange shores, because of the revenge that might be exacted by the men of their society.

Phillip was right, for the trouble that carnal lust, or, perhaps more justly, suspicion of unlawful acts of this nature committed by his gamekeeper, McEntire, led to disastrous consequences and a turning point in relations between the colonisers and the people of the land.

THE TURNING POINT

The night of 10 December 1790 was fateful. At the Georges River, the Bediagal leader Pemulwuy speared John McEntire, Phillip's gamekeeper. McEntire reached Sydney about 'two o'clock the next morning', where Phillip had arranged the 'surgeons' to attempt to remove the barbed spear and a clergyman to deliver last rites. 'On the wound being examined by the surgeons, it was pronounced mortal. The poor wretch now began to utter the most dreadful exclamations, and to accuse himself of the com-mission of crimes of the deepest dye; accompanied with such expressions of his despair of God's mercy, as are too terrible to repeat.'[42]

He was their trophy. Bennelong was the ultimate trophy to prove that
they'd created a colony, had befriended the natives and brought a
native back to court, and to exhibit Bennelong in the same way that the
returning Roman soldiers exhibited lions and tigers and elephants and
golden trinkets.

Professor Marcia Langton, historian, Yiman/Bidjara nation

It was suspected that McEntire had invited revenge for
raping one, perhaps more, local women. McEntire died painfully
on 20 January 1791, and Phillip was enraged. His response
showed his exasperation, and his tactics changed from tolerance
to reprisal, an abandonment of the measured justice he had
meted out to wrongdoers; he instituted measures he had scrupu-
lously avoided in his command of the colony. He sent two revenge
expeditions led, reluctantly, by Tench and Dawes to Botany Bay
with hatchets and head bags and orders to take Pemulwuy's head.
The hapless revenge party returned empty-handed.

The search for Pemulwuy continued, and this may have
been the cause of the grand tour arranged for Bennelong and
Yemmerrawannie. On Monday 10 December 1792 they departed
for London with Phillip, who had retired, on HMS *Atlantic*.
Arriving in London in 1793, they lodged in Mayfair, where they
were cared for by William Waterhouse, and met Lord and Lady
Dundas and other notables from the royal court. Ensign G Bond
of the New South Wales Corps reported: 'When he arrived in
England he was humanely introduced to the King at St James's',
and noted that they lived 'in the European manner'.[43] In the
Oracle and Public Advertiser, on 19 April 1794, it was reported
that 'Two Sooty Natives of New South Wales went to the Houses
of Parliament where they were introduced to several persons
of consequence'.[44]

Two letters from Hunter (then living in London but still acting on behalf of the colony) to the Home Office in August note Bennelong serving as a colonial trophy and amusing society with the stark contrast he presented: although he was apparently a 'savage', his verbal jousts were as sharp as the dilettantes and minor aristocrats seeking the attention and favour of ruling families. On Bennelong's part, he wanted the sartorial finery of the gentlemen of London society, and he wrote requesting a variety of items. In a letter dated 5 August 1794, to the Home Office from Hunter,[45] bills were presented which had been sent to Hunter for Bennelong and Yemmerrawannie's expenses in England, for £63 'at Eltham' in Kent and £96 'in town', presumably London, and there were bills 'paid by Mr Waterhouse on the account of two natives; two pairs of knee buckles–3 shillings, two pairs of gloves–4 shillings, a boat for the natives bathing– 2 shillings.'

At a soirée, Bennelong's wit struck those present sufficiently for them to report it in mock admiration. Baron Charles von Hügel reported that, 'On taking his leave, Bennelong asked the Prime Minister for permission to kiss his fair daughter's hand, to which her father agreed. The young lady held out a hand encased in a glove. Bennelong, however, declared in a loud firm voice: "Madam, I received permission to kiss your hand, not your glove".'[46]

Hunter expressed his concern for Bennelong's health. Delays in returning to his home have 'much broken his spirit and the coldness of the weather here has so frequently laid him up that I am apprehensive his lungs are affected'.[47] It was not Bennelong but Yemmerrawannie who succumbed. He died in England of a chest complaint and was buried in Eltham, a long way from home.

In 1795 Bennelong returned from London with the new
Governor of New South Wales, John Hunter. Bennelong was
'delirious with joy' at his return home,[48] but his life was shor-
tened by alcoholic excess and violent revenge ordeals. He was
tolerated by Governor King, who demoted him from the
Governor's table to the dining room. He returned to his own
society, but the scourge of alcohol abuse, not only for him but
also for many of his people, exacerbated the accelerating round
of violence and revenge in which they indulged during their
bouts of drinking.

**They are universally fearful of spirits. They call a spirit 'mourn'. They often
scruple to approach a corpse saying that the 'mourn' will seize them
and that it fastens upon them in the night when they're asleep. When
asked where their deceased friends are, they always point to the sky.**
Watkin Tench

Bennelong died in 1813. He was buried, with one of his
wives, in a grave in James Squire's orchard at Kissing Point. His
obituary in the *Sydney Gazette* was a vicious tract that failed to
mention his services to the colony.[49] With his death came the
end of the brief period of peace that he negotiated and managed
with Governor Phillip. Bennelong and Phillip were colleagues in
an extraordinary adventure. Bennelong was as much responsible
for the colony's affairs as Phillip, and in their tango of strange
intimacy, deceit and manipulation, they created a short-lived
period of friendship and tolerance. Both were courageous and
shrewd and, at the same time, flawed, succumbing to their pas-
sions and rages. With Phillip retired to England, Bennelong was
left to survive in the profoundly changed circumstances of his
country. He had changed, too, not least because of his alliance

with Phillip. At the end of his days, his mood of increasing bit-terness and alcoholic decline reduced him from his warrior's countenance to a weak, defeated man.

PEMULWUY AND THE BIDE-A-GAL RESISTANCE

Many shots have been fired at him and he has now lodged in him, in shot, slugs and bullets about eight or ten ounces of lead, it is supposed he has killed over thirty of our people, but it is doubtful on which side the provocation has been given. John Washington Price, surgeon[50]

While Bennelong was in London, suffering from the cold and pining for his home, the colonists, in their search for better ter-ritory to support their growing but malnourished population, had found fertile country for their crops to the west on the banks of a river, called Derebin, which they renamed the Hawkesbury. The land lay within Pemulwuy's domain of influence in the estate of the Gandangarra and the inland Darug, and extended to the mountain ranges in the west. Pemulwuy was member of the Bediagal clan. Unlike Bennelong, Pemulwuy had no wish to find an accommodation with the British. They had no great regard for Pemulwuy and regarded him as 'a riotous and trouble-some savage'.[51]

The colonists set about burning the forests, clearing them for farmland. Within a year, many more colonised the area and were soon in the majority. They escaped starvation in Sydney, but their land-clearing soon caused the Gandangarra and inland Darug the same fate. Instead of native yams and other staples, the colonists' crops covered the most fertile parts of the valley. In May 1795 Judge Advocate David Collins reported that their crops were at risk: 'The natives appeared in large bodies, men, women, and children, provided with blankets and nets to carry off the corn ... determined to take it wherever and whenever they could meet with opportunities.'[52] The settlers retaliated violently, and the traditional owners fought back. Collins described the ensuing conflict on the Hawkesbury as an 'open war'.[53]

In May 1795 the acting Governor, Captain William Paterson, aware of his responsibility for the food security of the colony, acted to save this vulnerable periphery from the rage of the traditional owners. He sent sixty soldiers to the Hawkesbury to destroy the Aboriginal people, and, as David Collins related, 'several of these people were killed ... but none of their bodies ... found'.[54] In contrast to the official records, the Reverend Thomas Fyshe Palmer recorded of the escalating violence: 'They seized a native boy who had lived with a settler, and made him discover where his parents and relations concealed themselves. They came upon them unarmed and unexpected, killed five and wounded many more. The dead they hang on gibbets, *in terrorem*. The people killed were unfortunately the most friendly of the blacks, and one of them more than once saved the life of a white man.'[55]

Like Arthur Phillip, Governor John Hunter tried and failed to secure an honourable peace, but the Colonial Office in London was not sympathetic. Hunter had failed to put down the native uprising; he had been unable to stop the rum trade; and he had had no success in stopping the power of the military. He was forced to resign. Pemulwuy had remained at large, although David Collins saw him at the man-making ceremonies held at Yoo-lahng—or Farm Cove—in February 1795. Collins made no attempt to capture him on this occasion, a decision he perhaps regretted later. Pemulwuy's reputation as an invincible opponent proved for a while to be true. With the mark of the sorcerer, a deformed left foot, he inspired admiration among his own and, for his ruthless attacks, hatred among the settlers. Before long, the troops were in battle with Pemulwuy and his colleagues.

Pemulwuy survived several attacks and, although wounded five times, he fought on at every opportunity. He burnt farm-houses and crops, starting the blazes several kilometres away. In another battle, Pemulwuy was captured after receiving seven bullet wounds to his head and body. Yet, a month later, still with irons on his legs, Pemulwuy escaped. John Washington Price, surgeon on a convict ship, who thought him 'brave and coura-geous', wrote in 1800, 'having killed some of our people an order was given to shoot him, yet few have attempted it ... [He] ... has been known to say "that no gun or pistol can kill him".'[56]

Philip Gidley King had become Governor with Hunter's departure, the latter defeated by the violent turn of fortunes in his colony. King opined about Pemulwuy's status as a man of supernatural powers and an unconquerable warrior, 'The strange idea was found to prevail among the natives respecting the savage Pemulwuy ... he could not be killed by our firearms.' He found it difficult 'to convince them ... that he was not endowed with any such extraordinary exemptions'. King 'gave orders to bring Pemulwuy in either dead or alive' and offered a free pardon to any convict who was successful: 'To a prisoner for life or four-teen years, a conditional emancipation. To a person already con-ditionally emancipated a free pardon and a recommendation for a passage to England.' On 1 May 1801 King also 'directed that natives be driven back from the settlers' habitations by firing at them'.[57]

Pemulwuy was killed in 1802 when he was shot dead by Henry Hacking, a seaman, explorer and robber, and, like so many others in the colony, a drunkard. Pemulwuy was beheaded and his head sent by Governor King to Sir Joseph Banks in London. In a letter to Banks, King wrote: 'Altho' a terrible pest to the colony, Pemulwuy was a brave and independent character, understanding that the possession of a New Hollander's head is among the desiderata, I have put it in spirits and forwarded it to you.'[58]

Everything about Pemulwuy is mythical in many senses because we only see him in the records occasionally.
Professor Gordon Briscoe, historian

The Darug requested that with Pemulwuy's head should go their promise of an end to resistance in return for being able to live on their own lands. But even the humiliation of the ritual beheading of this warrior could not put an end to the hostilities.

Tedbury, Pemulwuy's son, continued the war. Soon Tedbury, too, was captured and imprisoned in Parramatta jail, where he was compelled to lead the British to his fellow rebels and the settlers' corn that they had stolen. His comrade Mosquito, however, refused to surrender. Rather, he 'saluted them in good English, and declaring a determination to continue their rapacity made off'.[59] A month later, in June 1805, the *Sydney Gazette* was reporting Mosquito's successes: 'The natives about the Hawkesbury and George's River still continue their depredations ... it is hoped the apprehension of the Native called Musquito might effectually prevent any further mischief in those quarters.'[60]

By July the Governor had conceived a plan for the Darug to trade Tedbury for Mosquito: 'For this service, two were accepted to go in search of Musquetta, who with one or two more of his desperate associates still keeps the flame alive.'[61] In August 1805 Mosquito was captured, but not without a fight. He, or one of his men, 'avowed a determination to set fire to the building, and destroy every white man within it'.[62] The Judge Advocate, Richard Atkins, was, like so many of the Wangal people, a victim of the rum trade, resulting from the practice in the colony of using rum for currency. Although probably drunk, he delivered a verdict that would result in Mosquito ending his days in prison on Norfolk Island: 'The Natives of this country are at present incapable of being brought before a Criminal Court, either as criminals or as Evidences ... it would make a mockery of Judicial Proceedings.'[63] John Easty, a marine, recorded his view of Mosquito's wretched fate: 'A poor miserable place and all manners of cruelties and oppression used ... flogging and beating the people to death ... it's better for the poor unhappy creatures to be hanged ...'[64]

In July 1806, when the food scarcity was as severe as ever, Governor King reported to London that 'none of the Natives' accustomed purloinment of Indian Corn has happened this Year', and gave assurances of the 'general good Conduct' of the natives and their 'peaceable demeanor'. He also took the opportunity to remind London of his firm control by referring to 'the two who were sent from here to Norfolk Island where they have behaved very quiet and orderly'.[65]

Thus, with the beheading of Pemulwuy and the imprisonment of Mosquito, the armed resistance in the Sydney region died, eighteen years after the British had arrived. Fighting with spears and clubs, and outnumbered by men with muskets, the warriors of the Derebin had delayed the expansion of the mightiest empire on earth.

Philip Gidley King tried to secure an enduringly peaceful settlement before his departure by promising to reserve land for the Darug and their families. King, under pressure from settlers in the district, received a memo, 'requesting they might be allowed to shoot the natives frequenting their grounds, who had threatened to fire their wheat when ripe'. The author had forged the signatures, King discovered. Yet, even so, he sent for Darug representatives to respond to these claims. They told him

> they did not like being driven from the few places left on the
> banks of the river where alone they could procure food ... if they
> went across white man's grounds the settlers fired upon them and
> were angry; that if they could retain some places on the lower
> parts of the river they would be satisfied and not trouble the white
> man again ... Their request appears to be so just and equitable
> I assured them that no more settlements would be made lower
> down the river.[66]

King's promise of the land grant was soon forgotten, and the river flat country was entirely occupied. There were new theatres of war when the British found a passage over the mountain ranges that had confined the settlement to the coast.

GOVERNOR MACQUARIE'S NEW ORDER

In 1809 the new Governor, Lachlan Macquarie, arrived in Sydney. Like his predecessors, he had a vision of a successful colony at peace with the natives: 'I need not, I hope, express my wish that the Natives of this Country ... may always be treated with Kindness and Attention, so as to conciliate them as much as possible to our Government and Manners.'[67]

Bungaree had assumed Bennelong's responsibilities for liaison with the British. Whereas the Gadigal, Wangal and other harbour clans were once the owners of their estate, under Bennelong's proud, fierce leadership, now their land was overrun. In addition to the British in ever-growing numbers, now the people from other tribes from the north and south also gathered in Sydney. Attracted to the excitement of the settlement, the alcohol, food and entertainment, and the chance to observe the white strangers at first hand, these transients further disrupted the arrangement between the traditional owners and the British. Here they were free to carouse and soon began begging from the British, whose contempt for all of them intensified.

> The ideas of self-preservation and having farms here and all these things were very romantic in the minds of contemporary white people because they love hearing that kind of history. What they don't like is the Aboriginal perspective that says that Aboriginal people were protecting their land and they did it continually.
>
> *Professor Gordon Briscoe, historian*

Macquarie wanted order and created yet another scheme to bring the First Australians under the rule of British law and government. He invented a chief system, creating gorgets to mark the wearer as a person of rank to be treated as someone authorised to speak on behalf of his clan. These crescent-shaped plates were worn around the neck on a chain. Bungaree, who had replaced Bennelong as the leader of the *eora*, was the first man to be awarded the status of Chief by Macquarie, whereupon Bungaree announced himself as the King of Sydney. Dressed in a European uniform, he requested payment from every ship in port as the King of Sydney, falling into mendicancy and humiliating himself with each crew. Such was the illegitimacy of the breast plates issued to appointed 'chiefs' that they served only to reduce the men who wore them to caricatures of themselves and to belittle and emasculate the leadership traditions of their own societies. This must have been the intention, and Bungaree was the first to fall victim to this sly practice.

Macquarie and his wife Elizabeth's names were given to newly commissioned buildings and towns and to rivers and mountains 'discovered' by white explorers. But his most remarkable endeavour was the establishment of the Native Institution, which gave form to his plan to educate Aboriginal children in the ways of Europeans. As a product of the Enlightenment, Macquarie sought to found his institution in the principles of Christianity and British civilisation as an expression of divine inspiration in human affairs. Some of the leading head men agreed to place their children in the institution, and some excelled there. The Native Institution opened on 18 January 1815.

When Aboriginal people are actually materially, emotionally, physically, philosophically equal with the whites, they're not interested in what the whitefellas have got to offer.
Professor Peter Read, historian

The institution impressed at least one visitor, Rose Marie de Freycinet, wife of the French commander of the exploration ship *Uranie*, who gave a glowing report: 'The boys cultivate the garden attached to the house they occupy. The girls are taught the tasks suitable to their sex ... We saw the house where these little savages are kept: the advances they have already made are truly astonishing and think how valuable a work! These children, thus taught will carry to the homes of their families the germs of civilization.'[68] Appearances were deceptive, however. Some boys had escaped and others had died. Only two months after the opening, Macquarie reported that by 'unaccountable caprice' six children had been taken away by their parents.[69]

Then, during the years 1814 to 1816, a drought affected the region, placing the wheat crops in jeopardy. Wheat farms and the grazing lands for the colony's precious herds of sheep and cattle were also drying out. A government outpost had been established in the midst of the most fertile area 90 kilometres to the south of Sydney Town, where the relationships with the local Dharawal people had been fostered since two bulls and four cows had wandered into their estate in 1788. The area was named after the herd that had grown from these wandering cattle: Cowpastures, and the Dharawal became known as the Cowpastures tribe. Pushed out of their own territory by drought, and seeking food and water, the Gandangarra came into Dharawal territory, where they also sought revenge for the murder of two Gandangarra familes of women and children by white settlers. Governor Macquarie reported this latest outbreak of violence to the Colonial Office:

> The native blacks of this country have lately broken out in open
> hostility against British settlers residing near Cowpastures and
> have committed the most daring acts of violence. No less than five
> white men have been killed. I have uniformly made it my study
> to do everything in my power to conciliate the native tribes by
> showing them on all occasions much kindness.
>
> Indeed I had entertained hopes of being able to civilise
> a great proportion of them by the establishment of the native
> institution and settling some few grown up men and women on
> lands in Sydney. But I begin to entertain a fear that I shall find
> this a more arduous task than I at first imagined. In the mean
> time it will be absolutely necessary to inflict severe punishments
> on the mountain tribes. Many of the settlers have entirely
> abandoned their farms in consequence of the latest outrages.

However painful, this measure has now become absolutely
necessary.[70]

The settler retribution was indiscriminate and brutal. Some
of the Dharawal people had sought shelter with a local farmer,
Charles Throsby, who wrote from Glenfield Farm on 5 April 1816
to acting Provost Marshall William Charles Wentworth about his
fear for his innocent friends, Bitugally, Duel and Yettooming.
Yettooming's wife and two children had been the victims of
barbarous treatment:

> The people not content at shooting at them in the most
> treacherous manner in the dark, actually cut the woman's arm
> off and stripped the scalp of her head over her eyes, and on going
> up to them and finding one of the children only wounded one of
> the fellows deliberately beat the infant's brains out with the butt
> end of his muskett, the whole of the bodies then left in that state
> by the (brave) party unburied! as an example for the savages to
> view the following morning, therefore under these circumstances
> I hope I may be pardoned asserting that I do not wonder at the
> savages then seeking revenge in retaliation. I am well aware that
> the fears and aversions of the ignorant part of white people will
> lead them to accuse the whole, indiscriminantly, therefore it
> is to be hoped, steps will as much possible be taken to prevent
> any friendly natives being injured, least the lives of some of our
> stockmen or others in remote unprotected situations may fall a
> sacrifice in retaliation.[71]

Like the vigilante farmers, Governor Macquarie was unable
to distinguish between the Dharawal and the Gandangarra, and
his orders were swift and brutal: '[T]hey are to surrender to you
as Prisoners of War. If they refuse to do so, make the least show

of resistance ... you will fire upon them and compel them to surrender ... Such Natives as happen to be killed, if grown up men, are to be hanged up on trees in conspicuous situations, to strike the survivors with the greatest Terror. Any women or children to be killed are to be buried where they fell.'[72] He also added an instruction to top up the numbers at the Native Institution while they were on their revenge raid: 'Procure twelve Aboriginal boys and six girls between four and six years of age for the Native Institution at Parramatta. Select and secure only fine, healthy and good looking children.'

Local Darug and Dharawal guides were appointed to find these 'hostile tribes', but they led the soldiers astray for a month before escaping. Finally Captain Wallis, leading one of two detachments, heard that a group was camped at a farm in Appin. His report to Macquarie was a disingenuous account, one of many to follow, which sought to justify the unjustifiable.

> A few of my men ... heard a child cry. I formed line ranks ... and pushed up through a thick brush towards the precipitous banks of a deep rocky creek. The dogs gave the alarm and the natives fled over the cliffs. A smart firing now ensured. It was moonlight. The grey dawn of the moon appearing so dark as to be able to discover their figures bounding from rock to rock. I regret to say some had been shot and others met their fate while rushing in despair over the precipice. Twas a melancholy but necessary duty I was employed on. Fourteen dead bodies were counted in different directions. I regretted the death of the old native Balyin and the unfortunate women and children from the rocky place they fell in.[73]

After this slaughter, the Dharawal, with the permission of Mrs Macarthur, now the richest woman in the colony as a result of acquiring their land, moved *en masse* to her farm at Camden, the last safe haven in their own homeland. Then the rain fell for two solid weeks, breaking the long drought and flooding the rivers. Crops, homes and stock were destroyed, and any evidence of the massacre was washed away in the floods. 'All Hostility on both sides has long since Ceased; the black Natives living now peaceably and quietly in every part of the Colony, Unmolested by the White Inhabitants.'[74]

Governor Macquarie rewarded the Darug and Dharawal guides even though they had misled the military during the most recent engagements, allotting them a tiny part of their own territory in land grants in the area west of Sydney known as Blacktown. Macquarie banned the carrying of spears and declared that groups of more than six Aboriginal people near farms or towns be treated as enemies and shot. The alternative for the traditional owners was to accept his offer of a grant of land and to live like a white settler. The Governor invited 'the Natives to relinquish their wandering idle and predatory lives and to become useful members of the community where they will find protection and encouragement'.[75]

WINDRADYNE, 'DREADED BY THE BATHURST SETTLER'

In 1813 the colony expanded into Wiradjuri territory, the land of the three rivers flowing across a vast area on the plains to the west of the Blue Mountains, which they intended would support the new colony. Eager to ensure a more secure source of food, Governor Macquarie ordered a road to be built over the mountains, beyond which, some in the colony believed, lay China, a quaint idea disproved by Gregory Blaxland, William Wentworth and Lieutenant Lawson, who were the first from the colony to find a way through the mountains. With a team of convict workers,

George Evans and William Cox completed the road in less than six months. The Wiradjuri, who had traded with their neighbours on the coast, the Gandangarra and Darug, whose resistance had failed, must have heard stories about the foreigners. Evans would have concluded as much, for he wrote: 'At sunset I saw some Natives coming down the Plain. They did not see us till we surprised them. There were only two women and four children. The poor creatures trembled and fell down with fright.' There is no hint that there was any threat from the Wiradjuri. Evans, Cox and Henry Antill saw few Aboriginal people, but heard them calling in the bush.[76]

In April 1815 Macquarie, with his wife and a party of fifty, went to see the new acquisition. After negotiating two of the great rivers, Macquarie's party encountered 'three male natives of the country, all very handsome good looking young men', resplendent in their possum-skin cloaks. It is possible that one of them, whose image was painted by Lewin, was Windradyne, who was remarkable for his extraordinary size and bearing. Macquarie's encounter with him involved a friendly exchange: 'To the best looking and stoutest of them I gave a piece of yellow cloth in exchange for his mantle, which he presented me with.'[77] Several Aboriginal people were among the crowd that turned out to welcome Governor Macquarie and his party on their arrival at Bathurst, according to Antill, who was impressed by the skill of the Wiradjuri in making cloaks of sewn possum skin. Wiradjuri men, but noticeably no women, visited their camp, entering tents, mimicking their English, 'and took what was offered them, but did not ask for anything'.[78] A week later, some allowed their hair to be cut and were given gifts of clothing and 'tommyhawks'. On 11 May the Governor urged his men who were remaining to maintain friendly relations with them.[79]

The colony had expanded, and Macquarie had established and maintained 'peace if not harmony'. By 1817 Macquarie's tenure was doomed when Earl Bathurst, Secretary of State for the Colonies in Lord Liverpool's ministry, established a commission of inquiry, and sent out John Thomas Bigge to conduct it. Macquarie had little knowledge of this decision and was humiliated by the manner of Bigge's appointment, and even more so by Bigge's less than scrupulous conduct of his inquiry. His reports were harshly critical of Macquarie's administration and recommended radical change.[80]

In December 1821, with the town of Bathurst established near the place where he had much earlier met three Wiradjuri men, Macquarie returned to bid farewell and was welcomed with great fanfare. 'I found a great number of the Natives waiting here for me for several Days, and they immediately came to see me at Government House—to the amount of fifteen Persons. We dined at five o'clock—the Baggage having all arrived about four o'clock. In the Evening the little Town of Bathurst was very neatly illuminated in honor of my arrival in it—and the Natives entertained us with a very good Karauberie [corroboree] at Night, which lasted till eleven o'clock.'[81]

He could not have suspected that another conflict, more violent than the last, would erupt soon after his departure. The next Governor of the colony of New South Wales had a starkly different approach. Sir Thomas Makdougall Brisbane took over from Governor Lachlan Macquarie on 1 December 1821. He developed his own plans for the colony, closing the Native Institution and ignoring Macquarie's promises to Aboriginal groups in the colony of land grants and secure tenure.[82]

In 1822 Brisbane began to organise land matters in the colony that would open the way for a flood of settlers onto the western plains. He set in place a system that discouraged land speculation and encouraged those with capital and a willingness to take up land with the intention of making it productive. Under the previous governors, only a few had land grants with formal titles, and squatting and claim jumping was rife. Under Brisbane, there would be, if not a land tenure system, at least a semblance of order. Instead of chits signed by unauthorised persons, tickets of occupation enabled graziers to occupy land without a preliminary survey and gave them security against trespass. In 1824 Brisbane allowed Crown lands to be sold for five shillings an acre. Between May and December 1825 more than 500 000 acres (202 345 hectares) were sold.[83]

Settlers moved out over the plains in the ensuing years, among them George Suttor, who arrived with his son William in 1822. Suttor and his family were guided to well-watered land by Wiradjuri people, and they called their new station Brucedale. There were few other settlers on this frontier. William, left in charge with instructions to treat the local Wiradjuri with kindness and respect, made friends and quickly learnt to speak their language.

One of the locals whom Suttor befriended was Windradyne, known by the name of 'Saturday' in the colony, and respected and admired by Suttor:

> Saturday is a very fine figure, very muscular and his limbs are of a
> beautiful symmetry, he has a mind not unconscious apparently of
> his superiority. I was much amused the other day, a fine winter's
> day, to see Saturday and his tribe, and friends seated on the
> ground in groups of men and women, exposing their persons to
> the warm rays of the sun and seeming to be enjoying their singing
> and making joyful noise for hours. I never heard the women sing

but they are at times great laughers. I give my opinion the cause
of the disturbances between us and the Aboriginal people to the
cruel conduct of some of our people. The natives are really fond
of the white people. I have always been friendly to them. We have
never suffered the smallest injury from them.[84]

Brisbane's schemes resulted in an uncontrolled land rush.
The huge increase in soldiers, farmers and convicts running sheep
was disastrous for the Wiradjuri, and soon their responses turned
from friendliness to violent opposition. The first generation of
colonists had lost patience, however, with Aboriginal people,
after 'twenty years of attacks on the Hawkesbury and Camden',
and the first signs of resistance from the Wiradjuri met with
'prompt reprisal'.[85] In January 1824 the *Sydney Gazette* reported
that 'Advice from Bathurst say that the natives have been very
troublesome'. The reportage reveals that the Wiradjuri were
starving and that Windradyne could be a formidable enemy: 'In
justification for their conduct, the natives urge that the white
men have driven away all the kangaroos and opossums, and that
the black men must now have beef. The strength of those men is
amazing. One of the chiefs, Saturday, of a desperate tribe, took
six men to secure him and they had actually to break a musket
over his body before he yielded, which he did at length with
broken ribs.'

Windradyne, who had been leading raids on the settlement of Bathurst, was captured and sentenced to one month's
imprisonment. After his release, settlers made it impossible for
Windradyne to lay down his arms. As Windradyne and his companions passed by a farm, the farmer gave them some potatoes
as a friendly gesture. The next day, they returned and, believing
that the farmer's generosity would endure in the manner of their

own customs, dug up potatoes and took them away for another meal. George Suttor had come to understand their customs and traditions, so very different from those of the English. With respect to their views on property he noted: 'These natives have some imperfect ideas of property, and the right of possession. They say all wild animals are theirs—the tame or cultivated ones are ours. Whatever springs spontaneously from the earth or without labour is theirs also. Things produced by art and labour, are the white fellows as they call us.'[86]

The farmer had no such sympathies, and organised a party of his neighbours to pursue them. They attacked, shooting at the group, leaving several of Windradyne's people dead. Windradyne, alive but embittered, began a campaign against the settlers, attacking their homesteads, pillaging and murdering. George Suttor, however, had maintained his friendship with his Wiradjuri colleagues, and he and his family were spared in Windradyne's campaign. His ability to converse with them in their language was an invaluable asset during the conflict. William Suttor recalled the events:

> Our hut was one day surrounded by a large party of Blacks fully equipped for war, under the leadership of their great fierce chief and warrior named by the whites 'Saturday'. There was no means of resistance so my father, then a lad of eighteen years, met them fearlessly at the door. He spoke to them in their own language in such a manner as not to let them suppose he anticipated any evil from them. They consulted in an undertone, and departed as suddenly and noiselessly as they came. They never molested man or beast of my father's.[87]

A bloody cycle of strike and counter-strike ensued, as starving Wiradjuri killed the shepherds' stock, stockmen rode out in indiscriminate raids and, equally indiscriminate, Wiradjuri slaughtered shepherds in the service of absentee station owners. The homestead of Samuel Terry, said to be built on a sacred *bora* ground (an initiation site) and who, it was rumoured, had fed the Wiradjuri poison, was attacked by Windradyne and his men. The *Sydney Gazette* reported, 'On the estate of Mr Terry at Millamorah, three poor men have been destroyed by Natives. When the hapless men were killed, the sable murderers then proceeded to break up and destroy every article of convenience about the place.'[88] The settlers had armed their shepherds and servants, and guns and ammunition were dispersed around the district, fuelling the unauthorised vigilantism. The hatred and blood lust was whipped up at meetings, such as the one at Bathurst, which the evangelist Rev. Threlkeld reported with horror: 'One of the largest holders of Sheep in the Colony, maintained at a public meeting at Bathurst, that the best thing that could be done, would be to shoot all the Blacks and manure the ground with their carcasses, which was all the good they were fit for!' It was at this meeting that the settlers decided to exterminate the local Aboriginal population. There were conflicting accounts of their success, Threlkeld writing about the 'havoc' that ensued:

> It was recommended likewise that the Women and Children should especially be shot as the most certain method of getting rid of the race. Shortly after this declaration, martial law was proclaimed, and sad was the havoc made upon the tribes at Bathurst. A large number were driven into a swamp, and mounted police rode round and round and shot them off indiscriminately until they were all destroyed! When one of the police enquired of the Officer if a return should be made of the killed, wounded

there were none, all were destroyed, Men, Women and Children! the reply was;—that there was no necessity for a return. But forty-five heads were collected and boiled down for the sake of the skulls! My informant, a Magistrate, saw the skulls packed for exportation in a case at Bathurst ready for shipment to accompany the commanding Officer on his voyage shortly afterwards taken to England.[89]

The *Sydney Gazette*'s version was highly partisan, although the facts must have been well known. 'A party went out in quest of the natives, but the only horde they fell in with comprised three women; and without questioning the propriety of such a step, immediately despatched the poor unoffending creatures, not withstanding they were females.'[90]

Five white storekeepers were charged with manslaughter for the murder of the women but were found not guilty. With the Wiradjuri resistance taking an even greater toll on the settlers, the Gandangarra attacked from the south at William Lawson's property, killing seven stockmen and slaughtering 500 sheep. William Lawson Jnr bemoaned their incapacity to wipe out the local Aboriginal population: 'There have been several Aboriginal people recently shot by soldiers ... we have now commenced hostilities against them in consequence of them killing a great number of shepherds and stockmen, but afraid we shall never exterminate them.'[91] With yet more stockmen being killed in the continuing Wiradjuri attacks, some settlers abandoned their properties. In Sydney the reports in the *Gazette* raised the alarm: 'The immense stock is being scattered over the whole country, the shepherds have necessarily abandoned their charges and thus the strength and wealth of the colony is, for the moment, exposed to destruction.'[92]

On 14 August 1824 Governor Brisbane proclaimed martial law and offered a reward of 500 acres to bring in 'Saturday', or Windradyne. For Major Morisset, commander in the district, the key words of the proclamation were: 'resort to summary justice has become necessary'. With seventy-five soldiers and armed settlers at his disposal, he initiated the bloodiest campaign of the colony's short history. The *Gazette* announced the grisly news on 14 October 1824: 'Bathurst with its surrounding vicinity is engaged in an exterminating war.' The mass murder shocked the longtime friend of the Wiradjuri, William Suttor Jnr.

Under this condition the blacks were shot down without any respect. The proclamation of martial law was as indecipherable to them as an Egyptian heiroglyph would have been. So a party of soldiers was despatched. Negotiations, apparently friendly but really treacherous, were entered into. Food was prepared. The blacks were invited to come for it. Unsuspecting, they did come, principally women and children. As they gathered up the white men's presents they were shot down by a brutal volley, without regard to age or sex.[93]

The Wiradjuri, their neighbours and the colonists, all were counting the cost of the relentless bloodshed and high death toll. Hunted to the edge of survival, hungry and desperate, some of the Wiradjuri people came into Bathurst to ask for peace. There was hope for a 'speedy reconciliation', the *Sydney Gazette* announced, 'between the settlers and the black natives, which will quickly be followed up no doubt with the abolition of martial law'. However, martial law continued because Windradyne remained at large, as the colony's newspaper observed in October 1824: 'Saturday, who has rendered himself so notorious in the Aboriginal annals, still thinks it's prudent to keep out of reach, and has not even been heard of.'[94]

Two months later, Windradyne marched for seventeen days across the mountain range into Parramatta at the head of his force of nearly 200 warriors to attend the Governor's annual feast. With the word 'peace' stuck in his hat, he surrendered. The settlers who came to see him were awestruck: 'He is the finest looking native we have seen in this part of the country ... which combined with a noble looking countenance and piercing eye, are calculated to impress the beholder towards a character who has been so much dreaded by the Bathurst settler. Saturday is, without doubt, the most manly black native we have ever beheld—a fact pretty generally acknowledged by the numbers that saw him.'[95]

Governor Brisbane, writing to the Colonial Office about their attendance at the feast, made light of the disastrous campaign of terror and its death toll, and drew special attention to his pardon of Windradyne. 'I am most happy to report to your Lordship that Saturday their great and most warlike chieftain has been with me to receive his pardon and that he with most of his tribe attended the Annual Conference.'[96] Martial law was repealed on 11 December, after four months of bloodshed, but Lord Bathurst in England was horrified at Morisset's murderous use of his military powers and relieved him of his duties. William Suttor Jnr's conclusion was incisive: 'When Martial Law had run its course extermination is the word most aptly describes the result. As the old Roman Tacitus said, "they made a solitude and called it peace."'[97]

A SOLITUDE CALLED PEACE

Within the short lifespan of a poor Englishman of that time, the Aboriginal people of the Sydney region had been reduced to a vulnerable existence on the edge of the colony. Once the citizens of thriving societies, living well from fishing, hunting and harvesting the bounty of their superb landscapes, their numbers had been greatly reduced by the end of 1824, and each person could count scores of their kin who had died from disease and violence, whether in drunken fights or at the hands of the settler vigilantes or the British army. From Bennelong's uneasy friendship with Governor Phillip to Windradyne's fierce resistance and surrender at the end of the war in the western district, the outcome was disastrous. At the end, one warrior still harboured the need for revenge. Mosquito was still alive and, released from the prison on Norfolk Island, he was headed for Van Diemen's Land. The 'rolling frontier' had not stalled, and there were more nations of the First Australia yet to meet the British.

Towlangany
TO TELL LIES

2

'WHAT BUSINESS HAVE YOU HERE?'
Aboriginal warriors, Bothwell region, 1830

James Boyce

Aboriginal people have lived in Tasmania for more than 35 000 years—more than three times as long as the human occupation of the British Isles. They have adapted to extraordinary climate change (including being the southernmost human beings in the world during the last Ice Age), vastly different environmental realities and, in very recent times, the brutal invasion and conquest of their country. Very little is known about this long and varied past. Thus, before newcomers (including me) reflect on human history in Tasmania, a moment's silence is needed. We need to let go of the burden of 'expertise' long enough to acknowledge the extent of what we do not and cannot know.

Humility, respect and compassion are owed not because this approach is 'politically correct' but because it is honest. Humility follows an acceptance of how little we understand; respect,

accepting the simple truth that we live in the homeland of one of
the world's most ancient and adaptive cultures; and compassion,
because—and this I know with a degree of certainty rare in the
experience of an empirical historian—during the past 200 years
terrible deeds have been done. But even with such care, there
is no avoiding the limitations imposed by cultural background
and discipline. Those who don't share these constraints—artists,
storytellers, community builders—have perhaps the more important calling, but it cannot be mine. I am a white man largely
writing about what white men thought (the group who almost
monopolise the written record). This too can be done with integ-
rity (relations with the Aboriginal people were after all integral
to white history, too), but it's a sad bloody business, really.

BEFORE THE EUROPEANS

Tasmania, because it is a large and diverse island (about twice the
size of Taiwan), contains many geographic regions, each with its
own climate, vegetation, animal species and so on. Before the
British came this was reflected in cultural diversity, including
variation in matters such as housing and boat design. Over the
whole period of human occupation of Tasmania, the environmental contrasts were much more extreme: during the last Ice
Age the climate was up to 7 degrees colder and much drier than
it is today, and country that is now temperate rainforest was
open tundra with vast glaciers and now extinct megafauna. Not
surprisingly, the archaeological records confirm that there have
also been marked changes in human society. The ten million or so
artefacts deposited during the long occupation of Kutikina Cave
between about 20 000 and 14 000 years ago provides 'evidence
of a marked changed in stone tool technology and raw material
usage'. The warmer and wetter environment becoming evident

from the end of this period (which resulted in the last closing of the land bridge across Bass Strait and the formation of the current coastline by around 8000 years ago) was another major period of adaptation. And about 2500 years ago there is evidence that Tasmanian Aboriginal people further 'widened their coastal economy to focus increasingly on the hinterland ... incorporated exotic raw materials into their stone tool kit, commenced rock art at Mount Cameron West ... opened up inland areas by firing the landscape, and moving on to offshore islands'. Some technology and cultural practices, however, remained consistent over 20 000 years. For example 'Darwin glass' (black silica used in knives and scrapers) from a deposit near Macquarie Harbour was already in use 20 000 years ago, as was red ochre.[1]

By the time the British arrived, climate change and land management had ensured that Tasmania was an extraordinarily bountiful land for human beings. The nine different language groups 'harnessed the technology of fire to manage the land, encourage new growth for the wildlife, [and] keep open pathways that networked the island for ease of seasonal movement ...' The people 'collected from rich supplies of roots, fungi, lagoon leaks, yakka bread, seeds, orchid bulbs and plant shoots that were harvested throughout the seasons'.[2] While the environmental challenges were obviously much greater in the west because of the rugged terrain, the main pasturelands of the Midlands region (stretching between present-day Hobart and Launceston), created and sustained through regular burning, represented some of the richest hunting grounds in Australia. Without the presence of the dingo (which had arrived in mainland Australia after the land bridge had been closed) and with abundant water throughout, the Forester Kangaroo (or Eastern Grey), Red-necked (Bennett's) Wallaby, Tasmanian Pademelon (Rufus

Wallaby) and other herbivores existed in prodigious numbers. Coastal estuaries were rich in swans, ducks and other bird life. The (now extinct) Tasmanian Emu wandered far through the grassy woodlands. Vast populations of Short-tailed Shearwaters (mutton birds) and Australian Fur Seals provided rich seasonal food sources from accessible offshore islands. Along the coast were easily exploited quantities of shellfish, including abalone and oyster, and abundant crayfish.

I'm an Aboriginal woman from Tasmania. I come from a very strong line of Aboriginal men and women. I come from a time when my old women would get ochre, when my old uncles would dance, paint themselves and our community belonged to country. I come from a very special mob.
Darlene Mansell, Tasmanian Aboriginal

Given its plentiful food resources, readily available fresh water, sheltered waterways and accessible fuel supplies, it is hardly surprising that the island known to Europeans as 'Van Diemen's Land' since 1642 (when it had been briefly visited by an expedition from the Dutch East Indies commanded by Abel Tasman) became a favourite refuge for eighteenth-century Europeans wandering in the southern seas.

EUROPEAN VISITORS

From the 1770s, the people of the south and east coast of Tasmania had a succession of European visitors, including such legendary names in English history as James Cook and William Bligh. Adventure Bay on Bruny Island was a particularly popular sanctuary, appreciated not only for its harbour but also for its ready supplies of water, food and fuel.

Unknown whalers, particularly from America, were, however, the more regular callers. They could spend months at a time in safe harbours and estuaries, hunting migrating whales and restocking supplies. However, although no doubt comprising the numerical majority of visitors, little is known about their experiences in Van Diemen's Land during this time. By contrast, the British and French explorers wrote reports and journals, which contain sometimes detailed accounts of their meetings with Tasmanian Aboriginal people and observations of their way of life.

Two French expeditions spent the most time with, and had the greatest interest in, the Aboriginal people. The first, commanded by Bruny d'Entrecasteaux, visited Tasmania in 1792-93. D'Entrecasteaux's official instructions included that he was to 'seek to know the ways of life and customs of the natives [naturels]'.[3] The next French expedition, commanded by Nicolas Baudin, spent many weeks with the local people during 1802-03 and had an even stronger scientific and anthropological focus.

Although violence occasionally erupted while curiosity rather than conquest remained the European motive, relations were generally peaceful and often friendly. It is perhaps the human images that transcend culture and time—playing with children on the beach, cooking around a camp fire, sharing music, exchanging unfamiliar technology and food, laughing at misunderstandings and bumbled attempts at communication—that seem most poignant in the context of the invasion to come.

SEALERS

Some European visitors by the turn of the nineteenth century were staying permanently. Tasmania is made up of hundreds of islands, and many of them, especially in Bass Strait, had long been devoid of human occupation. The larger of these had dense populations of native animal species, which had no knowledge of predators (or how to escape them); others contained vast mutton bird rookeries; and scattered throughout were immense colonies of seals. The easy food, quick profit and good access (the sea was the British highway) in territory not occupied (and thus defended) by Aboriginal people ensured that the Bass Strait islands became the first site of European colonisation of Van Diemen's Land.

The women walked into the water in couples and swam to three rocks about fifty yards from shore, the women went through the same motions as the seals holding up their left elbow and scratching themselves with their left hand, taking and keeping the club firmly in their right ready for the attack ... all of a sudden the women rose up on their seats, each struck a seal on the nose and killed it.
Captain James Kelly

From 1798 seal skins from Bass Strait became the first major export from the British settlements of what is now called Australia. Men were left on the islands for months at a time to bludgeon the defenceless animals to death. Hundreds of thousands were slaughtered in a killing frenzy that made some large merchants of Sydney very wealthy but also ensured that most of the easily accessible seals were soon gone.

When the big capitalists left the industry, the little men stayed on, embracing a life of freedom and independence far from the surveillance, economic dependence and social subservience demanded by British civilisation. They killed the remaining seals, wallaby and wombat—selling skins and eating the flesh—and even had small gardens. Some were runaway convicts for whom the islands were a refuge from hell.

The men who were still called (somewhat misleadingly) 'sealers' traded with the Aboriginal people, especially those living in the northeast of mainland Tasmania. By about 1810 the sealers' economic and cultural ties extended to relations with Aboriginal women. Violence and probably the transmission of disease were never absent from these encounters, but in the early years self-preservation and self-interest mitigated brutality. As will be explored later, although savagery intensified as the conquest of mainland Tasmania accelerated during the 1820s, by the mid-1830s the stable island communities that would underpin the continuing resilience of Tasmanian Aboriginal culture were already evident.

'FIRST' SETTLEMENT

The officially sanctioned settlement of Tasmania began with the arrival of three invading parties during 1803–04, all of whom were meant to provide proof to the French (with whom Britain was engaged in an interminable war) that the British crown 'owned' Van Diemen's Land. Two of the new British settlements were at the estuary of the Derwent River in the south of the island, one on each side of the river, and the third at the mouth of Port Dalrymple in the north (which within a few years moved to the site of present-day Launceston). The British territorial claim was bizarre even to some Europeans, especially when it was recalled what the colonisers intended to do with the territory. Baudin, who witnessed the first of the ownership ceremonies (actually held on King Island during 1803), wrote to Governor King in Sydney:

> To my way of thinking, I have never been able to conceive that there was justice or even fairness on the part of Europeans in

seizing, in the name of their Governments, a land seen for the
first time ... it appears to me that it would be infinitely more
glorious for your nation, as for mine, to mould for society the
inhabitants of its own country over whom it has rights, rather
than wishing to occupy itself with the improvement of those
who are very far removed from it by beginning with seizing the
soil which belongs to them and which saw their birth ... [Had]
this principle been generally applied you would not have been
obliged to form a colony by means of men branded by the law
and made criminals by the fault of a government which has
neglected them and abandoned them to themselves. It follows
therefore that not only have you to reproach yourselves with
an injustice in having seized their lands, but also in having
transported on to a soil where the crimes and diseases of
Europeans were unknown, all that could retard the progress of
civilization ... I have no knowledge of the claims which the French
Government may have upon Van Diemen's Land, or its designs
for the future; but I think that its title will not be any better
founded than yours.[4]

There is no eyewitness British account of the first post-
invasion contact with Tasmanian Aboriginal people, but in 1831
the 'conciliator of the Aborigines', George Augustus Robinson,
recorded the recollections of Woorady, a Neuonne elder, concerning the British landing at what is now called Risdon Cove in
September 1803:

He saw the first ships come to Van Diemen's Land when they
settled at Hobart Town, called Niberlooner; that [the] natives
speared some white men who landed in a boat, one man in the
thigh; that white men went after the natives, the natives see them

come but did not run away, saw their guns and said white men
carry wood; that by and by white men shoot two blacks dead,
when they all became frightened and run away.[5]

The subsequent behaviour of the unruly, mutinous, often
drunk veterans of the New South Wales Corps occupying Risdon
Cove supports the likelihood of an aggressive landing party. On
3 May 1804 these men opened fire with muskets and a carronade
on a very large group of Aboriginal people, including women
and children. Three bodies were collected by the British once
the three hours of shooting had finally stopped (some of these
became the first body parts exported from the colony in the name
of science), and one infant was left behind, but it is not known
how many Aboriginal people died in all. One witness, the convict
Edward White, later recalled that 'a great many of the Aboriginal
people [were] slaughtered or wounded. I don't know how many.'[6]
It is not surprising that the Risdon massacre resulted in a break-
down in relations with the Paredarerme or Oyster Bay people,
which was a major reason for the British evacuating Risdon Cove
shortly after.

The commander of the Marines occupying the western shore
of the Derwent was David Collins, who had been a senior officer
in Sydney and knew from his experience there how important it
was to minimise conflict. Collins was fortunate that the Derwent
was a tribal boundary and he was therefore able to maintain
better relations with the South-east or Neuonne people whose
territory he lived on. Self-interest was a powerful motivator for
avoiding provocation. The British lacked the military power
to secure territory much beyond their established beachhead,
yet were soon almost entirely dependent on the rich Aboriginal
hunting grounds for food and clothing. The British Government,

consumed by fighting Napoleon in Europe, never sent supplies, and Sydney was scarcely more forthcoming. The result was that many of the approximately 300 convicts resident in the 'camp' (as it was colloquially called until the 1820s) were let free to hunt in order to feed the settlement, or simply wandered away to live semi-nomadic lives far from surveillance. The result was that by 1810 Britons lived from Hobart to Launceston in country that still remained Aboriginal territory. While conflict was never absent, the vulnerability of sole convicts meant that violence was comparatively limited at this time; blankets, flour, sugar and, above all, hunting dogs being exchanged for land access. Kangaroo dogs (a cross between traditional British hunting breeds and the greyhound) proved very effective hunters in open country against animals that had never known the dingo. These dogs were quickly adopted by Aboriginal people and, for white and black hunters alike, proved more effective than guns or spears in killing large game. During this time cross-cultural influence was also evident in other changes to both Aboriginal and frontier British culture.[7]

THE TASMANIAN WAR

From the early 1820s a new type of British settler moved into Aboriginal hunting grounds. Free settler land grantees were granted British title over the best pasturelands in proportion to the wealth they already possessed (the wealthier you were, the larger the handout). This country was ideally suited to sheep and, as wool exports began to boom, little investment was needed to make a quick fortune utilising the 'free' grasslands and assigned convict labour. For several hundred self-proclaimed gentry and land speculators, the only barriers to rapid economic and social 'advancement' were the itinerant whites (bushrangers and stock

thieves) and the Aboriginal people. A reformed and increasingly savage penal system brought the former largely under
control by the late 1820s, but the Aboriginal people proved a
more formidable foe, and fighting escalating from about 1824.
Responsibility for the expanded conflict was initially slated to
Musquito, a New South Wales resistance leader transported
to Van Diemen's Land (via Norfolk Island), but the defence of
the homelands only increased after he was captured and executed
in 1825.

The height of the well-documented 'war' (the word used
by the colonial government at the time) was between 1828 and
1831. Aboriginal advantages in the conflict were many and well
documented. In an era when guns were of limited accuracy, and
in an environment where horses were of limited utility, the main
hunting grounds and sheep country of the Midlands (which were
fringed by hills and thick scrub) proved difficult to monopolise.
In his journal Robinson summarised some of the other factors
favouring the Aboriginal people:

> The natives have the advantage in every respect, in their sight,
> hearing, nay, in all their senses, their sense of smell also ... They
> are at home in the woods, the whole country with few exceptions
> affords them concealment ... They can perceive the smallest
> trace, much less the plain footmarks of white men. They can
> trace small animals. They can also do with small fires, the smoke
> of which is scarcely perceptible ... They can subsist on roots and
> small animals and they know the passes and are well acquainted
> with the topography of the country. They will travel over the
> rocky ground where no traces are to be seen ... Their mode of
> attack is by surreptition. They lay in ambush for some time before
> they make their attack.[8]

The success with which the Aboriginal people fought for their country is reflected in the casualty figures: 187 whites are confirmed to have been killed and 211 wounded between 1824 and 1831 alone. After fire was employed against crops and property, the general view was the country districts would have to be abandoned if the 'hostile Aborigines' could not be killed or captured. In March 1828 east coast settlers sent the Lieutenant Governor 'a statement of the danger ... of being ultimately exterminated by the black natives' because of the 'new system which these people are adopting, namely, burning our stacks [the year's harvest] as well as our houses and making their attacks in the night'. A settler of the Clyde, John Sherwin, testi-fied in 1830 that men had called out, 'Parrawa parrawa—Go away, you white b—g—rs. What business have you here?' as they burned his property. Sherwin warned that if 'something is not speedily done, no one can live in the bush'.[9]

However, what such settler hysteria can obscure is how few Aboriginal people survived in what were termed by the British the 'settled districts' (the open grassy country suitable for sheep) by the time the final guerrilla war broke out and the colonial government had taken to detailed recordkeeping. Although large groups of Tasmanian Aboriginal people were still being seen in these regions in the mid-1820s, when the fighting stopped in the New Year of 1832 the combined population of the Lairmairrener or Big River people and Paredarerme or Oyster Bay people (the most feared British enemies) numbered only twenty-six in all. Some people lived on the Bass Strait islands, and there were a few refugees in other areas, but the disputed question remains: what happened to the others?

The suggestion that disease killed the large majority of the people in this short period is difficult to sustain. Although disease must have had a large impact over time (it is possible that many deaths occurred before official settlement had even commenced), the fact that there is not one documented observation of an Aboriginal person being afflicted by disease (outside confinement) during the 1820s, and that Robinson generally reported their health to be good, means that it cannot account for the speed of the people's demise. The more probable explanation is that the majority of the population were massacred, as some nineteenth-century historians (who drew heavily on oral testimony) believed. In recent decades Henry Reynolds and other historians have questioned, on the basis of evidence that largely pertains to the final phase of the fighting, whether the British were capable of doing such damage. However, while it was difficult to track down small mobile bands of guerrilla fighters, this was not true of clan groups still living a traditional life. By the mid-1820s white bushmen knew Aboriginal pathways and seasonal movements, and when large numbers of these men were conscripted to pursue communities that still included children, the elderly and the disabled, they could have a quick and devastating impact. What has been accepted by all historians (other than Keith Windschuttle) since 1834 is that most Aboriginal casualties were never recorded and that violence played a significant role in the rapid collapse of the Aboriginal population.

Although much of the fighting remained 'private', the final phase of the Tasmanian War is noticeable for its official nature. The declaration of martial law on 1 November 1828 in the vaguely defined settled districts legalised the killing of Aboriginal people. The declaration followed the Executive Council decision that 'the outrages of the Aboriginal natives amount to a complete declaration of hostilities against the settlers generally' and that 'to inspire them with terror ... will be found the only effectual means of security for the future'.[10] One instrument of terror was the government-sponsored roving parties. One of these was led by John Batman, the (later) 'founder of Melbourne', who described the 'success' of his roving party during the spring of 1829:

> In pursuit of the Aborigines who have been committing so many
> outrages in this district ... we saw some smoke at a distance.
> I immediately ordered the men to lay down; we could hear the
> natives conversing distinctly, we then crept into a thick scrub
> and remained there until after sunset ... and made towards them
> with the greatest caution. At about eleven o'clock p.m. we arrived
> within twenty-one paces of them the men were drawn up on the
> right by my orders intending to rush upon them, before they
> could arise from the ground, hoping that I should not be under
> the necessity of firing at them, but unfortunately as the last man
> was coming up, he struck his musket against that of another
> party, which immediately alarmed the dogs (in number about
> forty), they came directly at us the natives arose from the ground,
> and were in the act of running away into a thick scrub, when I
> ordered the men to fire upon them, which was done, and a rush by
> the party immediately followed, we only captured that night one
> woman and a male child about two years old ... next morning we
> found one man very badly wounded in the ankle and knee, shortly
> after we found another ten buckshot had entered his body, he was
> alive but very bad, there were a great number of traces of blood in
> various directions and learnt from those we took that ten men
> were wounded in the body which they gave us to understand were
> dead or would die, and two women in the same state had crawled
> away, besides a number that was shot in the legs ... We shot
> twenty-one dogs and obtained a great number of spears, waddies,

blankets, rugs, knives, a tomahawk, a shingle wrench etc etc. on Friday morning we left the place for my farm with the two men, woman and child, but found it impossible that the two former could walk, and after trying them by every means in my power, for some time, found I could not get them on I was obliged to shoot them.[11]

In both government and private military parties, current and former convicts, seeking indulgences and rewards, were the most effective British force. To encourage their efforts, from February 1830 a reward was paid for the capture of Aboriginal people, whether or not they had been involved in hostilities (and regardless of how many were killed or wounded during the operation). Nevertheless as resistance was sustained, settlers and the press agitated for even stronger action and, in August 1830, the Colonial Government resolved that it was necessary to bring to 'decisive issue a state of warfare which there seems no hope of ending by any other means'.[12] The new plan was to drive the Aboriginal people into captivity on the Tasman Peninsula through enlisting all available convicts and settlers to form a continuous line, or more accurately lines, of men crossing the island and pushing all before them. The justification for and operation of the six-week military campaign was described by a senior government official, GTWB Boyes, on 31 October 1830:

> Our papers were filled weekly with the atrocities of the Blacks and it has become apparent that unless means were devised for making them prisoner body in some well adapted part of this country, or, otherwise exterminating the race, that the country must be abandoned ... we have all been obliged to contribute in some way or another. The Lt Governor has taken the field with almost all the military—the Ticket of Leave men, Constables and as many assigned servants as could be spared, have been

marshalled, equipped for the field, and distributed like soldiers along the line, or formed into parties scouring the bush. Many of the young men, Clerks in public offices, have put the knapsack upon their backs, rations in their pouches and guns upon their shoulders and have marched in charge of ten or twelve men, each to the destined scene of action.[13]

The 'Black Line' proved to be an expensive failure, but this again largely reflected how successful the relentless pursuit of Tasmanian Aboriginal people had already been. There were, in the much-contested 'settled districts' at least, few Tasmanian Aboriginal people left to be captured.

CONCILIATION AND CLEARANCES

From 1830 to 1835 a government emissary, George Augustus Robinson, sought to negotiate an end to the fighting. Much confusion about the nature of Robinson's embassy, and particularly whether the Tasmanian Aboriginal people agreed to a settlement or treaty with the British, is due to the fact that the conciliation work changed so dramatically over time. Three main phases can be identified.[14]

The first mission was a nine-month journey of geographical and cultural discovery through the west coast in which the Aboriginal people travelling with Robinson arranged many friendly meetings with the local people. One influential member of Robinson's party was the young Nueonne woman Truganini, who in her short life (she was probably then about eighteen) had already experienced her mother being killed by sailors, her uncle shot by a soldier, her sister abducted by sealers and her fiancé murdered by timber getters.[15] It is not surprising that Truganini and other members of the conciliation expedition experienced with the reality of the British conquest, including her husband, Woorady, and Kickerterpoller (known to the British as Black Tom or Tom Birch) believed that there was no option remaining but to negotiate with the invaders. As Truganini later reflected: 'I knew it was no use my people trying to kill all the white people now, there were so many of them always coming in by boats.' She believed that the only option was to work with Robinson to try to 'save all my people that were left'.[16]

> Truganini in particular first realised that you could not beat the white man. That the people living out in the bush might only have seen small groups of white men. Truganini lived on Bruny Island, she had visited Hobart, she knew that there were far too many white people, that they were constantly arriving, and that to fight them was futile.
>
> *Professor Henry Reynolds, historian*

However, equally understandably, it proved to be the case that none of the west coast people wanted to be removed from their comparatively safe homeland. If it was not for the fact that the friendly relations developed at this time with the west coast people were to be critical to Robinson's betrayal of them three years later, the 1830 mission would have had no political impact. It was not until Robinson reached the northeast late in that year that he had his first 'success', and the second phase of the mission, in which a negotiated settlement was reached with the people of the settled districts, commenced.

In November 1830 an Aboriginal group agreed to Robinson's offer to give them a few weeks' protection on Swan Island, where they would also be able to obtain a good supply of a much-appreciated seasonal food source, mutton bird eggs. This group was led by Mannalargenna, an elder of the Oyster

Bay people who had more than twenty years' personal experience
in negotiating with and fighting the British and had become an
influential leader of the resistance. Mannalargenna understood
Robinson's status as an emissary and advised that he 'wanted to
go to Hobart Town' to meet Lieutenant Governor Arthur.[17]
However, Robinson instead kept Mannalargenna and his people
in secure detention while he went to the capital alone in early
1831 in order to put, without risk of contradiction, the absurd
claim that the 'natives generally would not object to be removed
to an island in Basses Strait' and would not 'feel themselves
imprisoned ... or pine away in consequence of the restraint, nor
... wish to return to the mainland or regret their inability to hunt
or roam about in the manner they had previously'.[18]

However, on leaving the capital and returning to the bush,
Robinson failed to meet up with any further Aboriginal people. In
August 1831 the humbled emissary was forced to resume direct
negotiations with Mannalargenna, who now agreed to join the mission on explicit terms that were spelt out in Robinson's journal:

> This morning I developed my plans to the Chief Mannalargenna
> and explained to him the benevolent views of the government
> towards himself and people ... I informed him in the presence
> of Kickerterpoller that I was commissioned by the governor to
> inform them that if the natives would desist from their wonted
> outrages upon the whites, they would be allowed to remain in
> their respective districts and would have flour, tea and sugar,
> clothes &c given them; that a good white man would dwell
> with them who would take care of them and would not allow
> any bad white man to shoot them, and he would go with them
> about the bush like myself and they then could hunt. He was
> much delighted.[19]

Robinson was elated at having secured Mannalargenna's co-operation as his 'influence amongst his people was great. He was universally admitted by all the native tribes who knew him as being the most able and successful warrior of all the Aboriginal people. Thus in him my hopes centred, in full antici-pation of a favourable issue to my endeavours.'[20]

Mannalargenna had again insisted on personally meeting Lieutenant Governor Arthur, and the delayed meeting finally took place in Launceston during October 1831 (after which Arthur could have been under no illusion regarding the basis on which Mannalargenna's cooperation had been achieved). It was soon after this, in the New Year of 1832, that a meeting with the only group still actively fighting the British was arranged near Lake Echo in the Central Highlands. These people, the remaining members of the Oyster Bay and Big River people, agreed to the terms put to them, and subsequently walked into Hobart Town to meet Lieutenant Governor Arthur, before setting sail for Bass Strait for what they undoubtedly believed to be a short sojourn only. The essence of the agreement with the colonial government—that the Aboriginal people would temporarily leave their homeland until peace had been restored and they could return protected and provided for—was never upheld. Instead, buoyed by 'success', and despite the fact that all fighting had virtually ceased, Arthur resolved to capture and remove every remaining Aboriginal person living on the Tasmanian mainland.

Colonial government policy had always been (and, as far as it was written down or communicated to London, always remained) to remove only 'hostile Aborigines' from the 'settled districts', but in January 1832, the government engaged Robinson on a new contract that would see him receive a large financial bonus if he removed all the Aboriginal people. Still hoping that their agreement might be honoured once this had been done, and with their bargaining options reduced by the almost complete cessation of fighting, Mannalargenna, Truganini and other Aboriginal people travelling with Robinson continued to co-operate intermittently as the mission moved into the northwest of the island. However, almost all the people removed in this third phase of the work (about two-thirds of the total) resulted from either Robinson's personal deceit or his arming of convict assistants. The Aboriginal people removed in 1832 and 1833 were captives who never agreed to a peace settlement, honoured or otherwise.

Self-defence is the first law of nature. The Government must remove the natives. If not they will be hunted down like wild beasts and destroyed.
Colonial Times, *1830*

During 1832 Robinson focused on the northwest, the area that, according to British title, largely belonged to the Van Diemen's Land Company. This region operated almost as an autonomous colony, with little government oversight or scrutiny. In the late 1820s the company's men had been responsible for some of the worst documented crimes of the war, including the infamous Cape Grim Massacre. The result had been that by the time Robinson's embassy revisited the region in 1832 the much-reduced population of Aboriginal people had retreated into remote country. After a large number of people were lured back to their lost hunting grounds with the promise of protection, Robinson (without informing his Aboriginal companions) tricked them into detention at Hunter Island, where many died, before forcefully removing them by a Royal Navy vessel to the more secure detention facility established in Bass Strait.

The next phase of the removals, conducted on the west coast during 1833, represents one of the least defensible crimes committed against an indigenous people anywhere in the British Empire during the nineteenth century. This was a region that had largely escaped the disruption of war: Aboriginal community life was still intact, and the people had a balanced demographic, including babies and young women (a marked contrast with the situation in the settled districts when Robinson undertook his work there). Robinson's journal entries also make it clear that no signs of disease were evident before the people were confined. Furthermore, during 1833 the small British presence in the region was being evacuated: the Macquarie Harbour Penal Station was in the process of being closed, and the Van Diemen's Land Company was removing its sheep and shepherds from almost all of the west coast, as this country had been found to be unsuitable for wool production. Thus, the west coast clearances were not motivated by competition for land or resources, and with the fighting having almost completely stopped, there was neither an economic nor a security justification for removing the people. Furthermore, even a pretence of negotiation was now abandoned. Armed convicts under Robinson's command brought the local people in by force before imprisoning them at the most notorious jail in the British Empire, Macquarie Harbour. The majority of the captives died at the penal station, some at Sarah Island and others at a rocky outcrop known as Grummet Island (where only the most hardened convicts were usually sent).[21]

The west coast clearances are deeply troubling not only because of the human horror they represented. While the benefits supposedly to be conferred on the Aboriginal people in the Bass Strait settlement—civilisation and Christianity—were talked about and no doubt believed, the government's policy was explicitly founded on the assumed desirability of Tasmania becoming 'native free'. This was no longer a 'war', private or public, but in its most literal sense 'ethnic cleansing'. It is this episode—rather than the well-documented fighting, which has been widely written about for more than 170 years—that is the real 'black hole' of Tasmanian history, never faced and still shrouded in denial.

The entire Aboriginal population are now removed.
George Robinson

Once the west coast people were removed, only a few Aboriginal people remained free. Most of these people, desperate to be reunited with family and community, agreed to be removed during 1835; some more may have been killed; and at least one family (which included William Lanne) stayed in the bush until 1842, when they too were taken to Flinders Island.

The British conquest of Aboriginal land was, however, by no means complete. As the west coast removals were being finalised and the last tracts of available sheep country were granted a private title, a group of land-hungry Van Diemonian land-owners, including John Batman, crossed Bass Strait to the Port Phillip district with shiploads of sheep. They were illegal squatters even under British law, yet their profitable invasion was eventually given retrospective sanction and the frontier experience of their battle-hardened former convict shepherds put to good use. From the mid-1830s the vast grasslands of western and northern Victoria effectively became the next terrible frontier in the Tasmanian wars.

The Betrayal

Darlene Mansell: The strategy was to remove Aboriginal people from the mainland, to smaller islands in what is called the Bass Strait. But their belief always was, that they could return to their country. But that didn't happen and that is one of the biggest lies in the history of Tasmania.

Aunty Phyllis Pitchford: They were stripped of their culture, they were stripped of their language, they were stripped of everything and the main of that happened at Wybalenna. They tried to teach them Christianity, trying to really push them into the white man's way of life and of course it wasn't going to work. They had their own beliefs, their own cultures, their own heritage and they wanted to maintain that but it was really traumatic, very traumatic for our people.

Darlene Mansell: At Wybalenna there's a big hill, and them old fellas would go and sit up on that hill, and they could see back, to the mainland, of Tasmania, and they were singing out to their old people, to the spirits of country, 'Take me home, take me back'. And it didn't happen. It just didn't happen.

WYBALENNA AND OYSTER COVE

In 1833 the Aboriginal settlement in Bass Strait was fixed at a Flinders Island site named Wybalenna (Black Men's Houses). While it is true that within their island confinement the couple of hundred residents had a greater level of freedom than was common in most Australian missions, Wybalenna is justly remembered as a prison where orchestrated attempts were made to destroy the people's culture and where the grief of exile killed body and spirit. Memories of the anguish and betrayal and the high numbers of deaths have survived to this day.

Most of the people removed to Flinders Island died from disease, and by 1835 the British openly anticipated that the others would soon similarly pass away. Nevertheless the government refused to return the people to the mainland, because of the threat they were still seen to pose to personal safety, prosperity and land prices. As Lieutenant Governor John Franklin informed Robinson (just before the latter left to become Chief Protector of Aborigines at Port Phillip) in December 1838: 'respectable settlers ... would not hear of it ... if the natives were brought [back]. Property would immediately fall in value very considerably.'[22]

Now those aboriginal women who were living there, they had children, generations of children, they were still living their cultural lifestyles, they were still speaking language, they were still dancing, doing ceremony, getting bush tucker, a thriving Aboriginal community. When Robinson took our people to Wybalenna there, they were forced to live the British way whitefella's way and it was harsh environment. It was a prison camp.

Darlene Mansell, Tasmanian Aboriginal

However, in 1847 the decision was finally made to close the settlement and transport the forty-seven survivors back to the mainland. The decision was made on the order of the Secretary of State for the Colonies in the context of the British Government's receipt of a petition to Queen Victoria from 'the free Aboriginal people Inhabitants of Van Diemen's Land now living upon Flinders Island'. While focused on grievances relating to a particular superintendent, they referred to 'an agreement' that 'Mr Robinson made for us and with Colonel Arthur ... which we have not lost from our minds since and we have made our part of it good'. As Reynolds has highlighted, while such matters carried little political weight in Van Diemen's Land, the situation was very different in London, where missionary societies concerned with native rights had considerable influence.[23] Moreover operating an Aboriginal settlement in such a remote location was expensive. Economy and prudence suggested it was time to close Wybalenna.

> The sad mortality which has happened among them since their removal is a cause for regret. But after all it is the will of Providence and better they die here where they are kindly treated than shot and inhumanely destroyed by the depraved section of the white community.
>
> *George Robinson*

The site chosen for the new Aboriginal settlement was a former convict probation station at Oyster Cove south of Hobart. Eight of the ten children were placed at the misleadingly named Orphan School in Hobart. This was neither a school nor just for orphans but was a large children's institution (part of the penal department) where convict and pauper children were moulded into labourers and domestics through a strict disc-iplinary regime.

Although some cultural practices were revived at Oyster Cove and two remarkable journeys were made (including a final six-week expedition to Port Davey in 1860), almost all the residents of Oyster Cove had died by the early 1860s. The two best known and longest living survivors were Truganini and Fanny Cochrane.

Mathinna
Professor Lyndall Ryan

Mathinna was probably born in 1834 on Flinders Island. Her father Towterer and mother Wongerneep had been captured at gunpoint by GA Robinson north of Port Davey on 20 May 1833. They were taken first to Macquarie Harbour, then transported to Flinders Island. Towterer was a chief of the Port Davey or Ninene tribe.

When they were captured Towterer and Wongerneep had a little boy, name unknown, who was sent to the Orphan School in Hobart where he died a few weeks later. Mathinna was probably born at Wybalenna late in 1834, but there is no record of her birth or her early life at Wybalenna.

The conditions at Flinders Island were traumatic—Towterer and his people were stripped of their customs and culture. Sickness was also rife. On the morning of 30 September 1837, Robinson recorded the following about Towterer, whom he had renamed King Romeo:

> I hastened to the spot and found a group of natives assembled and in their midst stretched on the ground was King Romeo and evidently in the last stage of affliction. He was dying. The hospital nurse was applying cold tea to his mouth. The doctor had been sent for and soon arrived. He said that it might be said the man died a victim of his own obstinacy. He thought it would be better to have him removed to his quarter, and I ordered four white men to the duty who conveyed him to the hospital on a shutter borne on their shoulders. He expired two hours after his removal. This afternoon some men were employed to dig a grave, and the carpenter and another man to make a coffin. (Quoted by NJB Plomley, *Weep in Silence: A History of the Flinders Island Aboriginal Settlement*, Blubber Head Press, Hobart, 1987, pp. 480–1)

On 1 October 1837 Robinson attended the post-mortem examination of Towterer.

> The spleen was twice the usual size, the lungs adhered to the chest on the right side so much so that in the opinion of

➤

the surgeon he could breathe very little on that side. Ulcers had formed in the intestines; this, surgeon thinks, was occasioned by his swallowing his spittle. They vomit a great deal of pus and when they swallow it is sure to act as a poison on the stomach. This, the doctor says, is generally the way consumption commences ... He attached himself to me when I first went to Port Davey. He has left a wife and infant child. (Plomley, *Weep in Silence*, p. 481)

Wongerneep, whom Robinson renamed Eveline, is also thought to have died around this time, although there is no record of her death. We think that at their deaths they were about thirty-seven years old.

Towterer's grave was later looted and his remains were sold to collectors, possibly in England or Europe.

In September 1837 Mathinna, now an orphan, was about three years old. Robinson introduced her to Sir John and Lady Franklin during their visit to Wybalenna on 26 January 1838. When Robinson left Wybalenna in January 1839 to become Chief Protector of the Aborigines in Port Phillip (now Victoria) the Van Diemen's Land government decided to send Aboriginal orphan children to the Orphan School in Hobart. The Franklins, however, were smitten with Mathinna because she was the daughter of an Aboriginal chief and decided to take her for themselves.

In February 1839 she was sent to Government House in Hobart. According to Plomley, she became 'a sort of pet in the household' until the Franklins left Tasmania in August 1843. During this period her portrait was painted by Thomas Bock. According to at least one Hobart newspaper, Mathinna was often seen in the Governor's carriage with his teenage daughter, Elinor. It is also believed that during this period she learned to read and write, and could recite English poetry.

When the Franklins left Tasmania in August 1843, Mathinna was sent to the Orphan School in New Town. In October 1847, then aged thirteen, she rejoined the remaining adult Aboriginal people who had been relocated from Wybalenna to Oyster Cove, opposite Bruny Island, about 30 kilometres southeast of Hobart. We know that she was invited with other Aboriginal people to Governor Denison's summer residence at New Norfolk over Christmas and New Year in 1848–49 and perhaps

➤

again over Christmas and New Year in 1849–50. It is also possible that she is represented in the drawing by Fanny Benbow of Aborigines at Oyster Cove, greeting Governor Denison and his family in 1848. At this time she was known as Armenia. She died from misadventure when drunk on 1 September 1852. She was aged eighteen.

Mathinna was probably buried in the Aboriginal cemetery at Oyster Cove, although as yet no record has been found. If so, her remains were dug up by Dr Crowther in about 1907 and removed to the Zoology Department at the University Melbourne, then placed in the Crowther Collection at the Tasmanian Museum and Art Gallery. Following a concerted campaign by the Tasmanian Aboriginal Centre, Aboriginal remains in the Crowther Collection were returned to the Aboriginal community in August 1984. The community returned the remains to Oyster Cove where, on 4 May 1985, in accordance with Aboriginal custom, a four-day cremation ceremony took place attended by 300 people, and the remains were cremated. Alma Stackhouse, chair of the Tasmanian Council of Aboriginal Organisations, said, 'The cremation ceremony has made the site more sacred.'

Oh father, bury me here. It's the deepest place. Promise me! Don't let them cut me, but bury me behind the mountains.
Truganini

Truganini, seen by many Europeans as the 'last' Tasmanian Aboriginal person, left Oyster Cove in the winter of 1874 when it was permanently closed, and spent the last two years of her life in Hobart Town. She was plagued by fears of her body being mutilated after her death, as had happened to William Lanne her friend. Despite the assurances she received, her fears proved well founded, her body being put on public display in the Tasmanian Museum until 1951. It was not until 1976, the centenary of her death, that the Tasmanian Aboriginal Centre succeeded in having Truganini's body cremated and scattered in the D'Entrecasteaux Channel near her home country of Bruny Island. Since then the Tasmanian Aboriginal community have been engaged in a long struggle for the return of the body parts of many other Aboriginal people held by museums around the world.

After Truganini's death only one former resident of the Oyster Bay station survived. Fanny Cochrane, born during the Flinders Island detention, had married a European named William Smith and was given a land grant in Nicholls Rivulet, inland from Oyster Bay, where she had eleven children and was prominent in the local community and Methodist Church. Many Tasmanian Aboriginal families today are descended from Fanny Cochrane Smith and another 'matriarch of survival', Dalrymple (Dolly) Briggs. Dalrymple, born about 1812, was the daughter of Woretemoeteyenner (whose father was Mannalargenna) and the sealer George Briggs, and raised her family in northern Tasmania.[24]

> By the 1860s there is a view that Tasmanian Aborigines might be the only primitive people on earth, and therefore there is an enormous trade in Aboriginal human remains that go to museums literally all over Europe. And to own an artefact from the most primitive people on earth becomes a trophy.
>
> *Professor Lyndall Ryan, historian*

THE ISLANDER COMMUNITY

As suggested earlier, the relations between the sealers and Aboriginal women changed over time. While negotiation was initially common, over time an increasing number of women were forcefully abducted and were effectively treated as slaves (slavery had yet to be outlawed in the British Empire, and the view that native people could become 'private property' remained widespread). Economic profit came from the women's ability to hunt, especially for seals and wallaby, but as the more easily killed animals were wiped out, Aboriginal women were also needed to survive long term on the islands.

During the 1820s, as the British conquest of mainland Tasmania intensified, Aboriginal women and children became highly vulnerable to forced abduction by marauding groups of former convicts. The women were removed to the Bass Strait islands and sometimes far beyond. Tasmanian Aboriginal people were taken to Kangaroo Island (where three contemporaries of Truganini were still living when she died), King George Sound and even New Zealand and Mauritius.[25] While renowned for their brutality, the sealers also offered comparative refuge and freedom for some women and children from the official and unofficial armed parties actively pursuing Aboriginal people after 1825. In the 1830s many women were to choose life with the sealers over the government-run Aboriginal settlement, although the possibility of 'losing' their women to the settlement (combined with the increasing dependence of the aging white men) seems to have dramatically improved the women's bargaining power and to have reduced abuse. Certainly by the late 1830s women were emerging as leaders of what were becoming stable, resilient and (in comparison with British society at least) matriarchal communities containing a large number of children and young people. The rapid change in the status of island women was particularly evident in the second generation.

Lucy Beedon, the daughter of Thomas Beedon and Emmerenna from Cape Portland, was the most prominent community leader for more than three decades until her death in

1886. Active in business and educating the children, Beedon was also an effective activist. The first campaign involved lobbying the government to provide a school teacher (Beedon suggested that the expense, like that of Oyster Cover, should be met from the revenue derived from the sale of Crown lands). School teachers were eventually placed at Badger and Cape Barren islands in 1871, although by then Beedon and the islander community were engaged in a more desperate struggle: the defence of their land. Facilitated by the 'Waste Lands' Acts of 1861 and 1870, Europeans were purchasing or leasing many of the islands occupied by the Aboriginal people and destroying mutton bird rookeries through over-harvesting and over-grazing. From 1867 the people conducted a sustained campaign, with the critical support of a few Church of England clergy (who articulated the ethical and historical obligations of the colonisers), to have some land and rookeries reserved for their use. However, the dispossession continued throughout the 1870s despite the fact that some rookeries were gazetted as game reserves. It is ironic that even as white Tasmania lamented the final 'extinction' of the Aboriginal people following Truganini's death in 1876, the last conquest of Aboriginal territory was proceeding almost without comment or concern. It was not until 1881 that the islanders, with the support of Canon Marcus Brownrigg, succeeded in having a part of Cape Barren Island reserved.[26]

The small Cape Barren Island reserve of 6000 acres became a critical community refuge that was central to Aboriginal identity and culture. It was also a site of perpetual struggle with white authorities. Although it was never a formal mission, during the nineteenth century the Church of England was heavily involved in the operation and management of the reserve. The Church saw it not as a means to preserve the way of life of what it termed 'half-castes' but a place where, as Bishop Bromby put it, the 'moral weakness caused by Aboriginal ancestry could be overcome' and the people could be made to 'relinquish the pursuit of mutton birds, properly attend to the soil and receive tuition in the sober virtues of respectable white society'.[27]

By the early twentieth century, residents of the reserve were boycotting the Church (which, anyway, now preferred to concentrate on the growing white population of Flinders Island), and the focus of the community's struggle shifted to the Tasmanian Government and the new Flinders Island Council. It is noteworthy that the Governor, the representative of the British Crown (with whom their ancestors had negotiated), remained the focus of petitions and advocacy. Land, cultural recognition, basic services and access to mutton bird rookeries were always insecure. This was a reflection in part of the reserve's ill-defined administrative status, which in turn reflected larger contradictions inherent in white society and government policy. On the one hand, the very existence of the reserve was a recognition of the survival of Aboriginal people; on the other hand, no Aboriginal people were deemed to exist. There were some major advantages to this contradiction—Tasmania was the only state without protection legislation—but people growing up in the islands during the twentieth century experienced the white community simultaneously denying their Aboriginality while purposefully discriminating against them.

The government's confusion about Aboriginality and the purpose and status of the Cape Barren Island Reserve resulted in a succession of inquiries and reports. In 1929 AW Burbury noted that the 250-resident population believed that the 1912 Act then governing the reserve had been passed 'in recognition of their claim that their country had been taken from them by the whites' (and, Burbury asked, 'if the Act was not the result of a recognition that these people were entitled to something, why was it passed?'). Burbury further observed that the people 'hate the whites, regarding themselves as having been supplanted and exploited by white men. They say that the whites took away their land and are now taking their kangaroos and mutton birds.'[28] The similarities with Aboriginal grievances documented exactly a hundred years before are obvious. In 1829 Robinson recorded that the Aboriginal people have 'a tradition amongst them that white men have usurped their territory ... killed their game and ... robbed them of their chief subsistence'.[29]

> Our community today is very saddened, or gets very upset with that global myth that Truganini was the last Tasmanian Aboriginal person, because generations have flowed from that time and will continue to flow. There will never, ever be no Tasmanian Aboriginal people. Never, ever.
>
> *Darlene Mansell, Tasmanian Aboriginal*

By the late 1930s the population of Cape Barren Island had increased to 300, and other Tasmanian Aboriginal people were spread through the Furneaux Group, coming together annually for birding. However, the population of the island fell after World War II when, in pursuit of assimilation, the Tasmanian Government revoked the reserve and endeavoured to force people to leave Cape Barren Island by running down health, education and other services. Many Aboriginal people did leave for mainland Tasmania, especially Launceston, in the 1950s and 1960s, but enough remained to keep the school open.

Community identity remained resilient through the challenges and hardships associated with assimilation, and in the 1970s Aboriginal people began to assert their claims in a public way. One aspect of this was the campaign for land rights, and in 1996 twelve sites were handed back by the State Government, including four mutton bird rookeries, Wybalenna, Oyster Cove and part of Cape Barren Island. A second round of land handbacks occurred in 2005.

The contemporary era has also seen a remarkable cultural renaissance in art, language and memory. This has included a reclaiming of the past. The debate in and outside orthodox history has been vigorous, but what is generally accepted is that traditional history provides only one way of understanding and learning. The study and interpretation of written records pertaining to Aboriginal–British relations is important, but perhaps everyone can be grateful that the constraints and pretensions of white history have not proved to be the final word.

Wurrbunj narrap
LAMENT FOR COUNTRY

3

HOW IT STARTS

Bruce Pascoe

White people just wanted the land. So did black people. They fought each other for it. The white people won. That's how history starts.

Someone wants what somebody else has, and they're prepared to murder to get it. The hands do the taking, but the hearts and minds have to justify acts that the Bible prohibits: killing and stealing.

To justify breaking your own religious laws requires your belief that the original owners didn't deserve possession of the soil, that they were beasts beyond God's love, that they had no intelligence and no attachment to the land.

Occupation of lands by violent invasion has an ancient history and was enabled by the development of weapons, but before the weapon came the desire to inflict harm on others. The decision to steal land was a later development and accelerated with the domestication of the horse and construction of sailing ships. Mobility allowed armies to take the land and lives of strangers.

Australia was no different. Or was it? The First Australians had all the same desires and abilities and could attack each other with efficient weapons, so why didn't they invade one another's territory to take possession of land, to become colonists like nations elsewhere in the world?

A man was almost in tears. He said, 'The white people have only left us a miserable spadeful of ground and now they want to take that away from us.'
Reverend Mackie

Is it too naïve to wonder whether the answer to that investigation may provide diplomatic tools for the modern world?

Long occupation of particular tracts of land is evidenced in the geographically specific vocabularies and the ancestral stories of geological events peculiar to that soil. The relatively small size of each nation and language is witness to the ambition to care for a particular region and no other. The negotiation of that decision across an entire continent required incredibly delicate and respectful diplomacy.

The violent European invasions of New South Wales and Tasmania were followed by an even more sophisticated war in Victoria. When hopes of driving the invaders from the soil had been dashed, the defeated black warriors retreated to camps and missions in order to protect the remnants of their people. The war and various introduced diseases reduced the Victorian population, estimated at 30 000 to 70 000 in 1836, to such a degree that by 1863 only 250 remained of the Kulin, whose nations had once surrounded Port Phillip and Western

> The place gets settled with extraordinary speed and there's just nowhere for people to go, for Aboriginal people to hide, there's no water that they can get to, there's no place that they can hunt kangaroo, there's no place that they can establish the way of life that they had developed over so many years.
>
> *Professor Janet McCalman, historian*

Port bays. Other Victorian districts had been depopulated to a similar extent.

In life you meet many whose actions cause inadvertent collateral damage but very few who actively seek to inflict harm on others. Angus McMillan was one of the few. McMillan led one of the most vicious campaigns of wanton murder and destruction this violent country has ever seen. The true story of the Gippsland war has never been revealed in its entirety, but the available records and the veiled references in other sources suggest a massive loss of Ganai lives. McMillan's calculated burial of the evidence of this war, quite often in a literal sense, indicates that the numbers known to have been killed by his Highland Brigade are a small portion of the probable total.

Some like to believe that a war never occurred on this land, but a dispassionate reading of the records of first contact is unequivocal. Spend some time reading the first-hand accounts of that period and note the deceptions employed by the squatters and colonial authorities to hide this silent war from an English parliament that had expressly ordered the colonists to ameliorate the condition of those they were dispossessing. The liberationists, who so passionately argued for the emancipation of Black America, hoped for some measure of colonial restraint in Australia without once considering that they should return stolen land.

It was a lot easier to embrace lofty sentiments in England than on the field in Australia where Aboriginal and Torres Strait Islander people were resisting the occupation. Obsessed with land and riches, the colonists pretended to believe that Indigenous Australians would welcome the light of British government and religion and that it was their moral duty to impose it. This shabby justification is mocked by the craven attitudes expressed in letters the colonists sent each other. They could fool London that civilisation was being exported to Australia, but they couldn't pull the wool over each other's pragmatic eyes.

The victor believed the defeated were inferior humans so, once the men with guns had left the victorious field, bureaucrats arrived with the same belief of superiority. How was that superiority manifested? Technology? Civilisation? Spirituality? Perhaps it was impossible for the colonists to consider those questions without invalidating their possession of the land.

A SPADEFUL OF GROUND

Once the war for possession of the soil had been lost, the Kulin nation experienced a period of intense privation as the survivors were deprived of access to watercourses and the usual sources of their sustenance. The yam daisy, as important to the Kulin as potatoes to the Irish, was almost completely eradicated by sheep and cattle in the first year of exposure. In war hunger is an important tool.

By war's end the Kulin nations were devastated and resorted to dwelling on the fringes of pastoral stations, where they could acquire work and food or, after the intercession of missionary groups like the Moravians and Wesleyans, on the mission stations.

> It's a double-edged sword because we lost so much. The churches
> convert our people to Christianity, which denied our lot the
> opportunity to carry on with our spirituality and our self-being, and
> that's something that affects me pretty deeply.
>
> *Jim Berg, Founder, Koori Heritage Trust, Gunditjamara Nation*

Many of these missions failed within years of their establishment, but some, like Cummeroogunga, Framlingham and Lake Tyers, still survive more than a hundred years later.

Victoria, burgeoning on proceeds of wheat, wool and gold, began at last to consider what it saw as the 'Aboriginal problem'. This was an era when Darwin's theory of the origin of species had gripped the European mind and convinced some that the Indigenous Australians were an inferior race on the way to evolutionary disappearance. It was a convenient explanation for the more venal minds intent on land acquisition.

All thought they were 'smoothing the pillow of a dying race' and that the measures soon to be introduced for 'Protection' would be short-term, inexpensive panaceas.

William Thomas was a different kind of colonist. He had the usual human failings, including a kind of squeamish bigotry, but most of his thoughts were for the welfare of others. Thomas was an English teacher in the Public Service and a fervent Wesleyan Christian. He was recruited to the Victorian Aboriginal Protectorate in 1839 and worked on behalf of Aboriginal people for the rest of his life.

The Protectorate system was created to bring Aboriginal people into centralised missions in return for rations, when the ideal of liberal egalitarianism was competing against conservative cynicism. Some thought a plan to provide for Indigenous health and education could best be carried out on missions under the benevolent gaze of Christian ministers, while the less generous and more pragmatic favoured the scheme as a way to clear the land of Indigenous people and eliminate any impediment to colonial expansion. The Protectorate system was ground down by the antipathy of local landowners and parliament. After the system collapsed, William Thomas was retained to act on behalf of the Kulin people.

William Thomas courageously maintained his defence of the Kulin even at the risk of his own reputation and income. He was a good Christian, but even he thought of the people as unenlightened savages. He learnt a great deal about the Kulin languages and culture, but his Christianity frustrated his understanding of the Kulin.

The entire population that now knows itself to be Aboriginal Victoria is descended from just that 300 or so people who were put on the reserves.
Professor Janet McCalman, historian

He never understood the intricacies of the moiety system, which divided the world between Crow and Eagle and controlled social, spiritual and cultural life. This ignorance of the Kulin rules of behaviour meant he often intervened clumsily in the processes of marriage, conflict resolution and mourning. Many of the cultural forms of the people disgusted Thomas and, while admiring the intelligence and general goodness of the Kulin, he gradually came to despair for their future and wondered at their reluctance to embrace European civilisation.

Charles Never

Murrumwiller was his original name and, like others, he adopted an English name, Charles Never, to operate in the new world. A pupil of the Reverend Edgar, a Baptist missionary, he had aspirations to be more than a labourer. He evolved a plan. If he were to join white society, Charles was determined to join its upper ranks, not the lower ranks as imagined by European humanitarians. Charles knew where power and status lie. 'I like to be a gentleman. Black gentleman as good as white,' Charles said.

To make his way in the world, Charles Never apprenticed himself to a tailor in downtown Melbourne, to gain indoor employment and learn to sew, so he could make his gentleman's clothes. But he refused to call the tailor 'master' like most apprentices should, and it was a short-lived arrangement. Now that he could make his own clothes, he wore only black clothing; black coat and trousers, tall black hat, black waistcoat, starched collar, black satin stock, black kid gloves, elegant cane and highly polished boots. Impressed by the Native Police uniform, he became their tailor.

Although it was hoped that the First Australians should behave like whites, when they sought to enter the higher ranks of society, and do it in style, they were laughed at, as Charles was. This did not deter his sense of the justice due to him according to his position as an Aboriginal Victorian.

> I mean to write to the Queen and ask her to give me a piece of land … to build a house on; and I mean to ask her for 400 pounds … to build my house. You say one time the Queen a good woman. And yet she send white man out here, take black fellas' land, and drive them away, and shoot them, and build planty [*sic*] house and garden on my land; and when I say, I ask her to give me back a piece of my land and money to build a house, you say she think I not know better. I know better. This land, my land first of all. Four hundred pounds not much to the Queen, and she take plenty land from me. (Charles Never)

Thomas' mood became jaundiced after the death of his friend the senior Kulin leader Billibellary. The two men were close, and much of what Thomas learnt about the Kulin was passed on to him by this man, who possessed enormous intellectual and diplomatic gifts and of whom he wrote: 'It may be said of this Chief and his tribe what can scarce be said of any tribe of located parts of the colony that they have never shed white man's blood nor have white men shed their blood. I have lost in this man a valuable councilor in Aboriginal Affairs.'[2]

Thomas' belief that no Kulin were killed by whites is not supported by the evidence, but it is obvious how highly he thought of Billibellary.

KULIN DIPLOMACY

When they had been defeated so crushingly by war, disease and dispossession, members of the Kulin nations sought to retrieve some tiny parcels of land as token reparation. Billibellary, the ngurungaeta or clan head of the Wurundjeri, and Derrimut, clan head of the Bunurong, chose negotiation over war; Derrimut even warned the Europeans of an imminent attack on the fragile early settlement of Melbourne. These men were conciliators and rationalists, and they employed diplomatic skills that had served so well in the past. While their countrymen fought a fierce resistance and died in the process, they pursued conciliation for more than half a fruitless century.

Billibellary, in particular, was an unusual man. In any civilisation he would have been a statesman and, as a ngurungaeta, was seen as a senior political figure by the Wurundjeri. His authority meant that he controlled the greenstone mine at Mount William from which stone axe blanks were quarried, a position of immense power owing to the importance of the axe in Kulin culture.

When Europeans arrived Billibellary's first instinct was conciliation. When John Batman sailed from Tasmania to acquire land he showed some sensitivity to Aboriginal custom and constructed his treaty negotiations for land acquisition in a way that resembled the Kulin tanderrum, a formal agreement that allowed visitors temporary access to Kulin lands and food resources. The crucial essence of this agreement was that the host must not suffer from the presence of the guest.

Batman, however, gloated on his return to Tasmania that his 'treaty' elevated him to the biggest landowner in the world. Batman prepared the document in advance of meeting the Kulin and sought to defraud the people by confusing his 'title' document with tanderrum. Alistair Campbell in his book *John Batman and the Aborigines* produces evidence that contests the validity of the document and Batman's motivation for producing it.[3]

Billibellary watched Batman carefully. He was a signatory to Batman's document, but some of the other signatories were less friendly to the Europeans after so many promises of reparation had been broken, and it became obvious that Batman had no intention of honouring the agreement. After the initial weeks of harmony in 1836 Kulin warriors began to avenge attacks on their camps, but Billibellary persisted in negotiations with the invaders.

Billibellary was a grave and courteous man, but his methods achieved little more success than those of his more warlike brothers. He may have lived for longer and educated some of his children, but he still lost his land. A Native Police force was established to help bring order to the colony, but order meant the quelling of Aboriginal resistance. Some praise this force as a civilising influence, but the official documents that commend the humanity of the scheme are overwhelmed by more pragmatic and craven connivance. Secrecy and deception were colonial tools used in India, China and Africa, always with horrible results and always to shield colonists from charges of murder and war.

Well in the Western District of Victoria they [Native Police] were used to hunt down our people. Tracking down the so-called renegades or, as we call them, our heroes, who were defending our home lands, depending on which side you're on. Depending on who writes the history and it's never the victims. It's always the victor. So the Native Police were an effective weapon. Kooris can read tracks and if you were using one of your own to hunt your own, you couldn't get a better weapon than that; trained hunters. Give them a rifle and a horse and a sword, that's a pretty good force. Bloodthirsty force.
Jim Berg, Founder, Koori Heritage Trust, Gunditjamara Nation

Billibellary was, at first, keen to join the Native Police as a way of maintaining some protection for his people, but as soon as he realised the real purpose of the corps he worked toward its disintegration. The captains of the force, like almost every other European, had no conception of the moiety responsibilities of Aboriginal people, which stretched their family obligations over a massive area. They refused to punish their kin for resistance to the invasion. As William Thomas wrote, 'When Billibellary learned that the police were employed to kill and capture other blacks he did all he could to break up the corps—one after another deserted, it was only kept up by recruiting or kidnapping from other tribes.'[4]

Thomas witnessed the readiness with which the Kulin adopted Christianity but perhaps didn't understand that it was a cultural refuge following the destruction of their spiritual life. Many Aboriginal and Torres Strait Islander people recognised in the Christian story elements of their own faith: a supreme being who dwelt in the heavens, the spirit life following death, and Jesus' words to protect the weak and needy. Thomas had the same mote in his eye as most Europeans in their relationship with Aboriginal people: he thought their culture disgusting and so inferior to his own that Aborigines could not expect salvation until they embraced the church and rejected their own culture.

The senior Kulin men and women did try to intercede through diplomacy in the destruction of their world. Much of what we know about the Kulin government and the intellectual and diplomatic skills of the ngurungaeta is explained in the work of Thomas, Green and others like George Augustus Robinson, the Chief Protector of Aborigines, and the ethnographer William Howitt. However, the contemporary understanding of the cultural roles is probably skewed because colonial historians were all men with little access to the intellectual and political roles of Indigenous women.

Margaret Gardiner and Joy Murphy, who are both senior Wurundjeri women in their community today, extol the virtues and dignity of the senior men of this period but also recognise the less well-known women like Louisa Briggs and Jessie Dunolly. Through Margaret and Joy the tradition continues. As Joy Murphy says, 'The ngurungaeta is a head man and usually selected by an elder who is passing on ... they are usually given that title because they have the knowledge and are seen to have the wisdom to be a leader of their people. They also take on the responsibility for the entire community and are very brave and become a spokesperson for their community.'[5]

Some of the traditional ngurungaeta were so highly regarded that they had influence beyond their own clans. In the aftermath of the war and their subsequent destitution, Billibellary, close to death, appealed to Thomas about the condition of the Wurundjeri and how the Europeans were hounding them from the fringe camps around Melbourne. Benbow, leader of the Bunurong, another of the Kulin clans, also urged Thomas to help them find 'a country to locate themselves upon'.[6] Derrimut, another signatory to Batman's document, who had saved the colony from imminent attacks by Wathaurong warriors, was rewarded with broken faith. In desperation he berated Thomas, urging him to retain their Bunurong reserve at Mordialloc. 'You have all this place, no good have children,' he said, then asked Thomas why he had 'let white man take away Mordialloc where black fellows always sit down'.[7]

We should be free like the white population. There is only a few blacks left now remaining in Victoria. We are all dying away, and we blacks of Aboriginal blood wish to have our freedom for all our lifetime. There is only twenty-seven Aborigines on the station Coranderrk, including men and women.
William Barak

His descendant Caroline Briggs recalls his appeal to a magistrate: 'Why me have wife? Why me have children? You have all this place, no good have children, no good have wife, me tumble down and die very soon now.'[8] 'That's the final betrayal, isn't it?' says Caroline Briggs. 'For a man that believed that they were going to walk together, but he had no more status any more.

They had been cheated.'9 In despair of his failure to protect the people as directed by his ancestors, Derrimut drank himself to death in the space of a few years.

None of the clan heads who signed the treaty saw any of their land returned in their lifetime. After Billibellary's death in 1859, his son Simon Wonga was appointed ngurungaeta of the Wurundjeri people. He and his brother Tommy Munnering led a deputation of Taungurung men from neighbouring Kulin clans to speak to Thomas urging him to help them intercede with the government in their search for land that they could farm. 'Marminarta [my friend], I bring my friends ... They want a block of land in their country where they may sit down, plant corn, potatoes—and work like white men.'10

Thomas approached the Surveyor General on their behalf and, as a consequence, the Central Board for the Protection of Aborigines agreed that they could select land. So far, so good— good men doing what their hearts and minds assure them is natural justice after years of neglect. But this brief flurry of honour and generosity from the government was subverted by greed and deceit.

Wonga, Munnering and the Taungurung selected a site at the junction of the Acheron and Little rivers in the Yarra Ranges in 1859 and, despite the age and sickness of most of the Taungurung and the Wurundjeri who joined them in their territory, they gradu- ally improved the land and began planting wheat and vegetables.

Then along came Stephen Jones, a largely incompetent farmer who sought permission to swap his failed station for the Kulin's Acheron reserve. Jones colluded with Snodgrass, a prominent pastoralist and politician, to persuade the government to shift the Kulin off Acheron and onto Jones' cold, bleak and unproductive Mohican Station.

The government wanted Acheron to be supervised by a group of trustees and, as one of these, Thomas chose Peter Snodgrass, whose father had been the acting Governor of New South Wales. Snodgrass, however, was implicated in a scheme used by some pastoralists to bribe officials responsible for land allocations.

Snodgrass and others worked tirelessly to undermine the good intentions of several parliamentarians keen to see the Kulin achieve a measure of justice. Part of the motivation of Snodgrass' group was outright greed, but at times it was a bloody-minded refusal to allow the Kulin land, especially land they had rendered productive by their labour. Perhaps Snodgrass was also avenging earlier attacks on his property by the Kulin resistance.

European prejudice eroded four years of intense physical and diplomatic work, and the Kulin had to watch in sorrow and diminishing faith as local graziers took possession of their pastures, sheds and houses.

GREENER PASTURES

After being forced off Acheron, the Kulin's hopes of claiming a tiny piece of their ancestral lands focused on a new reserve at Coranderrk.

Ultimately, the story of Coranderrk is of that fundamental failure to consider another's humanity. It has all the elements of any drama: pride, cruelty, honour, grace, religious tolerance, religious blindness, love, hatred, jealousy and generosity, good guys and bad guys. All the elements that make history. Read the original sources and wonder about your country. Don't despair, just wonder.

The lay Presbyterian minister John Green joined Wonga and his people at Acheron and then at Coranderrk, where he was appointed manager. He was probably even more benevolent than

Thomas and was greatly loved by the Wurundjeri, but, despite his good intentions, he looked on the Kulin as childlike and doomed to disappearance.

> Black fellow now throw away all war spears. No more fighting but live like white men, almost.
>
> *Simon Wonga, Head Man of the Wurundjeri*

Green worked beside the men in the field and had such high regard for their abilities and honesty that he included them in planning the new settlement and trusted them to such a degree that he left the stores unlocked for much of his time with them.

> My method of managing the blacks [he wrote] is to allow them to rule themselves as much as possible. When there is any strife among them this is always settled at a kind of court at which I preside. Had a long court today about Buckley, Locket, Dick, Davey and Andrew drinking a bottle of grog; and there was a law that everyone would be fined 5s; for the second offense 10s; for the third offense, if a young man he would forfeit all right to a wife from among the young women on the station—and for married men one pound. Agreed by all the Aborigines on the station, 110 in all.[11]

Mary Green had at least as much influence as her husband, but the period in which they lived hardly credited the work of intelligent women. Her tolerance and generosity were remark-able, and the Kulin had a high regard for her willingness to share their life and to allow her children to mix with theirs. John Green's initial success at Acheron was built on the humanity with which his wife embraced the people. If Mary Green could be a Christian, then so could they. Up to that point the reputation of Christianity had been advanced almost exclusively by people with sheep and guns.

The British Parliament, expressly commissioned by the Queen, had for years been warning the Victorian administration to protect Aborigines. While the colony was celebrating the marriage of the Prince of Wales in 1863, the Kulin, looking to the Queen's benevolence, decided to send gifts to the Prince in a deputation at the Governor's public reception. They were able to speak directly with the Governor, Sir Henry Barkly, who was said to be impressed by their claim.

The uniqueness of Coranderrk was still maintaining community and family and maintaining connection to their landscape. And it's a beautiful place.
Carolyn Briggs

The Kulin's decision to attend the Governor's levee was a final effort to bypass the Central Board for the Protection of Aborigines and directly influence the government. The Kulin's appeal to the Governor assumed that, as the Queen's representative, he would have the power to allow them a scrap of land. As Simon Wonga said, 'Blacks of the Tribes of Wawoorong [Woiwurrung], Boonorong [Bunurong] and Tara-Waragal [Taungurung] send this to the Great Mother Queen Victoria. We and other blackfellows send many thanks to the Great Mother Queen for many things. Black fellow now throw away all war spears. No more fighting but live like white men, almost. This is all.'[12]

The Dja Dja Wurrung of Mount Franklin Reserve sent gifts for the occasion, the Coranderrk residents sent rugs and baskets, and Ellen Richards crocheted a lace collar, which was specifically mentioned in the Queen's reply: 'The Queen trusts that ... she may be encouraged not only to seek her own improvement but to acquaint the other aboriginal inhabitants of their interest that their Queen, however distant from here, will always feel in their advancement and welfare.'[13]

The meeting with Sir Henry Barkly appeared to have been a great success because Coranderrk was formally gazetted in June of that year, and this encouraged the Kulin to believe that direct appeals to government would be more fruitful than reliance on the benevolence of the Protection Board.

The drawing depicting this meeting, however, pits European pomp mercilessly against Aboriginal poverty. The fur cloaks that protected the people from the cold and were tailored with such attention to luxury and style had long been sold or stolen and replaced by old blankets. Many European correspondents revelled in descriptions of the ragged penury of the Kulin's economic decline as proof of Indigenous inferiority.

The Coranderrk Reserve was established in 1863 during this mood of economic euphoria, racial superiority and residual Christian guilt. Green credited much of their success in gaining permission for the reserve to the gentle diplomacy of Simon Wonga.

The Kulin set to work on Coranderrk with amazing energy, and in four months had built nine huts and begun work on the pastures. 'Coranderrk' in the Woiwurrung language means the branches of the tree used to make drills used in the process of fire lighting, a crucial ability in the Victorian climate.[14]

Green worked beside the Wurundjeri in tireless determination to turn Coranderrk into a permanent place of comfort and refuge, but the people of Victoria, ambitious and restless with the riches of their booming economy, hardly gave the Kulin a moment's thought. Oh, they might wander up to Coranderrk for a Sunday outing to stare at the residents as if at animals in a zoo, but debate about the dispossession of the original owners hardly rated a paragraph in the newspapers unless to mock the dissolution and desperation of the remnant Kulin.

They formed this settlement at a place of their choice. And they were all young men, and I think idealists. They were all men that developed a vision together that Aboriginal people could have land of their own in this sea of European control.
Associate Professor Richard Broome, historian

In forty years of the Victorian Parliament Aboriginal people were rarely mentioned, and the Bills affecting them were often introduced in the last minutes of the last session, when members were hilarious with their evening beverages and the prospect of a holiday. The Aborigines Act of 1869 and its amendment in 1886, two of the most important Bills relating to Aboriginal people, were passed in this mood of irreverence with opposite sides of the house yelling salacious accusations about the parentage of Kulin children.

Most parliamentarians had never been to Coranderrk, never encountered any of the residents, but were keen to malign their morality. Even some members of the Central Board, charged with administration of the reserve, never visited. The secretary himself went rarely and, when he did, arrived late in the afternoon, never spoke to residents, and was gone shortly after. The country had turned its back on the Kulin nation.

Administration of schemes to benefit the Kulin were always funded with reluctant parsimony. Squatters designated to hand out food and clothing often pocketed the goods themselves, so the Central Board searched for someone in the field to monitor the church missions and government reserves. Thomas was too old, and the capable but overbearing Protection Board Secretary, Robert Brough Smyth, was too busy in his employment with the Mines Department, so more and more of this work fell to the responsibility of John Green, who was appointed Inspector of Reserves and Missions in place of Thomas, as well as his role in managing Coranderrk (for which he was never paid). The reserves and missions were scattered across Victoria, which meant Green was often away from Coranderrk.

> Since we began to settle and live in our own houses, we have improved much. We are now happy and glad to see so many children about us. Some are coming home. They are now tired of the bush. It is better to live here, than to go about and drink.
>
> *Simon Wonga, Head Man of the Wurundjeri*

Some European men were scandalised that he would leave his wife and children alone with black men, but both he and Mary had absolute trust in the Kulin, a trust that never wavered. Mary was so capable and trained the women so well that the work of Coranderrk proceeded harmoniously in a community of equals.

Mary Green was relaxed in her role, but John Green, burdened with the extra work and travel, became more harassed. Not least of his burdens was growing board resistance to the way he administered Coranderrk.

BOARD GAMES

Robert Brough Smyth had been a supporter of Green because he admired his energy and commitment, but the relationship soured when Green began criticising board policies and its interference with Kulin self-determination. As Smyth wrote, 'The Board is under no obligation to pay wages to the Aborigines ... they must be attentive and civil to all persons otherwise they will be sent away ... all persons sheltering or feeding the protestors will be removed as well as anyone using threatening or offensive language.'[15] Coranderrk was a prosperous station due to the enthusiasm of the Kulin, Green's collaborative administration and the quality of the land.

The Kulin demonstrated their ability to farm, as had the residents of the Lake Keilambete Reserve during their brief occupation under the administration of one of the Assistant Protectors of Aborigines, Charles Sievewright. Cummeroogunga Mission was also renowned for its produce, and Coranderrk won gold medals for its horticulture at the Melbourne Exhibition. Farming was not a mystery to Aboriginal and Torres Strait Islander people, but this was one of the necessary myths promulgated to sustain the argument that European occupation of the land was justified by the original occupants' failure to utilise it.

Grain cultivation, irrigation, harvesting and storage were important staples in the lives of Aborigines inside the Great Dividing Range, while in the more fertile coastal regions yam gardens were cultivated with intense care. Fish aquaculture and other types of food production added to the reliability and variety of food supplies. Terms like 'hunter gatherer' do not sufficiently describe Indigenous food production in Australia but are part of the prejudicial and politically loaded vocabulary of the invader.

Green's employment of the Kulin's established skills allowed the farm to develop with speed and success, and it paid a dividend every year, but the Protection Board intervened in search of even greater profits and insisted that Coranderrk concentrate on the production of the profitable crop of hops. Victoria was already beginning its love affair with beer.

The board's preference for hops cultivation affected the welfare of residents. Hops production is very labour intensive, which meant that production of dairy items, poultry and vegetables suffered. Green objected and Smyth bridled.

Green complained on behalf of residents about the wages and treatment at Coranderrk, but the board was incensed and determined not to take advice from Green or uppity blackfellas. The Coranderrk 'pioneers' (a term devoted to them by Diane Barwick, the person most responsible for recording their history) objected to the profits from their crops being used to pay white contractors doing work they could have done themselves. Green had been protesting to the board about this inequity for years and had a righteous temper when his pride was piqued.

In a hasty exchange at a board meeting in August 1874 Green offered to be relieved of Coranderrk if he didn't have the board's confidence. It wasn't a resignation so much as a plea for understanding and support, but Smyth leapt on Green's exasperated outburst and accepted his resignation. Then and later some on the board viewed this as a mistake, but gentlemanly pride was of much greater importance to most of them than the pursuit of competent and sympathetic administration.

Smyth's manner had earned him enemies, and this dispute erupted in the press, consequently affecting his work on the board. Smyth's arrogance and the ability of men to act more like wasps than legislators brought an end to his career and administration of the board. He wrote a long account of Kulin culture, the most thorough attempted at the time, but, true to his nature, he hardly credited the fact that most of the information it contained had been supplied by Thomas, Green, Barak and Billibellary.[16]

Captain Page replaced Smyth as board secretary. Page didn't have Smyth's enquiring mind but did have his bullying capacity. He was also a good hater and spent the greater part of his energies plotting the demise of his enemies. The captain was one of those people whose lives are devoted to the revenge of slights most others wouldn't notice. Beware the proud man.

A large part of his life was spent hating Anne Bon, an experienced grazier who learnt to respect Aboriginal people and counted many as her dearest friends. Yes, she was unusual in the colony of Victoria. She took an interest in the work of the board and, because of her wealth, influence and reputation for success, was able to approach the highest levels of government in search of justice for the Kulin. This search led her to query Page's administration. He detested her for it because she was a woman, and he viewed her intelligence and interest in government as an offence to male honour. It didn't occur to him that she had a moral imperative to expose his sloth and malice.

Page frequently referred to Bon as 'that interfering woman' and to her 'unladylike' interest in things that should not concern someone of her sex. He had a willing accomplice to his misogyny in the parliamentary Member for Healesville, Ewan Cameron, to whom Page turned for support when complaints about his administration reached the parliament. Page wrote to Cameron in his own defence in 1886: 'it appears that a Black man's word is believed before mine', and urged Cameron to 'put a stop to this outside interference'.[17]

Page managed to combine his sneering contempt for both women and Aboriginal people when he blamed Bon for the persistent resistance of the Wurundjeri, refusing to believe they were capable of mounting a sophisticated campaign against the board's mean-spirited management. Captain Page took a very different view of the abilities of the Coranderrk residents from that of Anne Bon: 'I am accustomed to discipline and control ... They are indeed, but hapless children, whose state was deplorable enough when this country was their own but is now worse, for they have adopted all the vices of the superior race, and gained nothing from the exhibition of its virtues.' Page never believed the Kulin could mount a protest of their own or write the letters that they sent to parliament, the press, Anne Bon and anyone else they perceived as sufficiently influential. He wrote: '... the Coranderrk half castes in particular can be led by any designing person male or female'. Page 'lamented their ingratitude' ('in the blood I suppose') and expressed his determination to quench all 'rebellious spirit'.[18] The senior Kulin studied the pecking order of European society with acute perception and applied their knowledge with uncanny dexterity despite their protests being met with sneering contempt and ruthless punishment on most occasions.

When protests occurred, so convinced was Page that the Kulin were incapable of mounting and articulating a campaign that he ordered police to go to Coranderrk and investigate hand-writing styles and grill residents for information about the white people behind the insurrection. Later the board encouraged the new manager, Strickland, to open residents' inward and outward correspondence in the hope of finding incriminating evidence against the Wurundjeri and their supporters.

True to the nature of human behaviour, some of those policemen were sympathetic and reported no conspiracy, but others on finding no evidence complained to Page of other things, usually the liberties Green and later managers were

allowing the 'natives'. And, true to the history of colonial
Australia, the well meaning were defeated hands down by the
treacherous and vindictive.

Page also hated Green because of the Kulin's persistent
requests for his reinstatement at Coranderrk. The Kulin complained of the arrogance and cruelty of Page's appointments
but possibly never realised they had been chosen for just
those qualities.

WHEN GOOD PEOPLE REMAIN SILENT

It wasn't just Page or Smyth or Green who manipulated the fate
of Coranderrk; it was also the overwhelming public opinion
that the Kulin were not fit creatures to possess the soil. If the
government or the press had mustered sufficient interest to
investigate the Central Board, Page could not have continued
to inflict such misery on the pioneers of Coranderrk.

Page was not content with his obstructions and deceptions
aimed at Green and Anne Bon; he particularly detested blacks
who complained. Two residents who felt the board's fury were
John and Louisa Briggs. They left Tasmania to work on the
Victorian goldfields in 1853. Louisa's grandmother was a
Bunurong woman who had been captured by sealers in 1833 and
sexually enslaved in Tasmania.

Louisa and John had spent reasonably stable lives in
Tasmania, where John learnt to read and write and Louisa to read.
They weren't intimidated by officialdom and lived quite inde-
pendently until they moved to Coranderrk in 1871.[19]

Louisa was a highly competent woman and, with Mary
Green, supervised the children in the dormitory. She was so
highly thought of as a nurse and midwife that she was
appointed matron in 1876, but her authority galled many

board members, who felt that a white woman should have control over her.

When Kulin petitions against mistreatment finally caused questions to be raised in parliament an inquiry was instituted in 1876. Louisa Briggs was questioned by the inquiry and conducted herself with unnerving aplomb—unnerving, that is, if you are convinced that all Aborigines are an inferior species. The board and Page never forgot her polite intransigence. John and Louisa had been forced off Coranderrk earlier when John protested about the wages and conditions, and now they were expelled again.

Over the years Louisa spent time at Ebenezer, Maloga and Cummeroogunga missions and demonstrated her competence each time. Her very success irritated many of her superiors, who accused her of agitating the population. Louisa's extensive experience of Europeans meant that she was able to anticipate their behaviour. Her 'agitation' and insubordination could also be described as the provision of good advice to a people at the mercy of colonial whim. Her confidence and knowledge infuriated the authorities and provoked jealous retribution from others with less ability.

WORDS OR WAR

The years of struggle ground down the spirit and bodies of Kulin leaders, and younger members had to heft the yoke of responsibility. With the death of Simon Wonga in 1875, William Barak became the pre-eminent ngurungaeta. Barak was Billibellary's nephew and was present at the signing of Batman's 'treaty'. Like his uncle, he had joined the Native Police in 1842 and remained in the corps until it was disbanded in 1853. As his descendant Joy Murphy says:

My great-great-uncle William Barak was at the signing of the
calculated treaty with Batman, and I think of a boy of about ten
years of age, standing proudly there at this moment ... maybe
he was able to understand from that meeting that there was
going to be a big change. Barak ... was an educated man from the
beginning, I think he knew about life and where it might go; he
had this vision for the future.[20]

The ngurungaeta were, as part of their political role, responsible for appointing young men to whom 'they gave their
words'. By the time William Barak had risen to the role of
ngurungaeta his spokesman was Tommy Bamfield. Bamfield
learnt a great deal from his elder and was involved in all the
Kulin's later attempts to hold on to their land.

Diane Barwick in her crucial history *Rebellion at Coranderrk*
describes the magnitude of the psychological adjustments Barak
experienced after witnessing the signing of John Batman's
fraudulent treaty: 'Death and dispossession had discouraged
the maintenance of many Kulin beliefs and practices and the
survivors had selected and adopted some of the alternative patterns offered by the European culture. For a generation they had
adapted to the demands of the European economy. At the end of
the 1850s the Kulin clans and their leaders sought to negotiate
better terms for this accommodation.'[21]

Barak had also seen the defeat of his people in war and the
broken promises of the government to allow the Kulin some
measure of independence. He was often disappointed, but he
never despaired. His courage was enormous, but his rewards were
few. Barak walked to Melbourne several times with the senior
Kulin in efforts to negotiate better housing at Coranderrk, the

reinstatement of Green and the dissolution of a hostile board, and to plead for retention of the reserve.

In 1882 agitation against board incompetence and failure to provide honest assessments about Coranderrk resulted in another inquiry into its activities. Barak gave his evidence:

> If they had everything right and the Government leave us here, give us this ground and let us manage here and get all the money. Why do not the people do it themselves, do what they like, and go on and do the work. We don't want any board nor Captain Page over us—only one man and that man is Mr Green and then we will show to the country that we can work it and make it pay and I know we will.[22]

But parliament succumbed to compassion fatigue, and Page's propaganda, and the result was a superficial reformation of the board.

The Kulin were not satisfied and decided once more on direct appeal to the government to censure the board, which was so clearly working against them. They set out on the long walk to Melbourne but had to adjust their pace as Barak by this time was old and lame. Younger members were still buoyant with hope, but Barak's heart must have been heavy. His countrymen may have believed their mission was to demand their due, or at worst bargain for a better deal, but Barak knew he was going there to beg.

Barak's diplomacy achieved some successes, only to have positive decisions overruled by other less generous parliamentarians or by Captain Page, who plotted against them in such malicious secrecy that some members of his own board weren't aware that he was working to spite the residents of Coranderrk.

The Kulin were pleading for the retention of their land
and the reinstatement of Green, but, as they had seen so little
of board secretary Page, they might not have realised that the
very mention of Green's name provoked the captain to drive
more nails into their coffin or, better still, their hands. It's hard to
accept that Page's heart was a blessed memorial to God's
generosity.

Once again the Kulin were disappointed and trudged back
to Coranderrk. The new manager, William Goodall, thought they
were chastened, but his reading of the situation was so superficial
he couldn't see that these were not naughty children admonished
by the headmaster but senior diplomats despairing for the future
of their people.

The board's indifference to the privations of residents at
Coranderrk is evidenced by the treatment of William Barak's
son David. The boy was gravely ill with tuberculosis and arrangements were made for his admission to hospital, but Page managed
to thwart the plans, so Barak carried the boy on his back to the
home of Anne Bon. Page showed no interest, as he was engrossed
in his plan to have Coranderrk closed. Barak was devastated by
David's death, perhaps realising that his direct lineage could
no longer be ngurungaeta. In the words of Margaret Gardiner,
'Just looking at the pictures [of Barak] before and after [David's
death] ... he didn't seem as strong, as vital as—as a—as a man. You
can see there's something missing in his eyes. You know his eyes
were tinged with heavy sadness.'[23]

In the last years of his life Barak turned to the pen and brush
to record life before white occupation, a life only he now could
remember. His paintings of corroboree and village scenes were
the bitterly nostalgic dreams of an old man, but they provide
crucial information about pre-colonial civilisation.

WOMAN OF HONOUR

William Thomas and John Green had worked selflessly on behalf of the Kulin in their capacities as employees of the government, but Anne Bon's commitment was generated solely by her morality. She was one of Victoria's largest landholders and among the most successful agriculturalists, and she had employed many Aboriginal people and learnt from clear-eyed experience to value their abilities.

Bon was an extraordinary woman for the period in which she lived. Her husband, John, had first proposed to her mother and then her sister before Anne suggested she should be his wife. She was wealthy, although she became more so with her marriage to John, but she still burnt with resentment towards the English for their occupation of the Scottish highlands.

John died soon after they emigrated and established their property, Wappan, near Mansfield. Anne continued to manage the property with the assistance of her sons and many Aboriginal labourers, and during that time she looked after Tommy Bamfield, who had become Barak's speaker. They shared not only a home but also an intellectual interest in Kulin culture. Their bond during the Coranderrk campaign was unbreakable, and when Bamfield died Bon lost one of her closest friends. Her many letters sent to those in power demonstrate her moral outrage on behalf of the people of Coranderrk. 'The blacks are neither slaves nor criminals, then why are they treated as such?' she wrote. 'You have power to reappoint the manager they love, to whom they always repair when invaded by sickness and death, and by doing so you will have the assistance of the House, the thanks of the outside public and the approval of Heaven.'[24]

Later in life she moved to the Windsor Hotel across the road from Parliament House, which may have seemed like the luxury she could afford but also allowed her strict surveillance of the board to which she was eventually appointed. Many board members were opposed to Bon's appointment, but others hoped this gesture of conciliation might mollify her. In fact she remained as critically involved as always and regularly attended board meetings well into her nineties.

This highly intelligent and resilient woman never failed to act according to her sense of moral obligation, but even this great warrior believed the pioneers of Coranderrk were being prejudicially affected by the growing number of 'half castes' seeking protection at the reserve. She was right in a sense because the trifling budget was stretched thinner as the population grew and the pioneers aged. The board and parliament refused to allow an increase in the budget, even as profits from the farm increased. One of the residents' most burning grievances was that their labours were not rewarded while managers and casual white farm workers were able to receive wages from the board.

Eventually Page was able to use parliament's frustration at the continuing complaints from Coranderrk to lobby for 'half castes' to be removed from the reserve. This was part of an assimilationist policy, which almost every Victorian saw as the answer to the Aboriginal problem: let the old 'full bloods' die out and immerse what they saw as the deculturated 'half castes' into the general community.

HALF CASTE ACT

The amendments to the 1869 Aborigines Act, more commonly known as the Half Caste Act, were passed by parliament in the last ten minutes before the Christmas break on 15 December 1886.

In the *Age* next day the editor's summary of the last day's typically hilarious sitting failed to mention the Bill destined to cause heartbreak for Victorian Aboriginal families. 'The other Bills which have been carried through their final stages are not merely of minor character when compared with those relative to water supply and irrigation, but would not have stood out as important in any session.'[25] Parliament seemed not to understand the destructive nature of its decisions and failed to give the issue sufficient priority or proper analysis.

The Bill allowed the board and Coranderrk management to disperse the mixed-race population and to separate families. Nothing could have been more successful in destroying family and community since the war of occupation. Residents were shifted from one reserve to another at the board's whim and prejudice. People from Lake Condah were sent to the other side of the state to Lake Tyers, and people from Tyers were sent to Cummeroogunga. In 1886 the Coranderrk residents sent a petition to the Premier of Victoria, Alfred Deakin: '... could we get our freedom to go away shearing and harvesting and to come home when we wish, and also for the good of our health when we need it; and we aboriginals all wish and hope to have freedom, not to be bound down by the protection of the board, as it says in the bill. But we should be free like the white population.'[26]

Dismissal from Coranderrk was often used as mean-spirited punishment for perceived crimes or simple insubordination. The Aboriginal community still remembers the pain of separation and the irreparable damage it inflicted on family.

Once again the failure of the general community and their political representatives to consider the humanity of the people they had displaced allowed a nation basking in the satisfaction of its wealth and democracy to indulge their views of racial superiority and to perpetuate vicious and contemptuous administrations.

The virulent policy of assimilation should have been enough to intimidate and suppress any civilisation, but the Aboriginal community refused to accept the future that had been planned for them. That defiance and resilience is consistently activated in our people's defence and is proof that you may punish dissent but you cannot defeat a people when they have etched on their hearts and minds the place where they were born and their responsibility for that land.

The Half Caste Act and its policy of exclusions and removals caused populations on reserves to plummet, but people still attempted to live close to their traditional lands and families, even if that meant living in fringe camps on riverbanks and rubbish tips. During the depression of the 1890s the parliament ordered the board to reduce costs, and from 1890 to 1918 Framlingham, Wimmera, Ramahyuk and Lake Condah were closed and many of the residents resettled at Coranderrk.

The Half Caste Act

Captain Page: It [the Amendments to the 1869 Aborigines Act] is the beginning of the end, which in the course of a few years will leave only a few pure blacks under the care of the Government Board of Protection for Aborigines.

Wayne Atkinson: It had genocidal intentions. The assumption was that the older members who were still living on the reserve would eventually sort of die out. And the end result would be that the Indigenous race would become absorbed into the mainstream population.

Twenty years after Barak's death the Coranderrk residents were still trying to hold on to their scrap of land, as this letter they wrote to the *Argus*, signing themselves 'Sufferers', shows:

> We are very much in sad distress thinking of how the board are breaking up our homes at Coranderrk and trying to transfer us against our wish. We wish to be here with our old people and near our loved ones in the cemetery. This is an estate given as a home to the natives. Remember we are no more slaves because we are coloured. We are under the British flag too. They might as well shoot us than shift us against our will. Will someone fight for us?[27]

Coranderrk was sold in 1948 to provide land for soldier settlers after World War II. Despite many Aboriginal people from the Coranderrk district serving in the war, none received grants of land on their home soil. The debate about breaking up the reserve was typically mean spirited and ill informed.

Bamfield died in 1893, Barak in 1903 and John Green, who had continued to farm on the outskirts of Coranderrk, in 1908. Only the cemetery had been reserved from the sale. Anne Bon erected its only gravestone, which stands to this day to commemorate Barak. Page died in 1890, but if residents believed a more benign rule would follow his autocratic reign, then his replacement, the Rev. FA Hagenauer, soon disabused them of such hope, as he was even more paternalistic and authoritarian than his predecessor.

The campaign by Barak, Wonga, John and Louisa Briggs, and their supporters, such as Anne Bon and John and Mary Green, to gain some foothold in the colony had been all but fruitless. The preference to negotiate and conciliate had proven no more productive than warfare.

Barak's thoughts on the relative merits of warfare and reconciliation as he painted his last images of his people must have been bleak and painful. His offer of peace in return for 'a spadeful of ground' had been met with almost relentless contempt. The refusal to consider the cultured humanity of another people still blights the relationship of black and white Victorians today. Of course there are many good-hearted agitators in the white community, but resistance to that goodwill frequently prejudices parliament and the media.

There is a future, but it requires an understanding of history and a refusal to commit the same mistakes. We are all people. Love thy neighbour as thyself.

Altyere
DREAMING

4
THE SEA MET THE DESERT, AND THE DESERT MET THE SEA
RG Kimber

The year 1890 was dynamic—a good year and a bad year in Central Australia. It was the year that the railway line was extended from its origins decades earlier in Adelaide and Port Augusta to Utnathata, the 'place of the mulga flowers'. Well, almost. The place of the mulga flowers was the originally planned terminus, about 20 kilometres north, so the name was dragged down to the rail-head and, as it was heard and written down for the first time, became Oodnadatta. So the sea reached the desert by way of the steel rails, and the first train arrived. Some of the first to marvel at the train were T Magarey, the manager of Crown Point cattle station on the Finke River, another station hand and a reliable old Southern Arrernte[1] stockman. They were examining the new 'iron horse' and its carriages, discussing its horsepower in terms of hundreds of horses, and were delighted when the old Arrernte man commented that the train driver must have had a very long stock-whip! The old Aboriginal stockman's response became a legend of the Outback for the next fifty years.[2]

We know our Altyere (Dreaming), there is no other law.
The Arrernte people were here from the beginning. This country was
Arrernte country. This Aboriginal law was given for eternity from
the beginning of time.
Herman Malbungka, Western Arrernte nation

Later visitors, understandably puzzled about its supposedly being 'the place of the mulga flowers', were less poetic in their descriptions. During a public lecture in Adelaide the Surveyor General of South Australia said:

> This little downship, dumped down nowhere so to speak, right in
> the heart of gibber country, does not impress one favourably as
> a holiday resort ... To see Oodnadatta in the drought season is to
> see a region as desolate as can be imagined, nothing but gibbers
> as far as the eye can reach. It has been said of Oodnadatta that the
> Devil made the place and even he was so disgusted with his work
> that he threw stones at it.[3]

That is a bit harsh! I first travelled to Oodnadatta in 1970, a drought year, with the perished cattle and brumbies showing only hide-and-hair backbones in the dry, sun-baked mud of the dams. I thought it looked more like a Bearded Dragon lizard, heat haze flattened out against the shimmering gibbers, but as in 1890 it was more than that. There were people there, and they were friendly.

The old dirt road still runs north of the chocolate and purple colours of the gibbers and the ancient sun-bleached

When the white men came, they began putting poles in the ground.
Telegraph posts. Initially people thought the noise the telegraph line
made meant it was some kind of monster, snaking across the country.

Max Stuart, Arrernte nation

yellow-flanked residual hills, largely following the route of the
mythological young Urumbulla men who travelled in the time of
the Dreaming, from the sea at Port Augusta to the Centre, then
north again. They in turn were unknowingly followed by the
explorer John McDouall Stuart, who in 1860–62 first made the
Centre known to Australians other than the Indigenous peoples
who lived there, then by the Overland Telegraph Line construction parties of 1870–72, and later the railway line. The answer to
why all of their travels, formalised routes and variations were so
similar, from the time of the Urumbulla youths onwards, is the
presence of precious, and rarely permanent, waters. The chain
of mound springs along the western side of Lake Eyre through to
the famous Dalhousie Mound Springs north of Oodnadatta leads
any traveller almost directly to the Finke River, or Larapinta (the
River of Salt), as the first Europeans heard the river's Arrernte
name. It is reached at its southernmost fragmented channels
in gibber and sand-hill country on the fringe of the Simpson
Desert. The infrequently filled rocky waterholes in its bed soon
give way to a broad white sandy riverbed lined by red gums, with
coolabahs further out in the floodout and billabong country,
then spiky spinifex-dominated land. Almost imperceptibly the
country rises from below sea level at Lake Eyre to a skerrick
above it at Oodnadatta, then to the 1500-metre height of the
MacDonnell Ranges, before again imperceptibly falling away to
the sea at Darwin. The Finke, its major tributaries and the Todd
River lead one north to the headwater country of the MacDonnell

Ranges; Ntaria (Hermannsburg Mission) is on the upper Finke, and Alice Springs is nestled in the ranges on the Todd.

I find it interesting that, with the exception of the explorer Ernest Giles in the early 1870s and Professor Baldwin Spencer in the 1890s, the first European explorers and later travellers looked at all in terms of landmarks, pastoral and mining potential, and timber for telegraph poles, buildings and yards. Although intrigued by the residual rock that Stuart called Chambers Pillar, on which many carved their names and dates of travel, they rarely commented on the fine details of the red sand landscape or beauty of the ever-changing colours of the ranges further north. (I guess that it helps if, as I am, one is privileged to call it home, and to be suffused by the light and the colours, hear the liquid silver of butcher-birds calling, listen to the wonderful silence, and lie on a swag at night and be dazzled by the brilliance of the stars.) However, those first new travellers and residents soon appreciated the more reliable rainfall of these central ranges, which, although fluctuating around an annual figure of 250 millimetres, was double that of Oodnadatta. It was milder, too, in summer than the country north through to the low, stony hills and scrubbier trees of Barrow Creek and Tennant Creek, and the Mitchell grass–dominated Barkly Tableland. Beyond the central ranges lay the dry deserts that offered little but sandhills and spinifex to any outsiders, although they were their dear homelands to the Aboriginal peoples who lived there.

I digress too much.

As though the Devil was still at work in 1890, it was also a year of increasing economic depression in South Australia, so the planned extension of the railway was shelved. As though to compensate, parliamentary franchise was conferred on the

> There is not a remarkable feature in the country without a special
> tradition. Tradition. Why, it is the very breath of their nostrils—that is—it
> was before the white man came amongst them and trampled tradition
> and everything else that was good out of them.
>
> *Frank Gillen*

people of the Northern Territory, with the Territory sending two
members to the Legislative Assembly of South Australia.[4]

Native Constable Billy was also prominent at the time. His
explorer friend of the previous year, WH Tietkens, stated of
him, 'a more willing, intelligent, industrious and skilful native
it would be impossible to have'.[5] As 'a reward for his valuable
services' Tietkens invited him to Adelaide, and so a man of
the desert saw the sea and was made a welcome guest at the
explorer's home. While there, a neighbour's prize fowls were
stolen, and Tietkens asked Billy if he could help to solve the
crime.

> As may be imagined the hard footpaths and metalled road
> retained no traces or footprints after a couple of days' exposure
> to the perambulations of the residents of a large suburban village.
> [After] a very long and patient search the tracks were seen in the
> water table to leave the road and go towards a grass paddock.
> [About] the middle of it Billy said the three men had separated,
> and he pointed out the spot to me, saying 'One fellow go that way;
> the other one go over here.' Close by Billy picked up a very small
> feather, which was the only tangible evidence that I had so far
> seen. After following the tracks of each man for a little distance
> ... [he] set off on the trail of the man he thought had carried
> the fowls, and very soon picked up some more small feathers,

showing that we were on the right track, but beyond the feathers my unpracticed eyes could detect nothing that could be taken for a footprint. The unerring skill of the black was, however, never at fault, and after following the trail down a small street Billy pointed out the side gate of a house, through which he said the man had gone. Looking over the fence we saw some fowls in a coop.[6]

And so the desert man's skills resulted in the arrest and gaoling of a thief. Shortly afterwards Billy returned from the sea to his family at Charlotte Waters, where the Rain Dreaming songs were sung.[7]

You have to be driven by some kind of mad vision, to leave Germany, and live in Central Australia and to create a settlement as they did.
Professor Marcia Langton, historian, Yiman/Bidjara nation

Another who had travelled down to Adelaide was Pastor WF Schwarz, who had served at Hermannsburg Mission, westerly from Alice Springs, from the time of its foundation on the banks of the Finke River in 1877. Sometimes he felt that he had been gathering salt rather than souls during his missionary endeavours. After more than ten years, he had the satisfaction of converting several Western Arrernte people to Christianity in 1890, including 'Tjalkabotta, who in accordance with mission custom chose a Christian name for himself, Mose (Moses)'.[8] He commenced the New Year in Adelaide by attending a meeting where the treatment of Aboriginal people was discussed.

His address to the group confirmed the belief that Aborigines were doomed to extinction, and that 'unless something were done to protect them they would soon die out'.

Although he did not name anyone, few in the audience would not have known that his early remarks referred to Mounted Constable Erwein Wurmbrand's patrol of November–December 1884. He stated his 'conviction' that three arrested cattle-spearers had been shot to save Wurmbrand the trouble of travelling 1200 kilometres south to Port Augusta, the nearest place then possible for a trial.[9]

There were resonances in these remarks with those that were recorded in February–March 1874, after the Barrow Creek telegraph station had been attacked. On that occasion two telegraph station staff were speared to death by Kaytetye warriors, and at least three other men were injured. In response the South Australian Police Commissioner had advised that 'close adherence to legal forms should not be insisted on', and a newspaper editor suggested, 'Retribution, to be useful, must be sharp, swift, and severe.' The evidence suggests that such advice had been followed. Eleven shooting deaths were accepted as unavoidable, but other unofficial accounts suggest that scores more Kaytetye people were shot.[10]

Schwarz continued his address, still without naming anyone, with further sensational claims:

> He also knew of a policeman being sent from Alice Springs to arrest some blacks, but instead of arresting them he shot them, and brought back against their will two young black women, who lived with him, and one of whom came to the city with him. There was hardly a station on which there were not half-caste children. Some of these were treated nicely, but the majority were not cared for at all. There were some on the Mission Station, and they were more intelligent than the pure blacks, but most of the half-castes were afflicted with a loathsome [venereal] disease.

One of the most serious complaints of the missionaries was that when they had young girls under their charge they were generally led astray by white men. Recently three young girls ran away from the station and they were now in the police camp in the neighbourhood. Very frequently blacks disappeared, and the other blacks came to the station to inform the missionaries that they had been shot. One young fellow disappeared suddenly, and the blacks stated that his throat had been cut by whites. He had not seen the killed blacks, but could rely on what was reported by the other blacks who regarded the missionaries as their friends. There were some atrocious offences against the natives, and some steps should be taken to further protect them.[11]

The shocked audience stated that a Commission of Inquiry should be sent to formally gather evidence, and that reserves should be established for the protection of the Aborigines.[12]

These comments, since they effectively condemned everyone except the missionaries, caused general offence in the Centre, particularly to Mounted Constable William Willshire, the policeman allegedly involved in 'atrocious offences'. As a journalist reported, he immediately responded with his own charges against the missionaries:

A very warm controversy is now being carried on between the troopers and the Lutheran Missionaries at the Finke River. Trooper W. H. Willshire has stated that the missionaries ill treat the natives, and he has known a lubra to have been chained to a log by them, and both boys and girls to have been hunted with whips and revolvers. He also states that the missionaries drive the old and infirm natives away from the station. J. A. Besley, a telegraph operator at Alice Springs, reports that the natives are ill-treated by the Europeans, and that large numbers die from pulmonary

> ## Men's Business
> **Mounted Constable William Willshire:** In March 1883 when coming through Emily Gap, three lubras followed. Three lubras followed behind my horse saying they were going to Alice Springs. Just as I reached the entrance to the gap, five blackfellows appeared and ordered the lubras to go over the range as no women were allowed to go through the gap.
> **Herman Malbungka:** Our men had some dangerous taboos, powerful and dangerous. People were killed who broke the law.
> **Mounted Constable William Willshire:** At first they assumed defiant attitudes, but I cleared them out and passed on, followed by the lubras, who to my great astonishment, picked up some rags, bushes and grass and made coverings to their faces and walked blindfolded.
> **RG Kimber:** Because the law was broken by the women despite the fact they were forced through and despite the fact they covered their faces, there was only one logical answer and the Aboriginal men later had to put them to death.

diseases, syphilis and hydatids. A full enquiry will probably be made into the statements of the missionaries and the police.[13]

The Commission of Inquiry found that, despite the presence of many children of mixed parentage in the Centre, they were unable to prove that fornication had been indulged in by the citizens, who protested their innocence, nor that there had been any unlawful shootings. On the other hand, the missionaries being honest men, and not being asked about all of their good deeds, admitted to the chaining up and whipping of Aborigines who broke the mission laws or the Ten Commandments. While the commission emphasised to Willshire that he must adhere to rules to do with his work as a mounted constable, they found that he had widespread support among the station owners. He might not have come out of the inquiry smelling like roses, but he was in at least as good odour as the missionaries.[14]

Willshire, about whom Mounted Constable South wrote that he had 'always considered him eccentric, with an inordinate love of Notoriety', celebrated a little too early.[15] Even as the commissioners were commending him, the South Australian Government's Attorney General was finding discrepancies in his recent reports. He ordered Post-Master Frank Gillen of Alice Springs, a Justice of the Peace, to gather evidence. Gillen began to hear stories from Aboriginal witnesses that appalled him.

While there was little doubt that Willshire's camp had been attacked in the course of intergroup Aboriginal feuding and a visiting Aboriginal man speared to death, the evidence also indicated that Willshire had lied about obtaining arrest warrants and that he had been involved in horrific deeds. These included, according to several Aboriginal witnesses, that he had ordered his native constables to shoot two Aboriginal men on Tempe Downs Station so that he could acquire one of their wives to satisfy his predatory sexual lust; that he had danced with excitement when this had occurred; that he had then cut the throat of one of the men, who had been severely wounded, to complete the murder; that he had then had the bodies burnt before enjoying breakfast; and that one of the widows, if not two, were living with him at his Boggy Waters police camp on the Finke River. Although the white station hands admitted that they had heard some shots, they claimed that they had not seen anything. However, the evidence that Gillen gathered from the Aboriginal witnesses was compelling. He sent it to the Attorney General and senior police officials in Adelaide, who ordered him to have Willshire arrested. Mounted Constable South, who made the arrest, wrote that, in addition to his previous reputation for being a larrikin policeman, he thought that Willshire must be 'insane'.[16]

Willshire was, however, sane enough to realise that he was in danger, so he coached his native constables to give accounts that were as identical as possible. They were to indicate that, in a dangerous frontier situation, he had followed correct police procedure.

After his arrest Willshire, to his intense anger rather than with any sense of shame, was put in chains and taken down to Port Augusta for trial. Illustrative of Native Constables Larry, Archie, Jack and Thomas's evidence against him was that of 'Archie, a native trooper':

> Been at Tempe Downs, along with Willshire and three other trackers. Got up daylight, go along station, Willshire and others go along too, down creek to Donkey's camp. Had a rifle and revolver. Had no neck-chains or handcuffs. Took rifle and revolver to shoot Roger and Donkey. Wanted to shoot Roger and Donkey because they take away Willshire's lubra. Her name Nabarong. That's why we shoot Roger and Donkey. Willshire yabber me shoot Roger and Donkey. Sit down along creek with Larry when Willshire tell him, Larry shoot Donkey. Willshire sit down close to the station then. Saw Roger and Donkey when they were dead. Their bodies were burned. Willshire, Billy Abbott, the two other [native police] troopers, and myself were present.

At this point the lawyer for the defence asked if this was a lie, whereupon Archie, although stating that he had not lied, indicated that Donkey and Roger had been shot because they had resisted arrest for the crime of cattle killing. He also contradicted himself on several other points as he gave further evidence.

Did tell Mr Gillen that Mr Willshire been yabber all the morning 'Take blackfellow, no shoot 'em.' Did tell Mr Gillen that he had a rifle and a pair of handcuffs, and Mr Willshire a neck chain. Told him that when they got to Donkey's camp he jumped up and tried to throw a spear. Tried to catch him, but did not speak to him, not knowing his language. Larry then caught him round the shoulders but could not hold him. Told Mr Gillen all that. Larry then spoke to him, but could not understand. While Larry held Donkey, Willshire tried to put on the neck chain but Donkey jumped away and knocked Willshire down with a yam stick; he struck Willshire on the head and hand. Before Larry dodged him he threw a spear that Larry dodged. When Donkey knocked Willshire down he ran away. Then Larry shot him. He tried to spear witness before he threw the spear at Larry. That, Mr Willshire was lying on the ground when Larry was shot. Him [Willshire] cocoa-nut very hard. Had Larry not shot Donkey him get away along a range. Knew Roger and Donkey killed old man Naemi. Told Mr Gillen, Willshire said, 'You no shoot Roger and Donkey, only catch 'em long a handcuff.' Thomas been have a handcuff. Said, saw Jack catch Roger long a arm. He been try get away. Thomas try put on handcuff. Thomas said let me put on handcuff—I not shoot 'em. Did not hear Thomas say any more. Said, 'Rogers throw two spears at Jack and one at Thomas.' Said, 'saw Thomas fire two shots, one striking Roger on the leg and one above the hip near the ribs.' Said to Mr Gillen 'I have not been told by anyone what to say.' Said to Mr Gillen 'I hear the bodies were burned by the blacks.'[17]

As each witness contradicted himself as much as did Archie, the jury took just fifteen minutes to find Willshire not guilty, without 'a tittle of evidence' against him.[18]

Well over a century later, it is clear that the conflicting evidence, failure to call several key witnesses, and formal advice to the jury by the presiding judge meant that the jury had little option but to declare him innocent. It is extremely doubtful that he was, but the reality is that a jury unanimously declared him innocent.

After he had celebrated, he was posted to the Top End of the Territory, where his booklet of the times indicates that he and his native constables continued their ruthless patrols and abduction of nubile young women.[19]

Life went on in the Centre, as the seasons came and went, and the rains caused a burgeoning of all life after the drought.

Most Central Australian Aboriginal groups whose country had been 'settled' or 'invaded'—the perceptions varied in the 1890s—came to an accommodation of the situation. They were invariably shocked and offended when, on returning to their last great drought fallback waters, they found them fouled by the hundreds of 'devil-monster' beasts and the 'bush tucker' destroyed all about. Initial retaliation was exciting as they speared horses and cattle, and challenged the police and station hands. By the late 1880s, however, the patrols led by Mounted Constables Wurmbrand and Willshire had resulted in the shooting of so many young men that various means of cooperative association were sought.

They were intelligent people, who found seasonal work in the stock camps interesting. During the musters the Indigenous men were acknowledged as the more expert at tracking animals, and teams of strong young men of both European and Indigenous ancestry worked well together. There were reciprocal benefits to be had for their work, with gifts of prized iron knives and axes, bottle glass that could be used to fashion knives and scrapers, other appealing gifts, meat from the regularly slaughtered animals, and other strangely interesting foods and billies of tea. And after the muster they were free to travel their country as they had always done.

There were also droving, police patrol or waggon travel journeys that took them to country and peoples beyond all previous knowledge other than that which was encoded in the Dreaming tracks. Some things were simply accepted in alert silence, and Willshire, for all of his faults, captures a sense of this:

> When the blacks who accompanied ... [me] across the northern half of this great continent came to Port Darwin, whatever astonishment there was, was not displayed by the blacks. Some surprise on their part was expected; but neither the unaccustomed big waters, the steamers, the ships, nor the houses, seemed to put them in the least degree out of their ordinary demeanor.
>
> In order to test them further, a monkey was bought and brought down to the natives on a man's shoulder. The animal had its hands full of bananas, and it was busily engaged in devouring the fruit. The trackers were fairly taken by the beast; they literally roared. Two of them were somewhat scared, for they thought that Jacko was the devil. They soon divested themselves of this idea, and of all the supernatural ideas they might have connected with the new phenomenon, and they employed all their spare time in cultivating the monkey's society. The animal was taken back to Alice Springs, a thousand miles away, on a pack horse, and he arrived in safety; but while his owner was away someone placed him on a horse and fastened him on with a chain, in order to test his riding capabilities. The result was that the unfortunate animal's brains were dashed out against some rocks.[20]

They caught three natives on the station, took them up to the
MacDonnell Ranges and shot them there. The dead men rest dead still
in their chains. With all the shootings that are taking place it is hard
to conceive that the native people have any kind of future. Our only
hope is that they are rescued from this intolerable situation. The male
population of the natives has decreased alarmingly.

Pastor Kemple, Hermannsburg missionary

Each new situation resulted in a considered response by
local Aborigines, with cautiously cordial relationships soon
established in most instances. On some occasions, however, such
as during the Arltunga gold rush from 1887 to the 1890s, when
hundreds of armed prospectors arrived, the adjustments by the
local Aborigines were, of necessity, almost instant. However,
any initial taking up of new pastoral country inevitably led to
tensions. Thus a relatively peaceful year came to an end in June
1891 when some sixty spearmen attacked the newly established
Frew River Station. The few white men present were fortunate
to survive. Station manager James McDonald, who was there for
seven years, was described as having 'been speared through the
left leg above the knee: his head shows where it once opened to
the none too tender advances of a stone tomahawk; the forehead
above the right eye has been fractured; his right arm hit with a
boomerang which penetrated up to the shoulder'.[21] Although
the local Aborigines fiercely resisted, spearing many cattle and
the white station men alike (although none of the latter fatally),
McDonald and his small band of heavily armed men retaliated,
focusing on the men. It is possible that some 400 or more warriors of the Alyawarre, Wakaya and Kaytetye were shot.[22] At
much the same time a large marauding band of Wave Hill country

warriors attacked and murdered scores of Warlpiri at a waterhole on the Cockatoo Creek floodout, 250 kilometres north-west of the Alice. Those few who escaped the massacre sent fit young men as runners to alert the Warlpiri groups to the south, west and east. They rapidly gathered together as a *walmalla* (fighting band), tracked the murderers and fiercely took their revenge. Many years later a prospector noted in his diary: 'saw plenty abo. bones; must be a battleground.'[23]

There were more peaceful and enjoyable times once the 'sorry business' mourning period was over. Charles Chewings, an interesting explorer and geologist of the Centre in the mid-1880s, and for decades afterwards a pastoralist and bush businessman, came to know and appreciate many Aborigines over the decades. Reflecting towards the end of his life, he remembered:

A bucking horse, a ferocious bullock, or a humorous episode will send them into roars of laughter. I have seen them laugh until the tears ran down their cheeks. Many years ago a police inspector journeyed far inland to see his police officers. At Charlotte Waters was a mounted constable who had been stationed in that district for many years. When he went there he was a fine, strapping, well-proportioned young man. Being of careful, saving habits he had packed away his regimentals carefully, they being unnecessary in such an out-of-the-way place ... The climate, good food, and little exercise agreed with the trooper, and he put on much condition.

The inspector, wishing to know whether his officers were keeping up practice in sword exercise, and knowing that formerly this officer was adept at the art, ordered him to don his uniform and give an exhibition. With considerable difficulty the constable got into his long-disused suit. All went well until those exercises requiring greater freedom came on, when a tear occurred here, and buttons flew off there!

Some of the onlookers were station natives. These, without exception, never moved a lip or a hair during the exhibition; but when it was over a native had got to work with a piece of chalk. On the walls of the house and on the tanks the whole proceedings were depicted in a series of sketches. The constable was there, sword in hand, with abnormal drop-chest development, the perspiration streaming from him, rips and tears in his regimentals, and buttons flying in all directions; the agony on his face was indescribable.[24]

The artist was probably Erlikilyika, known as Jim Kite to the Charlotte Waters telegraph station staff. He was the first Central Australian artist to be recognised Australia-wide for his artistic talents, being appreciated for his carved likenesses of animals in soft stone rather than his drawings, although Frank Gillen, who had been on the staff at Charlotte Waters for twelve years before his transfer to Alice Springs, collected some of the latter, too.[25]

In 1894 the Horn Scientific Expedition, led by experienced Central Australian explorer, surveyor and bushman Charles Winnecke, traversed much of southern Central Australia. Other members of the thirteen-man party included scientists Professor (Sir) Edward Stirling (anthropologist and medical officer) and Professor Baldwin Spencer (biologist and photographer). Professor Spencer's collection of zoological specimens, photographs, paintings, sketches and writings, complemented by all other scientific records, provides a remarkable, unmatched record of the era. And although explorers William Gosse, Ernest Giles and William Tietkens had all previously described Uluru (Ayers Rock), with Tietkens being first to take a (relatively poor) photograph of it, Spencer includes the first truly popular scientific account of 'the Rock', accompanied by a superb black-and-white photograph:

> Ayers Rock is probably one of the most striking objects in central Australia. From where we stood the level scrub stretched away monotonously east, west and south to the horizon. Above the yellow sand and dull green Mulga rose the Rock—a huge dome-shaped monolith, brilliant venetian red in colour. A mile in length, with its sides rising precipitously to a height of eleven hundred feet above the plain, it stands out in solitary grandeur against the clear sky. Its otherwise smooth sides are furrowed by deep lines of rounded holes rising in tiers one above the other and looking as if they had been hollowed out by a series of great cascades down which for many centuries the water in the rain seasons must have poured in torrents from the smooth dome-shaped summit.[26]

Much as the sand in the vicinity must have appeared yellow at the time, it is the one descriptive element that would now be challenged; red is universally given as the colour these days. Further details are given, and he also considered that the nearby mulga scrub, where he saw numerous mounds of earth left by women digging for honey ants, 'must be a favourite hunting ground of the blacks'.[27]

Spencer also acknowledged Frank Gillen, whom he met for the first time in Alice Springs, as providing him with an example of an Arrernte myth and the first translation of the sacred Arrernte word *alcheringa*:

> The blacks have a rather curious myth to account for the origin of the pillar. They say that in what they call the Alcheringa (or as

Mr Gillen appropriately renders it the 'dream times'), a certain
noted warrior journeyed to the east and killing with his big stone
knife all the men, he seized the women and brought them back
to his own country. Camping for the night on this spot he and
the women were transformed into stone, and it is his body which
now forms the pillar, whilst the women were fashioned into the
fantastic peaks grouped together to form what is now known as
Castle Hill, a mile away to the north.[28]

However much he was now intrigued by Aboriginal cultures,
Spencer's focus was biology, and it was Professor Stirling who
wrote the volume entitled *Anthropology*, including in it a
contribution written by Gillen.[29]

During the expeditioners' time in Alice Springs, however,
Spencer had immediately recognised the value of Gillen's friendship with the Arrernte. The two men became good friends, and in
1896 and again in 1901–02 they recorded numerous Aboriginal
activities and collected many artefacts. More significantly, they
were the first people in the world to use both film and sound
recordings, as well as photographs and the written word, to describe the cultures of the peoples with whom they interacted.
Included in that which they witnessed were the most extensive
and elaborate ceremonial cycles ever recorded in Australia,
among them the famous Mudlunga, or Tjitjingalla corroboree.
This great public corroboree had originated in southern
Queensland, been carried from group to group down the east
side of Lake Eyre (all of the time being adapted to local situations
with regard to ceremonial body patterns and decorations), looped
north about Lake Eyre to reach Alice Springs and eastern Lake
Eyre in 1901, and later reached Ooldea on the Nullarbor Plain. It
had a number of revivals through to the 1950s.[30]

In 1899 they published *The Native Tribes of Central Australia*. It instantly became one of the most influential anthropological books in the world, and was followed by several other significant publications, including *The Arunta* in two volumes in 1927. This later publication appropriately acknowledged all of the 'chief men of the Engwura Ceremony' (a festival of more than sixty dreamtime acts performed in corroboree) of 1896, the oldest of whom, Erikenkintera of the Achilpa (Native Quoll) totem, had probably been born around 1820.[31] Almost overnight the Arunta, or Arrernte as their language and name is now mostly spelt, became the most famous Indigenous nation in Australia.

The Horn Scientific Expedition was not without its reprehensible side, for, with the reluctant assistance of two local Aboriginal men, many sacred men's objects were stolen by Charles Winnecke, the leader, and Dr Stirling, the anthropologist, from a cave far to the west of Alice Springs. That Winnecke believed that, by leaving behind almost half of the wooden items and also leaving 'a number of tomahawks, large knives, and other things in their place, sufficient commercially to make the transaction an equitable exchange', suggests that he had heeded concerns by the two local men. However, one of the Aboriginal men who showed the particular expedition members the cave was later murdered by fellow warriors as punishment for this crime. This appalled Gillen, who, although he had purchased such sacred objects himself when he had been offered them by old men, realised that he had been 'in ignorance of what they meant' in life-and-death terms.[32]

In 1895 missionary Carl Strehlow arrived at Hermannsburg. He found it recently abandoned, so he began the hard work of re-establishing it as both a viable pastoral property and a christianising influence. Despite almost twenty years of endeavour by

Tywerrenge

RG Kimber: Tywerrenge in the conventional way of using it is an Arrernte word and is also a sacred word. It relates to sacred objects, which can be in the landscape themselves. However, they are also mainly referred to as stone or wooden tablets of a different kind which may be plain but are often inscribed with totemic devices which relate to the totemic ancestors of a certain part of the landscape, and therefore every person who was born in the landscape also inherited these sacred objects.

Max Stuart: It's a little bit like Moses. He went up the hill. The Ten Commandments. We received the Tywerrenge from the Altyere (Dreaming), in the beginning of time.

RG Kimber: There was a widespread interest in these Tywerrenge stones which are very difficult to understand, but they have got symbols upon them in many cases, and it really fits in with a sense of there was a Rosetta Stone sort of a thing, if you could only, this must be Aboriginal writing, how do we understand it, there was some sense of a talisman or almost like, here's the holy grail if we can only grasp this we'll get a better understanding of Aboriginal culture.

Herman Malbungka: The Tywerrenge is our number one priority for the people. All our children learn this. They learn about our Tywerrenge. We have not abandoned this. Never. We are here to this day.

the foundation missionaries, he felt that a 'thorough improvement would be brought about if the blacks would become Christians not only in name, and if the whites would act as Christians'.[33] Moses Tjalkabotta, one of the earliest converts, was a man who fulfilled his hopes in becoming a strong Christian.[34]

While Carl was rejuvenating Hermannsburg, in 1897 Jerome J Murif became the first man to ride a push-bike from the sea near Adelaide to the central desert and onwards to the sea at Darwin. At Oodnadatta the Arabana and Southern Arrernte Aborigines gave him advice. 'A council of the dusky ones called here to adjudicate upon my chances of getting through to Darwin arrived at the following decision:—"Wild blackfellow big one frightened. Him think it debble-debble an' run away all right. One time 'nother one think it [the bicycle] debble-debble, and throw it spear."'[35]

Moses was a good leader. He was a blind man but he knew every Tywerrenge and he never let on. He was a Ngkarte, a church leader, but he was also an Ngkarte, a senior leader in the traditional way, for us Aboriginal people.
Max Stuart, Arrernte nation

Mostly, however, because so few Aborigines had seen a bicycle, the reactions were of astonishment, and interesting expressions were invented to explain the phenomenon, some by those who had come to know trains and some by others who had not. As Murif rode into Horseshoe Bend Station, south of Alice Springs, an Aboriginal ran to the station store, and Murif recorded:

> Here it was that one of the encamped blacks on spying me rushed helter-skelter to the storekeeper to breathlessly inform him that whitefellow come along ridin' big one mosquito.
>
> Previously blackfellows had described the bicycle as a 'piccaninny engine.' 'Big pfeller engine come alonga bime-bye, I suppose?' questioned the blackfellow, having in mind a Transcontinental railway doubtless. 'One-side buggy' had also been a native's not inapt description of the novel vehicle.[36]

The drought time came again, and all suffered mightily in the first great recorded Central Australian drought of 1897–1906. Numbers of stations were now either abandoned or sold at huge losses, and the recently arrived rabbits died out until regular rains again fell.[37] And although the Wankangurru and other Simpson Desert peoples had experienced few direct pressures until now, they left their homelands for the dependable waters on the fringes of the desert and the new food supplies available at stations and Killalpaninna Mission in South Australia. Many never returned, and all others visited less frequently than before their time of association with white people.[38] The desert dwellers of the Gibson and Tanami deserts, and the sand-plain desert between the Simpson and the Barkly Tableland, also found themselves in peripheral contact with the strangers. Treasured items of glass and steel found their way through the brief contacts, or through gift exchange along the Dreaming trails, deep into the deserts. Explorer David Carnegie found steel and glass items over the border in Western Australia; and in 1898 Mounted Constable Ernest Cowle reported that the butcher's knife was 'ubiquitous— for many miles West [of Illamurta police camp] and at least as far South as Ayers Rock', and that steel was being used in their adze-tips.[39]

> Water is the crucial answer to everything here. In the desert it's extreme, so these waterholes are so significant, and they, in a way, hold a lot of the essence of the landscape in them.
>
> *RG Kimber, historian*

During the great drought Frank Gillen was promoted, and in 1899 he and his family moved to Moonta in South Australia. He was replaced by the Bradshaw family who, while not having Frank's deep interest in Arrernte culture, nonetheless had good relationships with the local people, coming to know many by name, regularly giving out rations and sharing many experiences.

When the Bradshaws left after nine years, the Aboriginal house-maids and other assistants remained lifelong friends.[40]

Meanwhile, the pastoral pioneers of the Centre had the same strengths and weaknesses as any other members of frontier society, some being benevolent and caring towards Aborigines who lived on their station properties, a limited number being cruel, and most being somewhere in between.

John Warburton of Erldunda Station, 200 kilometres south of Alice Springs, was not unusual in the era in considering the Aborigines who lived on the station inferior. However, as a letter he wrote indicates, he clearly had a feeling of responsibility for them:

> We teach them cleanliness first, and afterwards we teach the boys
> to earn their own living as stockmen, for they are not born with
> a knowledge of their work. We teach them to ride, to work hide,
> to fence, to handle an axe etc.; and we teach the girls to wash, to
> cook, to sew, and to take a pride in keeping themselves clean and
> neat, all of which requires much patience and time upon the part
> of the white instructor.[41]

Tom Coward, who fifty years previously had been a member of an exploration party in northern South Australia and, as a policeman, had done his 'share of "nigger hunting"' on behalf of the government, had earlier taken a much broader, thoughtful approach:

> We have driven the blackfellow away from the water, we have
> denied him the right to secure game, from all fertile fields he is
> prohibited, and generally speaking there is less care for him than
> for a horse or a beast. As a 'tenant in right' he has been evicted.
> Nothing in Irish history where evils ought to be redressed is

more flagrant than that which today presents itself with regard
to the blackfellow. We have gained his possessions by might, and
without some degree of reparation we cannot conscientiously
establish our right.

In Australia the rights of the blackfellow as first occupier
have not been considered. He has been driven from pillar to
post, his 'gins' have been contaminated and disease has been
spread broadcast, and if he rebelled (which in the natural order
of things he would) he has been met without hesitation by
powder and shot. There are certain reprisals which ought to
be made; the fast decaying race call for some assistance; and
a Federal Government, if not alive to this first duty, will be
unworthy of its position.

I am anxious to see him well cared for, and desirous to
give him the opportunity of occupying his time in such places
as he can gain a livelihood in without the severe interference
of an unscrupulous white man, who does not understand his
habits, characteristics and aspirations, and cares nothing for his
feelings. The blackfellow is human, and he was the original owner
of Australia, and the undercurrent of demand is that his rights
should be appreciated at their true value.[42]

While there were those who could idealistically agree with
him, in practice small reserves, ration depots and protectors were
the best any government managed at the time. This was illustrated
on the 'historic' day of 30 March 1901 when, as Professor Baldwin
Spencer and Frank Gillen were travelling across Australia,
the vote for 'the first election—for the Federal Parliament' was
held.[43] However much Gillen perceived it as a turning point in
Australia's history, it had little real impact on the Centre at the
time. Melbourne was the distant location for the Federal

Parliament, 'on the other side of the moon' in pre–motor vehicle and pre-aeroplane years, and voluntary visitors to Oodnadatta were as rare as feathered frogs. Rarer! Adelaide and Darwin, the city and port with responsibility for administration of the Territory, were each 1500 crow-fly—or, as some would say, fly-crow!—kilometres from Stuart town. And if Oodnadatta was a terminus in the 'middle of nowhere', Stuart town and the Alice Springs telegraph station were like a distant mirage beyond 'nowhere'. Thus in the middle of the 'Federation drought' in which almost all stock died, Stuart town was 'in a moribund condition', as Gillen put it.[44] Oodnadatta rail terminus, Hermannsburg Mission and, for a brief few years, Arltunga goldfield, were the only places in Central Australia with a score or more of voters. Even the Territory as a whole, still administered from South Australia, was nothing but a drain on that state's resources, universally regarded as a 'white elephant'. And as the scientist Gregory termed it after his travels through drought-stricken northern South Australia, in the year of Federation the Centre was all part of the 'Dead Heart of Australia'. It would be another thirty-five years before naturalist HH Finlayson called it the 'Red Centre', the name by which it is now appreciatively known.[45]

Spencer and Gillen's Southern Arrernte assistants, Parunda (Warwick) and Erlikilyika (Jim Kite), did not vote in this first federal election because they had no right to vote, being Aborigines, viewed as doomed to extinction. There is, however, no indication that they or any other Central Australian Aboriginal people had any knowledge of the significance of the election, or that they believed that they were doomed. They remained dynamic interactors with their country and the people they met.

Although the drought continued, and all of the Indigenous people were stressed, they prevailed. As they had always done, they retreated to their major drought fallback waters, some of which had been developed into timbered wells during construction of the Overland Telegraph Line. WR Murray, an experienced surveyor and explorer who prospected the country west and east of Barrow Creek for five months in 1906, commented: 'But few natives were seen in country back from the telegraph line, they being mostly on the wells on the line, or in the vicinity of the stations where rations are available. All told, we only saw ten men and women, and no children.'[46]

These concentrations of people during the drought assisted Spencer and Gillen to contact people during their travel from the sea to the desert, and from the desert to the sea, right across Australia. While their main focus was on recording all cultural aspects possible, Spencer recognised, as did Charles Chewings and ornithologist Captain SA White, that Aborigines, in knowing 'the habits of every living thing around them', were 'the most competent naturalists that ever were, or ever will be'.[47] As a consequence he encouraged every man, woman and child to bring him natural history specimens. Gillen delighted in the 'five or six' children's exploitation of Spencer during their stay at Barrow Creek, with a small boy called Tchanama a favourite at the game:

> [Tchanama] is attached to our staff in the capacity of beetle
> hunter and picker up of zoological trifles such as frogs and small
> lizards. He doles out specimens one at a time and generally
> succeeds in extracting some lollies although we have tried our
> level best to make him understand that we prefer the day's
> collection being brought to us in one lot. Like the wily Chinee,
> him no sabee and in an hour's time he returns with another

beetle. Spencer lectures him and vows that never again shall he
have a lolly until he brings in 'big fellow mob'. Tchanama smiles,
his eyes sparkling, his teeth gleaming beautifully white and even,
and with a lolly in his mouth and two or three in his little black fist
he trots off joyously; Spencer comes in and assures me that he has
made the little beggar understand this time. I am not sanguine
and in an hour or so the little ruffian appears again, this time
accompanied by his little sister Nun-galla each hanging on to a
frog for bare life ... Spencer's face is a study as they come forward
with their offering, two of the commonest of froggies, he dare not
refuse to take them for fear of discouraging the kiddies so again
they go off with some lollies.[48]

While Tchanama was enjoying his lollies, another gold rush
was occurring at Arltunga; and at Hermannsburg Mission, Moses
Jalkabotta continued to assist Carl Strehlow—as he did until
Strehlow's death in 1922, and then helped his replacements,
notably the 'Straight-out Man', Pastor Friedrich W Albrecht.[49]

Moses Jalkabotta, along with other senior men acknowledged by Carl Strehlow, helped Strehlow to understand the
language so that he could better preach the gospel and translate
the Bible into Arrernte as well as record the culture of his people
over the period 1907–20. This wonderful research was published
as *Die Aranda- und Loritja Stamme in Zentral-Australien*. Moses
had become blind by this time, but became one of several wide-
ranging evangelists and, as with Carl and Friedrich, a legendary
figure in Central Australia's history. Together with his wife, Sofia,
he travelled by donkey into Alice Springs, and south for hundreds
of kilometres down the Finke River to Charlotte Waters. They
had even confidently travelled to the far south-west, through

the Luritja and south-eastern Pintupi desert country to the Pitjantjatjarra country of the Petermann Ranges. At all times he had carried the Christian message that pastors Schwarz, Strehlow and Albrecht had given to him.[50]

In reflecting on these times, of which I have read and yarned about with a rare few old Aboriginal and other Australian characters (now long deceased) born in the late nineteenth century, or their descendants, I have felt as though I have shaken hands with the people I have mentioned. Like the Boer War and World War I soldier-survivors of my childhood, most lived long and good lives most of the time. We all have feet of clay, some with just a smearing and some with bloody great clod-hoppers, but mostly we don't look at them. Even if I judge those people I have mentioned harshly now, whether for shooting people; for being paternalistic or having Darwinian beliefs about 'primitive stone age Aborigines'; for replacing Aboriginal belief in 'the Dreaming' with Christianity; or for taking away their lands, their livelihood and their women, there is more to them than that. Even Willshire, a megalomaniac whom I think was a murderer and sexual predator, was never convicted of any major offence, made friends with some of the Aboriginal people and some of the other Outback people, married 'down South' and had some children, and was considered a hero by some in his time. And if the opportunity offered, I'd like to meet him, along with all of the other good people whom I've mentioned, have a yarn about a campfire at night. Of course I'd need to keep him unarmed on one side of the campfire, and missionary Schwarz, Frank Gillen and the native police who gave evidence against him on the other.

Were I of Aboriginal descent, would I think the same? Doubtfully so. However, I have had Aboriginal friends who lived through the 'bad old days' of shooting, or of family members being speared to death, or dying (before contact with the wider world) of thirst and starvation because of severe drought. They have accepted that the world has changed, often for the better, and judged people individually rather than condemning all who are not Aboriginal. And probably every Aboriginal land claim and native title claim in Central Australia has benefited immensely from the records of Spencer and Gillen, Carl and TGH Strehlow and those of many other early recorders.

The sun still comes up in the morning and goes down at night. The ranges are still red against the intensity of blue sky. The stars still scatter their dazzle every night, and the moon still rises. My wife and my children and the people they married are all still alive, as are nearly all of my friends and acquaintances. And I cannot do anything about the weather, so every day I enjoy it for whatever it is.

Yes, every day I wake up is a good day—the alternative isn't all that flash.

Rather than ramble further on these matters, I think I'll just jog along with Frank Gillen for a while. His brief notes of April 1901 capture something of the era:

> Blacks preparing for an elaborate corroboree ... In the morning Spencer and I visited blacks camp collected some beetles also procured from the blacks some edible tubers called Ilya-kamana ...
>
> The beetles collected are called by the blacks Ilyanilyana from the fact that they feed upon the Ilyana plant a species of Claytonia.
>
> In the afternoon got kine and photo records of Lubras Corroboree called Unintha. Women decorated with much taste

various designs painted on bodies otherwise naked as Mother Eve but perhaps somewhat shyer though certainly not ashamed.[51]

As they travelled north of Charlotte Waters Gillen daily cursed the myriad flies, but also recorded all of the Arrernte place names on their route, and wrote in his diary: 'It is a lovely mild night, still with the peculiar stillness of the bush, occasionally the horse bells ring out with startling effect, a cricket chirrups to his mate an invitation to come out of her retreat, a weird old Mopoke utters his harsh note, the boys sit poking sticks into the fire while they chant in low tones a corroboree song ...'[52]

Marda-marda
TWO BLOODS

5 BLOOD HISTORY
Steve Kinnane

LIFE IN THE VALLEY

Fitzroy Crossing has been in the news again. Front-page news-paper images of women carrying slabs of VB home on pension day mirror the scenes outside the window of my donga in the centre of town. It's Big Pay day in Big Pay week.[1] More than this town's fair share of community members are gripped in the teeth of grog. At night, children hover in groups of five and six along the main street, buzzing around streetlights as the sound of competing ghetto-blasters echoes through the town. This is punctuated every so often by the desperate seagull-shrill sounds of men and women shouting at the top of their lungs. Later, groups of children peel off, heading down to the river to light little fires and get some sleep away from the humbug, the noise and the threats of violence.

> God made the white man
> God made the black man
> And the devil made the half caste.
> *Helena Murphy, (née Clarke), Yawuru*

Fitzroy Crossing exists at the edges of Bunuba Country, the country of Jandamarra, the legendary resistance fighter. Four main language groups are represented in Fitzroy Crossing: Bunuba people, whose country stretches to the north and the west; Gooniyandi people, those from river country to the east; Wangkajungka people, from country to the south-east, towards the desert; and Walmajarri people, those from the south side of the Fitzroy River, the country that stretches out into desert beyond the scattered backbone remnants of the stunningly beautiful St George Ranges.

In 1968, when award wages were finally granted to Aboriginal pastoral workers, hundreds of families found themselves dumped in Fitzroy Crossing by white station owners.[2] Entire language groups were removed from the commercially leased stations on which they had worked, building them up for almost a century, and the lands that they own and had worked within for centuries before. Fitzroy is not remarkable in this regard. Its story is that of dozens of towns with large Aboriginal populations living a diaspora existence in country not their own. Peoples with different languages, different geographies and different dreaming are bound by their shared history, that of colonisation. They are bound, too, by the aftermath of decades of misguided, paternalistic government policies aimed at socially engineering the diversity of Aboriginal peoples of the Kimberley and throughout Western Australia into an imagined mirage of unified Western whiteness.

Of course, it is not only history that has produced this reality, which is not the reality for all of the people of Fitzroy Crossing, or the other fifty-four remote communities clustered around significant sites and historical meeting places throughout the Fitzroy Valley. Leaders of the Kimberley Aboriginal Law and Culture Centre have worked for decades to uphold law, culture and language in the face of incredible poverty and the mute witness of hand-tied government bureaucracy. Mangkaja Arts Agency represents internationally renowned artists and supports the cultural vibrancy of the Fitzroy Valley, living side by side with entrenched poverty, poor educational outcomes and under-resourced health services. There is a collection of Aboriginal-controlled and -run organisations throughout the Fitzroy Valley. They are engaged in a social reconstruction of their own choosing, slowly reconstituting their own values and visions for their families and their country, beyond the social engineering of almost a century.

ANOTHER INQUIRY

At the insistence of Aboriginal leaders in the Fitzroy Valley the State Coroner is holding an inquest into the twenty-two alcohol-related deaths that have occurred in the Kimberley in as many months. Eleven of these took place in the Fitzroy Valley within the last twelve months.[3] The stories are shockingly similar: stories of young men and women without hope, of alcohol and drug dependency, of a lack of follow-up support services and a woeful neglect in government service delivery. Positive things that happen in the Fitzroy Valley happen because key leaders and their supporters simply work harder to make them happen. They have set up refuges, small businesses, large community enterprises, community-owned cattle stations and community-run schools.[4]

In the courthouses and makeshift hearing spaces erected for the inquest, families come forth to speak of their pain and suffering, repeating their calls for support and opportunities for their young people. In the face of such an onslaught of grief and the seemingly never-ending cycle of arm's-length, scaffold-thin support, people draw deep into their spirit to overcome shyness, shame, sadness and anger, and speak up in the search for answers.[5] In the Killing Times,[6] it was an overtly powerful colonising force that had to be contended with. In the twenty-first century, it is an internalised violence, cold pressed into the competing forces of remarkable leadership and hard-up apathy, stunningly beautiful country and knockabout style with over-crowding, poor sanitation and unsteady or non-existent economies. History is not the sole reason for this layered, contradictory community existence. We each have choices to make about our lives every day. But history counts.

The violent beauty of the ancient Devonian limestone reef outcrops of the Oscar, Napier and King Leopold ranges attracts tourists in their thousands. More than 30 000 take the Windjana Gorge-Tunnel Creek road each dry season to follow in the footsteps of the Bunuba and, particularly, to hear the story of Jandamarra, the Bunuba resistance fighter who led his people in a historic battle against the forces of colonisation.[7] For many, they follow the well-trodden path of tourist buses, gasping at the freshwater crocodiles that bask in the sun at one of the key battle sites of the Kimberley Region, Windjana Gorge. Stepping through the narrow passage cut into the gorge by thousands of years of erosion, they pass through the wall of the

Napier Ranges into the historical turning point of Aboriginal and non-Aboriginal relations in Western Australia.

Further on, they will marvel at the opening of Tunnel Creek, a massive cave complex and underwater river stretching for almost a kilometre, venturing no further than the day-lit opening or beyond the ankle-deep cold, dark waters within. This was where Jandamarra evaded capture for three years. It was where, after being wounded, he remained in the safe, dark world of the tunnels, before emerging and choosing to stand and fight. Jandamarra was fighting more than the Western Australian police force and Aboriginal troopers that day. His stand has come to represent continued resistance to the lac- quered gloss of pseudo-scientific theories of racial superiority and ingrained inequality bound in imaginary portions of blood.

BLOOD SCIENCE

Having occupied the southern portions of Western Australia, the latter half of the nineteenth century saw the colonists move further north into the fertile river valleys of the Kimberley.

Speculators in the south focused especially on the western and central Kimberley region. The Swan River Colony was estab- lished in the south-west of Western Australia in 1829. Investigating successive expeditions into the Kimberley by George Grey and Phillip Parker King, historian Cathie Clement found that, 'to the explorers of this era, the fertile country on rivers such as the Victoria, the Glenelg and the Fitzroy appeared to be crying out for colonisation'.[8] The most recent and famous of these early expeditions was led by Alexander Forrest in 1879. Forrest followed the Fitzroy River through the central Kimberley. Forrest's expe- dition and the development of steamships led to the instigation of commercial survey parties in search of good pastoral lands.

By 1881 news of the success of the Forrest expedition and other private expeditions had spread. By 1884 the entire region had been remotely apportioned to distant speculators, thus beginning the dysfunctional imposition of government at great distance.[9]

In the Kimberley during the Killing Times, from 1889 to 1905, British imperialism expanded rapidly. From Darwin's scientific theory of evolution the pseudo-science of social Darwinism was spawned. This mistaken and popular belief held that colonisation was an inevitable process in which peoples deemed to be 'inferior' were doomed to die out.[10]

However, such misconceptions of supposed Western superiority were about to be tested. Aboriginal people did not simply lie down and die, and the frontier was a much more complex place than the theorists and commentators could ever have imagined from their drawing rooms and libraries. Ideas forged at great distance have driven men (invariably men) to great violence within acts of appropriation, theft and opportunism. Wherever such powerful ignorance exists, resistance will also always be found.

THE JANDAMARRA TRAIL

Dillon Andrews is a Bunuba elder. His softly spoken voice belies the strength of his six-foot four-inch stockman's frame (six-foot eight in his hat). When he walks his country he does so with conviction and an easy rolling comfort across the limestone outcrops embedded in red earth held together by paint-pattern stands of spinifex. This is Leopold Downs Station, a Bunuba-leased property out of which Dillon's own community, Biridu, has been carved, the land in which he was tossed up from a boy.

Dillon is showing Kartiya[11] tourists through his country. He has built up a successful cultural tourism business, Bungoolee

Tours, in the heart of Jandamarra country. It has taken him years with little government support. He has not wavered. The cattle that formed the backbone of Aboriginal economies in the Fitzroy Valley no longer provide for a growing and youthful population. In seeking a way to uphold culture, bring young people through their difficulties and be free of government, this kind of independent business offers people some hope. In this regard, Dillon is a stand-out. Having been out on Bunuba country with Dillon and having learned of his country and its history, 'cultural tourism' doesn't quite describe the experience. It is like an exchange, an act of respect. These exchanges enable a deeper sense of country to permeate this history, winnowing Kartiya misconceptions through experiencing traditional ownership of country in contemporary Australia.

Jandamarra was getting to know two things here. He was getting to know the magic of his own country and at the same time getting to know the whitefellas, and he was very good at knocking around with the whitefellas. He was noticed very early for being something different.
Professor Howard Pedersen, historian

For Dillon Andrews the stories of Jandamarra live on in the waters of Tunnel Creek and the Oscar and Napier Ranges that have cradled him throughout his own life. Within Dillon's country, 'Jandamarra will always be a hero to the Bunuba people. Doesn't matter how people see it as good or bad, he'll always be a hero ... who fought for the Bunuba People and for his country,' he says.[12] Jandamarra's story is also one of survival in the face of massive change to community culture, ancestral country and a collective sense of spirit in ancestral heroes. It is also a story of broken boundaries and the consequences for all concerned.

PAYMENT IN BLOOD

Frontier cultures breed frontier values, frontier justice and frontier violence. Jandamarra's story often revolves around two
competing themes: that of Jandamarra the freedom fighter,
and that of Pigeon (his European name) the violent outlaw.
This polemic does not rest only with black or white tellers
and listeners. For the Bunuba who tell this story, Jandamarra
is indeed a freedom fighter as well as an outlaw. In the Bunuba
sense, Jandamarra was an outlaw for crossing Bunuba law, being
with women of the wrong skin, and for this he was punished with
a form of banishment.[13] In the Killing Times, this fracturing
of connection to his people possibly aided his transition into
settler society as a well-regarded police tracker. In the lead-up to
his choice to rebel against settlers, he is painted as being torn,
caught between two cultures and choosing, in the end, to follow
Bunuba law, to live on his country independent of settler society
and to make a stand for Bunuba land. Within settler histories, he
is seen as an outlaw and murderer, a rebel of individual action and
responsibility only, the leader of criminal acts, not a revolutionary
and resistance fighter. For Dillon Andrews, Jandamarra's story
is, quite simply, his people's history, framed against the reality
of these very real Killing Times and the resultant tide of blood
wrought by those in the south intent on occupying this country.
As is often the case, it is also the story of relationships struck amid
the fray of colonisation that are unable to straddle the divide. As
Dillon Andrews relates:

> [Jandamarra] ... grew up at Leonard River station ... this was
> in the 1800s ... Quickly, Jandamarra picked up the skills as a
> stockman, a drover, a shearer, and very skilled craftsman ...
> And he became from a stable boy to a station hand, and then

during that time there was ... a European stockman called
Richardson. And he, Richardson, was the head stockman, and
then he befriended Jandamarra. They became close friends, very
good mates. And later on, Richardson then became Constable
Richardson. And when he became a policeman ... Jandamarra
became his right-hand man.[14]

Howard Pedersen has traversed this story from all angles,
sifting through the archives and walking through Bunuba country
learning from Bunuba people. Through his work with Bunuba
elders, he has collaborated in telling Jandamarra's story in all its
complexity. The years spent delving into the records of the police
and Colonial Secretary's offices added to the community stories
handed down among Bunuba people to reveal the tensions at play
in these frontier lives. As Howard Pedersen relates, 'In early 1894
Bill Richardson had an established relationship with Jandamarra.
They'd worked together; they knew each other. The general
popular story was that Jandamarra walked into the breezeway of
the Lillilmooloora, the old homestead Lillilmooloora that was
... operating as the police station—it had been abandoned—and
shot Richardson and released all sixteen Bunuba people from the
chain. And together ... those prisoners and others joined up with
women and children and they walked to Windjana Gorge.'[15]

The life of a tracker was an uneasy compromise, a borderline
crossing of opportunity and subterfuge. It was unusual for police
to have a tracker working in his own country. It was considered
wiser to have people from country elsewhere without relationships to those they would have to track and imprison. Jandamarra
was an unusual man: incredibly adept by any measure of
European skills, and exemplary in Bunuba ways of living within
his country. However, as more southerners encroached on

Bunuba lands, and as he came into greater contact with his own people in his work as a tracker, difficult choices were placed before him. For Dillon Andrews, no greater dilemma could have faced Jandamarra than to have to arrest his own elders in their own country and, in particular, to have to arrest Ellamarra, a greatly respected Bunuba leader:

> Jandamarra and Richardson captured them ... put handcuffs, chained them up and walked them ... to Lillilmooloora, [which] they call Fairfield Station ... They were held for nearly ...seven days in chains. But ...meantime ... Ellamarra was talking words of wisdom to Jandamarra. He probably told him, 'Look, I grew you up, I look after you, I cared for you, I'm the only one who raised you up, your mother didn't look after you, I did.' Ellamarra probably said that, you know, 'I even carry you on my back, I fed you, show you how to hunt, I look after you, I put you through the Bunuba law.' And here, you see, poor Jandamarra was caught in two worlds. One was his tribal elders, and another was his friend and partner Richardson. And this kept on for a few days until Jandamarra started to realise [that] next day they were going to walk them to Derby. That night, Jandamarra shot Richardson. And set his elders free.[16]

What followed moved the colonial establishment to take action, releasing a wave of violence and retribution that would result in a guerrilla war waged by Jandamarra and his followers for more than three years. Howard Pedersen documented the build-up in colonial forces before Jandamarra's rebellion. As he relates, 'In 1888, the Western Australian Government responded to the incidents of resistance right throughout the Kimberley by putting a whole range of ... police stations, a whole network of

police stations, to try and quell this growing Aboriginal opposition to European settlement. By the early 1890s a quarter of
the whole Western Australian police force is based in the
Kimberley, where there's only one per cent of the European
settlement population.'[17]

In the immediate aftermath of Richardson's murder,
the Bunuba collected weapons and the women, including
Jandamarra's mother, became key members of his outfit, making
bullets and loading weapons, hunting, providing food, providing
intelligence and acting as scouts' decoys. The initial resistance
was clear and decisive. Dillon Andrews tells of Bunuba ways of
understanding Jandamarra's success in evading capture from
overwhelming forces:

> The police ... hunted him for nearly three years, three and a half
> years. And then Jandamarra, being a Bunuba man and knew that
> area so well, his main hideout was Tunnel Creek. And he stayed
> there and it's a beautiful spot. And the police couldn't track him
> down. It was a place that only Jandamarra and the Bunuba people
> knew ... Hid there for three and a half years. Still eventually
> they track him down, and many times he was shot and wounded.
> But with him he had a few elders who used to heal him. The
> bush medicine; black magic. And the police knew that this man
> Jandamarra he was someone special [who had] special magical
> power ... that Marban man, we call them.[18]

Regardless of his personal powers and abilities, Jandamarra
could do little to stop the butterfly effect of his own resistance
as the colonial authorities acted swiftly to put down any further
resistance. Following the shooting of Richardson and the
ambushing and killing of two pastoralists entering Bunuba
country with more than 500 head of cattle, a decisive historic

> It would be a good time for the Western Australian Government to
> shut its eyes... and let the settlers... teach the niggers the difference
> between 'mine' and 'thine'. It would only have to be done once and
> once done could easily be forgotten.
>
> Derby Correspondent to the Northwest Times

battle was waged at Windjana Gorge, a sacred Bunuba site and
prominent water source. Howard Pedersen describes this event
as 'a full-pitch battle' in which guns 'had been secured, quite a
few at that; at least there were three or four repeating Winchester
rifles, shotguns, single-load breech rifles. I mean, there was a
significant amount of arms ... in the hands of the Bunuba ... and
... all evidence suggests they were out to inflict a serious military
defeat on the West Kimberley police force.'[19]

Had it not been for a contingent of Queensland Aboriginal
troopers who had been secured to subdue and kill Jandamarra,
the element of surprise would have gone the Bunuba way.
However, having found Jandamarra's and Ellamarra's positions,
the Queensland troopers turned the tide.

> The shooting then lasted from early in the morning until late in
> the afternoon [as Pedersen relates]. Ellamarra was shot ... and
> ... seriously wounded and probably died as a result, [and] never
> appears again at all. Jandamarra was also seriously wounded—
> he'd been hit a number of times by police bullets—and withdrew
> into the back of the cave. In a fairly courageous act of leadership
> ... he came out, began firing at the advancing police ... and kept
> them at bay until the women and other members of the Bunuba
> group had been able to withdraw into the myriad of caves at
> Windjana Gorge. So it was an amazing act of bravery on the part
> of Jandamarra. But he, in doing so ... got wounded quite a few
> times. And he was thought to have died as a result of his wounds.[20]

When Jandamarra resurfaced, to the colonists' surprise, the authorities wasted no time in sending a clear and direct message to any further resistance. As Dillon Andrews sees it, settlers feared that more people would rise up as Jandamarra had:

> Yeah, well, there was ... a massacre going on right throughout the Bunuba country, along the Fitzroy River, you know. And probably they were doing that just because [settlers thought] 'We'd better do something now, otherwise we'll get more people like Jandamarra.' And I think ... more killing was going on because of what Jandamarra was doing. And they were afraid ...the European was afraid [and thought] 'We may as well start wiping the Aboriginal people away because otherwise they will end up being like Jandamarra.'[21]

As Howard Pedersen discovered in the colonial record, the wider story fits closely with Bunuba oral testimony, except in regard to numbers, motives and outcomes:

> And it wasn't any part of Western Australia; it represented the new frontier of development. So it was strategically very important to Western Australians. Forrest basically sent up ... reinforcements under the command of ... Inspector Lawrence, someone who Forrest knew, had grown up with in Bunbury ... and what was required was ruthless action ... Just before Christmas they began ... a ruthless journey of bloodshed, all the way from the upper reaches of the Fitzroy River ... around a very famous station called Fossil Downs, pretty much all the way to the mouth of the Fitzroy River. In his diary, he mentioned seventy-nine Aboriginal fatalities. Now, you know ... the Aboriginal people have always indicated a much higher figure than that, several hundred. But one will never know. But it was ... one of the most horrific incidences of mass murder in the history of this state ...

It was a ruthless campaign designed to inflict mass fatalities; men, women and children ... They were not [only] Bunuba people; most of them ... were Unggumi people or other ... language groups that were not in any way ... related to the Bunuba, but they suffered.[22]

After repeated skirmishes and reprisals, as Dillon Andrews says, the police brought in an Aboriginal tracker to equal Jandamarra's skills:

> So they bring in the best black tracker in the whole of the Pilbara ... Micki ... he is older, much older, than Jandamarra, but he's had a similar background. He's ... worked on stations. He's gone back to live the lifestyle of an independent Aboriginal country. He's been in prison, he's escaped, he's been imprisoned again ... He's remarkably clever. When Micki arrives at the end of 1896 ... and at the beginning of 1897, there is a real attempt ... to capture or kill Jandamarra.

Dillon Andrews' telling largely concurs with the record of the events in the archives, with an important distinction— Jandamarra's courage under fire:

> Well, Jandamarra, he was near a place called Six Mile Lake at Tunnel Creek and that's where he got wounded. And he was losing a lot of blood. He came back to ... the back end of Tunnel Creek to a place called Dingo Gap. And there, I reckon, because of loss of blood he fainted. And still they were tracking him down. And it was ah, Mingo Mick, I think, that one, yeah, who tracked him down. And couple of times they said that Jandamarra fainted because of loss of blood.[23]

Police accounts reveal Jandamarra, wounded but still moving, making for his home in Tunnel Creek. Pedersen takes up the story:

The police write about how Micki is giving chase to Jandamarra and firing. And he's marking him on several places of his body, but Jandamarra continues to run. Jandamarra collapses, very close to Tunnel Creek. He's home and the place where he can be safe. Blythe [a pastoralist who was set to gain from Jandamarra's death] instructs Micki to hold back ... he wants to fire the final shot ... to end this war ... He knows that once Jandamarra's gone, the Bunuba mountains are his and his family's. So he ... rode up to Jandamarra, who is lying face down, and suddenly, as Blythe leans over on his horse to fire the final shot, Jandamarra turns with his Winchester and fires simultaneously. And Jandamarra's shot hits Blythe in the hand ... and takes his thumb off. Jandamarra is actually hit in the groin. But he still manages to escape into the grass ... and then into the Oscar Ranges.[24]

The wounded police party and prisoners returned to Derby. Within two days, Mingo Mick returned to track down a badly wounded Jandamarra at Tunnel Creek. Jandamarra was being tracked by a Marban of high degree, someone of similar skill and ability. It is when they are away from the police that Jandamarra's final hours are counted:

The Bunuba oral history [Pedersen continues] is that ... early in the morning on 1 April 1897, Jandamarra came out of ... Tunnel Creek and stood on the top of a very tall rock pillar ... and looked at Micki. There was some exchange through eyesight, of respect, according to the Bunuba oral testimony. And Jandamarra with his last bullet takes a shot at Micki and misses. And then Micki shoots back to a defenceless Jandamarra, [who] falls dead at the bottom of the rock. And then shortly after the police arrive ...

and ... decapitate him, and bring his head back to Derby in a sack ... amidst the scenes of jubilation and celebration in Derby. And there's a very big drunken party to celebrate.[25]

Jandamarra's body was buried in his country, but sadly, as with so much of that period of colonial conquest, his story is far from over, as Dillon Andrews attests: 'Well, like, it was a really sad loss for the Bunuba people ... But he fought for his country. Yeah, after all that, it's about a hundred years, after Jandamarra done all the fighting and things for the Bunuba country. Again, the Bunuba people still haven't got a strong native title, we still don't own the land. It's our traditional country, but we still don't own it.'[26]

The fact that Aboriginal people were prepared to stand and fight and had organised and had strategically thought out an ambush was a real shock to Western Australia, and that's when the official declaration of war came from the government.

Professor Howard Pederson, historian

Jandamarra's death coincided with the greater expansion of colonists into the Kimberley and throughout the state. The state's population exploded with the gold rushes of the 1880s. In the Kimberley, gold, land, water and pasture were regarded as open for the taking. Jandamarra was killed while a relatively young man, barely out of his twenties. Had he lived, he would have witnessed the declining fortunes of his people; his country was too attractive to colonisation. Having perceived the 'battle' won, colonists considered what the next steps were to be for the increasingly impoverished and disenfranchised Aboriginal peoples of Western Australia. Their solution was simple: let them bleed out.

CREATING THE DYING PILLOW

Today, the old offices of the Aborigines Department are ironically used by Lifeline, a service created to help people in desperate need. The three simple interconnecting Edwardian offices are disarming in their stillness. It was from here that the individual lives of thousands of Aboriginal people of Western Australia were managed in minute detail. It was from here that, from 1915 to 1940, Mr AO Neville was installed as Chief Protector of Aborigines. From the corner of the largest room in the complex, tucked against the back veranda of the Colonial Secretary's Office, Neville oversaw the imposition of some of the most racist and damaging legislation ever inflicted on a civilian population.

The means by which Aboriginal Western Australians were managed was scientific in nature. The department used carefully numbered personal files about its charges and thematic administrative files to manage larger populations and wider issues of relevance. Such issues as cohabitation between black and white were watched and monitored here. Reports gathered by the police about the management of people's wages, which were taken from them without permission and withheld to be managed for them by the state, along with the secret identities and whereabouts of thousands of children, were stored here. The children of focus were those who, if of mixed descent, were taken away from their families and placed in institutions, such as the Swan Native and Half-Caste Mission, the Salvation Army Girls' Home, Dullhi Gunyah Orphanage, New Norcia Mission, Beagle Bay Mission, Sister Kate's, Forrest River Mission, the Derby Leprosarium, the Carrolup River Settlement and the Moore River Native Settlement.

The rooms are now bare, but they resonate with the pain of our history, sucking the air out of my lungs, leaving me

Mixed descent

Steve Kinnane: Files record an increasing number of children of mixed descent. Now sometimes from oral testimony of people who I've spoken to, who were alive at that time, these were through liaisons that people had chosen. For the large part the stories that people tell, though, are of abuse of Aboriginal women, are of rape.

Marcia Langton: This is a breach of the code of racial hygiene and the children of such unions must be removed both from the black races who they would pollute and also from the white race who they would also pollute.

Steve Kinnane: There was a saying, 'God created the white man, God created the black man and the Devil created the half caste'.

shockingly breathless and somewhat emotional. Ghosts rise up to meet me, of women who never found their mothers, children abused in institutions, families kept apart for decades. There is a sense of isolation, fragmentation and the minutia of government intervention in people's everyday lives. My anger becomes palpable, but at who or what: at these silent rooms now used to save people's lives; at the people long gone who carried out these policies; at the very stupidity of their power and ignorance, their brazen racism; or at the cumulative foundational impact of the weight of this history on our communities? Here are the foundations of problems in towns like Fitzroy Crossing and of race relations that were set down in these three simple rooms. This is the place where race relations in Western Australia were solidified, like some nineteenth-century chemistry experiment, the laboratory from which the results of these pseudo-scientific experiments were applied to Aboriginal people with the public's blessing. It does not have to remain so.

As the last of the Aboriginal resistance to pastoralism in the Kimberley by the Bunuba became recent memory, Western

Australian governments of the early twentieth century applied a simple formula to a complex issue. Within the Petri dish of public policy imposed on Aboriginal lives, eugenic racial policies designed to manage and cultivate an imagined whiteness took hold. Neville was not the chief architect of this policy, but he became its advocate. It would not take many years for every Aboriginal person in Western Australia to feel the cold touch of Neville's decisions in their lives. By 1938 Neville would enter the national stage, whereby his ideas would be welcomed and largely embraced by other states and territories for use across the entire nation.

It's not a kindly, charitable, evangelistic act that's embodied in this idea of protection. It's the idea that, well the natives are going to die out anyway, and so to make it more convenient for them and more convenient for us let's segregate them from our colonial outposts so we can just get on with it and let them die peacefully over there.
Professor Marcia Langton, historian, Yiman/Bidjara nation

INSTITUTIONALISING FIRST AUSTRALIANS

The *Aborigines Act 1905* (WA) was created as 'an Act to make provision for the better protection and care of the Aboriginal inhabitants of Western Australia'.[27] As the twentieth century took its first shaky steps, so too the colony of Western Australia took its first false steps into self-government. The Killing Times continued in the Kimberley region. There were still many groups, desert peoples and people in the northern central Kimberley who were aware of Kartiya but remained independent on their country. This was largely due to their isolation as well as their resilience. Having completed pastoral expansion into the Fitzroy

Valley, failed attempts to place cattle in more marginal, rough country would prove to be a dividing range, a saving grace for some Aboriginal peoples.

In the world of colonial Western Australia, concentrated in the city of Perth, it was considered that all that remained at the turn of the century was a mop-up operation for those Aboriginal peoples, mostly of mixed descent, who had been disenfranchised by settler society. Before acting on this growing belief, it was decided to hold an enquiry, to gather evidence and steel the debate that was raging in the popular press, largely about the perceived 'Aboriginal Problem'. Many Aboriginal families were doing it very hard. Some, usually those who had managed an accommodation of some kind on their own country, working on stations or completing work treks along former trade routes and seasonal harvests, had managed to remain fairly independent. However, being black, being poor and generally being outnumbered, they were watched very carefully, and their lives were considered to be a problem to be solved.

The Roth Royal Commission was completed in 1904. Similar to the Coroner's Inquest into Alcohol Related Aboriginal Deaths in the Kimberley in 2007, it sought advice from government agencies, welfare groups, concerned citizens and those charged with overseeing the welfare, in particular, of Aboriginal Western Australians.

Professor Anna Haebich is a historian who broke new ground in the 1980s with her insightful, detailed and community-informed approach to this history. Professor Haebich's first book, *For Their Own Good* (1988),[28] changed the way Aboriginal history was understood in Western Australia, revealing the human frailties at the heart of these events, as well as the political and historical contexts that drove people's actions. For Professor Haebich, Roth's character also influenced the findings and recommendations of his report:

> Roth was a very interesting individual and he had a lot of sympathy ... for Aboriginal women and children in particular. And he showed this in his early years in Queensland. When he came back and wrote his report, he put this material into his report. But when this went to parliament there was, again, a furore and the pastoralists attacked him and said that he was perhaps inventing this or cast aspersions on his evidence and his capacity to report correctly ... So this evidence was there, but it was attacked and undermined by parliament in Perth.[29]

Commissioner Roth focused on police abuses of Aboriginal prisoners and the reported slave conditions under which Aboriginal workers lived on northern stations. The commission was considered to have 'crystallised the already existing differences of opinion between the north and the south, in regard to the treatment of Aboriginal people'.[30]

Western Australia had been an independent colony since 1897. The colony had previously been unable to obtain self-government from the British Crown due to its treatment of Aboriginal people. Slavery may have been abolished in other regions of the empire, but bonded labour, black-birding of women as pearl divers and blatant maltreatment of Aboriginal workers was common in Western Australia. In *For Their Own Good* Professor Haebich revealed that the evolution of the Acts controlling or influencing Aboriginal peoples from the 1840s to the *Aborigines Act 1905* (WA) were focused on the notion of the 'soothing of the dying pillow'. Distorted Darwinian theories of the superiority of Western races infiltrated popular thinking and colonial and state policies in all aspects of

Aboriginal lives. As Professor Haebich outlined, the various acts of legislation concerning Aboriginal people were based on the 'pseudo-scientific theory of Social Darwinism, which postulated that Aborigines were the least evolved race in the world and as such they were doomed to pass away'.[31] Little had changed since the Bunuba Resistance of 1894–97.

> Very clearly there was violence, and rape, and sexual assault, but I think also women became free agents able to wield political power because so many men were killed and the women were the last adults left standing. And women used their ability to move easily between societies as a part of their survival strategy and I'm sure that they did that in order to ensure that their own people survived.
>
> *Professor Marcia Langton, historian, Yiman/Bidjara nation*

The Aborigines Act was to have particular influence in advocating the greater removal of Aboriginal children of mixed descent from regional Western Australia. Had the authorities significantly resourced the department responsible for this damaging legislation, the situation could have been even worse. However, even with their limited resources, the effect was devastating.[32] With statehood came the creation of new boundaries, the absorption of Aboriginal territories and the segregation of Aboriginal peoples. Within the Aborigines Act areas known as reserves were created to which Aboriginal people could be removed without trial for an indefinite period. Aboriginal children were now under the guardianship of the Chief Protector of Aborigines and could be removed without permission from their parents, their homelands and their rights and responsibilities to their country. Aboriginal labour was to be regulated, and people could work only under permits given at the discretion of the Chief Protector.[33]

SUFFER THE LITTLE CHILDREN

Auber Octavius Neville, the son of an Anglican rector, was raised in the expectation of going far in colonial service. He was a contradictory man in many ways, someone who appears to have been very well loved by his immediate family, but who seemed unable to pass such care on to the children who were his official charges. My judgement of this aspect of Neville does not come from his family or acquaintances, but from the testimony of older women and men, aunties and uncles, who did know him, albeit as charges under the various incarnations of the Aborigines Act.

These people met Neville in many places: in his office at his command, waiting outside in lines stretching around the corner of the back entrance to the Colonial Secretary's Office; on stations, where he surveyed them as children, planning for their eventual removal; at settlements and missions, where he was a dignitary, a man of importance to be impressed by the overseers, and in his home, where women worked as servants for himself, his wife and his children. Auber lost one of his children, a daughter who died at around the age of the children whom he preferred to take away from Aboriginal parents: five or six. And so, while he also met our family members as entries in the personal files that he meticulously kept about our families, we met him on more occasions than he may have realised; met him, judged him and his work, and found him to be wanting.

Within the files and the cards that he used to document the lives of Aboriginal people of Western Australia, calculations of race could be as focused as one 132nd. This kind of obsessive documentation was often at odds with the mismanagement of the lives of the people who had been placed in his charge. This is not to say that Neville was solely to blame for the contemporary realities facing Aboriginal people throughout Western Australia.

The violent skirmishes, massacres, enslaved workforces and removal of children were as much the responsibility of the non-Aboriginal population who had individually and collectively supported the building of such corrupt foundations of control and subjugation. However, Neville was an unusually fastidious and obsessive man, seemingly unable to reflect on the effect of his own actions, and this was to be our undoing. 'Mr Neville was ambitious,' says Anna Haebich, 'and I think that's the key to Mr Neville ... Mr Neville was there to carry out the agendas of his master, and his masters were the politicians and the public. And they wanted him to implement the 1905 Aborigines Act and that's exactly what he did ... He's not a visionary, he's not a reformer; he is carrying out his duties as a public servant. But as time goes on ... my feeling is that he starts to enjoy the feeling of power that he has over the people.'[34]

> I was about five or six when they took me away. I remember that day when the police came and picked me up. My mother, well, she just stood there. I can see her crying you know, just standing there, nothing she could do, nothing at all. I never see her again.
>
> *Elizabeth Ray Dalgety, from* Sort of a Place Like Home

As Professor Marcia Langton argued in regard to Neville's contradiction of wanting to 'save' the best elements of his mixed race charges and, at the same time, control the growing population of people of mixed descent, this was based largely in the racist ideology of the time as well as within a set of pseudo-scientific ideas: 'People like him believed there was a place for the half caste, three-quarter caste, quarter caste, octoroon peoples in manual labour and domestic positions if they could be trained properly. And the idea was to separate them from their native contexts, and to put them into Western institutions and this was regarded as all for the best ... He was applying a kind of scientific approach to controlling these, this coloured race that had emerged on the frontiers.'[35]

If Neville was the gardener and 'whiteness' was what he wished to cultivate, the settlements would be the hot houses in which he would tend his most ambitious socially engineered crop, *Albus aborigine submitto*. Aboriginal children taken from their families were to be the root stock of this imagined creation of a submissive Aboriginal population, and thousands of Aboriginal mothers, fathers, siblings and grandparents would suffer the consequences.

Before supplying Gladys with the things for which you ask,
I should like to have another report as to her conduct and progress.
It is not worth spending money on this girl unless she is going to
profit by the training she is getting.
AO Neville

THE SETTLEMENT EXPERIMENT

For the first half of the twentieth century the only members of white society who came into direct contact with Aboriginal people were the police, pastoralists and other primary industry workers, and missionaries. Neville did not trust church-based missions. The Act was to be administered by his department, and he was to be responsible for any major decisions in the lives of the people. Instead of independent, smaller missions over which he had no control, he would manage the lives of Aboriginal inmates within a wider settlement system. By removing the government subsidy provided to missions per child per annum by the government, Neville forced the closure of almost every Aboriginal mission by 1921. With the missions in decline, he set up the Carrolup River

Settlement in 1916 and the Moore River Native Settlement in 1917. In 1922 Carrolup River was closed to effect economies, and its inmates were transferred to Moore River, massively increasing the Moore River Native Settlement's population and stretching its capacity to provide any form of assistance.[36]

Anna Haebich's study of the settlement scheme was based on thorough research of the Aborigines Department files, and interviews with community members who experienced its influence:

> Mr Neville saw them as clearing houses. First of all you would
> take in people who were in need. And they could be dealt with
> in a centralised way, given rations or whatever care they needed
> there, hospitals and so on. So particularly older people, the elderly
> people, would be moved to these settlements, and they would stay
> there and eventually pass away. Meanwhile you would bring in the
> children, take them away from their families, bring in the children
> and put them in dormitories, teach them [the] basic three 'Rs' and
> [provide] some training in domestic service or in farm labouring
> work and then send them out to work ... During the thirties there
> were over 500 people there. And the facilities were overused and
> run down, and there was very little for the adults to do, and the
> conditions for the children were appalling.[37]

If cemeteries are the gardens of the dead, the cemetery at Moore River (also known as Mogumber, a Noongar word meaning 'place of clouds') is a very subtle yet also menacingly silent garden. The site was chosen in 1921 because of its cultural foundations, the presence of moodjar trees, resting places for the spirits of the dead. After a time the spirits would leave the trees, travelling through underground streams to a resting place under the ocean (Wardandi), far to the west. This 'garden' is subtle for this fact alone, subtle to many who do not recognise the power and significance of the moodjar trees, beautiful, big moodjar trees that glow burnt orange in the setting summer sun. It is also subtle because the hundreds of graves of the Moore River Native Settlement and the Mogumber Mission inmates are hidden from view.[38] Of the more than 400 people buried here, more than half are children younger than five. The mounds of earth that may belie the location of an adult grave are not visible for such young bodies. The reclamation of this gentle sloping plain by the undergrowth of wattle, woolly-bush and salt-bush also obscures their existence.

BACK TO MOGUMBER

On Back to Mogumber Day hundreds of former inmates and their children and grandchildren would return here to place flowers or bailer shells on graves, a Noongar tradition linking the dead with the ocean. The annual Back to Mogumber Day commemorated the hand-back of Moore River Native Settlement lands to Aboriginal control in 1990 via a ninety-nine-year lease from the Western Australian Government. What separated the fate of those who survived and could return free from those who died incarcerated? I would like to think resistance, resilience and courage. However, these traits will get you only so far. They are necessary traits if you are going to survive, but they are no guarantee of survival. There are many resisters buried here.

Returning to the remnants of the settlement, researching the files that were kept on our families, reading the revelations of historians and sharing our oral histories can reopen old wounds and fears. So too can it act as a means to redress injustice, through understanding what took place and bearing witness to other people's similar experiences. Many of Noongar–Yamatji elder Sam

> Are we going to have a population of one million blacks in the
> Commonwealth or are we going to merge them into our white
> community and eventually forget that there were ever any
> Aborigines in Australia?
>
> *AO Neville*

Dinah's family were inmates of the Moore River Native Settlement,
as was Sam himself. His experience of redressing the past through
opening the files kept on his family is unsettling and restorative,
and a common experience for many who have taken this step:

> I started reading Mum's file after I got the file from DCD
> [Department of Community Development]. And as I started
> to read it I started to get a picture of what ... my mother had
> to endure. She ... wrote letters to the Protector, A. O. Neville,
> asking that she be released ... She asked to go back to stay with
> her father, my grandfather, down at Mount Barker ... Even my
> grandfather wrote letters to the Native Welfare Department
> asking that she be released ... That never eventuated. She
> eventually died there, and two years before the ... Moore River
> Native Settlement was disbanded ... I get angry when I read
> Mum's files ... You know, I certainly am not going to allow for
> that to ever happen again. And I will stand up for the rights of
> my people. And for the policies that may be introduced to try and
> bring about a demise ... to our people. And I'm quite adamant and
> I'm quite strong in that feeling. I'm prepared to put my life on the
> line so it will never happen again. There was no need for it in the
> first instance.[39]

Doris Pilkington's powerful book *Follow the Rabbit-Proof
Fence* is one such story that tells of the escape of her mother
and aunt from the Moore River Native Settlement. This book

and the subsequent film that was made of it have done more to inform a wider audience of this history than any of the valuable documentaries, books and exhibitions that have been created previously. Against incredible obstacles, including the actions of Neville and the Western Australian Police Force to capture them, Doris's mother and one of her aunts made it back alive. The film of her book has alerted international audiences to the conditions that her family and other Aboriginal families suffered. Through choosing to escape, their story has become a symbol that has exerted an influence greater than anything they could have imagined as young girls travelling thousands of miles on foot, simply to return home. Doris's own story in tracing this journey is an act of courage in itself, of dealing with the unfinished business of these past policies:

> It was when I began to write ... *Follow the Rabbit-Proof Fence*,
> I went to the libraries and studied the past history of the
> Aboriginal affairs and so on. And that's where I read about
> Mr Neville and his grand ideas. Of making these changes, so he
> thought, for Aboriginal children. So when I read that, you know,
> I was horrified when I thought. You know, here's this man
> making a decision—this is an adult—a decision for Aboriginal
> children.
>
> You know, as a writer I've travelled and, promoting the film
> *Rabbit-Proof Fence*, I've travelled to many countries, and where
> I saw evidence of ... fighting for the rights of children. WE didn't
> have that. WE just followed along because the government said,
> what the government said, we do; what the government gives, the
> government takes.
>
> So that was that ... I learnt from that reading, researching
> and learning about Mr Neville.[40]

By the early 1930s, news of the deplorable living conditions at Moore River began to surface in the press. As with 1905, there was vigorous debate in the media about the conditions under which Aboriginal people suffered. Neville engaged the public in a campaign to provide him with the resources and the legislation he believed necessary to achieve his unfolding plans. Segregation and separation were no longer an option in Mr Neville's view, and his new approach, founded in those very same false race theories of the nineteenth century, would be his most controversial. As Anna Haebich relates:

> So, in the lead-up to, in pushing for changes, Mr Neville had a
> vision. As I said before, he wasn't really a visionary but in this
> case he had a vision of a new way of dealing with the Aboriginal
> problem that we've now come to call the policy of biological
> absorption. And basically it was about the State intervening
> in Aboriginal lives to, as Mr Neville said, make the people
> become lighter. So it was a policy that combined manipulation of
> Aboriginal race and of Aboriginal culture to basically erase both
> from the community. So you would have no more people who
> looked Aboriginal, you would have no more Aboriginal culture.
> That was the idea.[41]

The policy of segregation had led to an increased number of reserves and communities existing on welfare hand-outs from the increasingly embattled Aborigines Department. As the cost of living increased and unemployment became a pandemic, Aboriginal Affairs received even less money and was expected to do more for a growing Aboriginal population. Debate in the media, often fuelled by Neville writing under a *nom de plume*, centred on issues of race, of assimilation and, with Neville's urging, biological absorption of Aboriginal peoples. However, in fanning this debate, Neville took the risk of encountering an adversary to his policies worthy of his own compulsive and impassioned approach. This adversary arrived on the scene in the form of Mrs Mary Bennett. As Anna Haebich relates:[42]

> Mary Bennett was independently wealthy, she was well connected, she was very intelligent, she was a feminist and she was involved in the international feminist movement. She lived in London for a long time, and she was also involved in campaigns for the rights of native peoples of the British Empire. She was outspoken and she attacked Mr Neville on numerous occasions for the policies that he was advocating for the department ... Mrs Mary Bennett believed in the ability of Aboriginal people to really learn ... and to be part of the nation if they wanted to be.[43]

Being independently wealthy, white and confident of her actions, Mary Bennett took the lead in progressing community calls for an inquiry into the state of Aboriginal Affairs. Similar to the Roth Royal Commission of 1904, the Mosely Royal Commission polarised community responses to the supposed 'Aboriginal Problem'. Neville had also worked hard to see such a review undertaken. Both Mary Bennett and Neville were seeking legislative changes to enable what it appears they believed would aid the welfare of Aboriginal peoples of Western Australia. Neville's view was that Aboriginal people would never be accepted by wider white society, so they should be transformed into white people without cultural connections to their ancestral past.[44] Reviewing this position, Professor Haebich found that Mary Bennett's view was that, given the chance, Aboriginal people had the ability, when free of the controlling manipulations of government, to manage their own affairs as useful members of a wider Australian society. 'Mary Bennet was instrumental in getting the

> The deplorable social and economic position of Aborigines...
> is caused by the victimization of the Aboriginal women... Many of
> these poor children are parted from their mothers... but first for
> years they suffer the misery of hunted animals, always running
> away from the police... always in fear that at any moment they
> may be torn away, never to see them again.
>
> *Mary Bennett*

Mosley Royal Commission appointed. It was her allegations of slavery still in ... the pastoral and pearling industries in the north that appeared in the British press that really riled the Western Australian Government and ended with the appointment of the royal commission.'[45]

Neville prepared for the royal commission by calling together the self-constructed evidence of his own personal and administrative files. Further, he was allowed such latitude in questioning criticisms of his department that, in Professor Haebich's view, it was questionable whether he was actually a part of the royal commission rather than an individual with responsibility in need of being reviewed.[46]

> At the hearings, Mary Bennett went toe to toe with Mr Neville ...
> He sat in on all the hearings, almost as a co-commissioner with
> Mosley, who was a chief magistrate. He sat up with him, and he
> also directed questions ... at people who appeared in front of the
> commissioner ... He was very vitriolic in his questioning of Mary
> Bennett. And she stood up to him, she wasn't about to be spoken
> down to by him ... She was also representing some Aboriginal
> people, presenting their evidence on their behalf because it
> was very difficult and a very daunting experience for Aboriginal
> people to appear before that commission, and particularly given
> Mr Neville's very active interference in what was happening.[47]

The debates about policy, legislation, the Mosely Royal Commission, all of these things were reported in the press. Now having established that fact, that the public could know, of course the big question is, did they care?

Professor Anna Haebich, historian

A number of Aboriginal witnesses also presented to the royal commission. These people found that their own personal files, created by Neville about them without their knowledge, were taken as serious evidence against them. 'Aboriginal representations to the Mosley Royal Commission ... from the south ... were principally directed at the appalling conditions at Moore River Native Settlement and the fact that children were being taken away from their families.'[48]

Instead of curtailing Neville's powers and the mismanagement of the state, the *Native Administration Act 1936* (WA) laid the foundations for some of the most devastating regulations and invasive controls on Aboriginal lives in Western Australia.

He increased his controls over marriage, so any marriage involving Aboriginal people had to have his approval ... then the controls over sexual contact. And he also, of course, had powers to take people to institutions, and he had the new children's institution, Sister Kate's, which was set up in Perth in the early 1930s to cater for and to accommodate and train near-white children, they were called then. And to turn them into white children, children who thought they were white and who were going to live as white people.[49]

'YOU BASTARDS, YOU'RE AS BLACK AS I AM'

The above immortal words were yelled, regularly, by an older Noongar woman at children of Sister Kate's Home for Quarter

Caste Children when they visited the city on an outing from the home. While Neville may have seen the role of Sister Kate's Home as being the segregating and sifting out of children of fair complexion so that they could be accepted into wider society, within the tiny population of Perth they were all too regularly and sometimes none too politely welcomed back into the Aboriginal flock.[50]

> What Australia's half-caste daughters need is their own mothers who love them, and their own homes among their own people, and teaching, until such a time as they shall have attained legal and economic and political freedom, and meet white people on terms of equality.
>
> *Mary Bennett*

My grandmother, Jessie Smith, would regularly visit Sister Kate's Home, checking on the children of women, friends and claimed family, who were out working as domestic servants and requested information about their children. My grandmother would prepare for the Sunday trips by saving bundles of news-papers, brought home by my grandfather, who worked at West Australian Newspapers as an electrician. These papers would be swapped in the Depression with 'Con the Grocer', who would provide fruit and lollies for the children. Loaded up with my mother and other Aboriginal children she was caring for, they would head out to Queens Park to the children's home in a borrowed taxi-truck. My grandmother was, at that time, under investigation by Neville for 'suffering' other Aboriginal women, men and children under her roof. Having married a white man, she was expected to blend into white society. This she did not do. My grandfather, Edward Smith, was being threatened with prosecution for this very same charge, and they were both being investigated, as were many mixed race couples during the Mosley Royal Commission.[51]

Sister Kate always wanted the family environment. Mr Neville wanted
the government dictates and there was a degree of tension between
them. I know that when Mr Neville came out he was horrified to find
the boys and girls in the dormitory sleeping together. He said, 'You'll
have boys over here and girls over there' and he indicated and Sister
Kate said, 'No, I'm bringing these children up in as normal a family
environment as I can' and it remained like that.
Gerry Warber, Noongar nation

Walking arm in arm with Kate Clutterbuck, my 21-stone
grandmother and the effete old nun, Sister Kate, whom my
grandmother and all the children called 'Gran', would spend
the day talking about the children of the women unable to care
for them, and allowing a sense of normality and community into
the children's life. It was true. My mother really had kicked the
football with Polly Farmer at Sister Kate's.

Such stories of friendships and celebration between the
cracks of control and manipulation by the department are not
uncommon. Sister Kate's might have been allowed to function
within Neville's graces because it suited his goals of biological
absorption. Similarly, my own grandparents were able to marry,
after being denied the opportunity for more than ten years, as
Neville saw advantage in people of 'colour' marrying 'white'
people. However, Aboriginality is more than colour, racially
imagined characteristics and biologically mythologised fan-
tasies. Community finds a way. Community, or communion,
knows the colour of its own bonds of belonging. Within the
earlier subtle space of Sister Kate's, it existed as a compromise
between Neville's perceived outcomes and Sister Kate's own
management of the lives of these children in her care. That Sister

Stolen children

Anna Haebich: The police come thundering in on their horses and they're looking for half-caste children. So there was this great flurry and crisis and fear.

Doris Pilkington: And the mothers had no rights at all, no rights to protest, or anything. All they could do was sit down and cry.

Sam Dinah: We were raised as white, and we didn't know anything about our customs or culture. I've spent the best of my life following that removal in institutions.

Gordon Briscoe: Their sole purpose of assimilating people was to change them, change their race, to change their culture, to change their language, to change their practices of living with other people, to change their religion.

Sam Dinah: Never saw mum after that. Matter of fact I didn't, I don't even, didn't even know what she looked like.

My own grandmother was born in the Kimberley region during the Killing Times. I've tried to imagine what it must have been like, finding yourself on a police escort walking a hundred and fifty miles, where she was housed with people who were chained at the neck, with other children who'd been taken away from other stations.

Steve Kinnane, historian, Mirriwoong nation

Kate may have seen the outcome as assimilation, may have been so. That she allowed for community contact against the policies of the Aborigines Department is clearly so.

In later years, many children who were placed with Sister Kate (who had since passed away) spoke of sexual abuse at the hands of visitors and some staff. This, in itself, shows the failure of such social engineering against the alternative: to support individuals and communities to be fully functioning members of societies of their choosing and cultures of their being.

AN IDEA UNDESERVING OF A TIME

The effects of the Native Administration Act were predictably damaging. It was akin to the destructive federal policies on Indigenous affairs of the Howard Liberal government's eleven years in power from 1996 to 2007. Aboriginal peoples of Western Australia were faced with enduring the impact of the Depression while continuing to endure the leadership by law of an individual whom none trusted or could have dialogue with. If anything, it was a period in which, like the end of the twentieth century and the beginning of the twenty-first, an incredible depression of a different kind overtook Aboriginal communities, and individuals found themselves marginalised and disenfranchised as never before. It holds resonance with the Killing Times, not for the outright slaughter and aggression against Aboriginal people but for the opportunities lost, for the constancy of the ignorance and the poverty and the miasma of enforced neglect.[52]

As the Native Administration Act was coming into effect, Neville was on a roll. Having achieved his greatest victory in almost two decades, as his newly created Native Affairs Department was preparing to act on its newly created powers, Neville was being courted by the federal sphere. 'In 1937, the Federal Government held the first national meeting of State and Federal authorities working with Aboriginal people,' as Anna Haebich relates. 'Neville succeeded in persuading the other representatives to adopt, as a resolution, his policy of biological absorption as a national policy.'[53]

Ironically, events in Europe, tied in part to theories of racial superiority, segregation, and social and biological engineering, would thwart Neville's plans to implement the legislation he had fought so hard to have passed. Watching the events of Europe from afar, overt aggression and fascist authoritarianism could be seen clearly through the lens of another society. However, as Professor Haebich found, such recognition was not without its ramifications for Western Australia:

> So after all of that, after they pass the resolution and Neville returns triumphantly to Perth, he has his 1936 Act, he has the 1937 resolution. And then of course it's the lead-up to the war, the war comes and the matter is dropped. And of course in the post-war years that sort of policy is anathema. People have heard about what happened in Nazi Germany and [its] race-based policies, and there was no way you would get any policy like that accepted in Australia.[54]

Neville finally retired in 1940 at the age of sixty-five. The legislation that he was instrumental in creating continued to have detrimental effects on Aboriginal populations in Western Australia for decades to come. However, without Neville at the helm, the same zeal was not evident and, with the coming of the war years, the state's grip on Aboriginal lives in Western Australia was loosened. Institutional and legislative change is an important goal in seeking social justice. However, without individual action and responsibility, the best laws are not worth the paper they are written on. Likewise, sometimes it takes a change at the top, a shifting of individuals who have not been able to accept that they, or their actions, are a major impediment to desired social change; cultivating democracy instead of imagined racial purity to appease an immature society.

THE APOLOGY

The Howard Liberal government was removed from power by a popular vote in November 2007. The newly elected Labor Prime Minister, Kevin Rudd, promised that his government would

The Native Union

William Harris was the centre of a political movement called the Native Union, which resisted the oppressive laws that bound his people in Western Australia. He wrote to politicians and newspapers, and in 1928 led a deputation to the Western Australian Premier. The Premier ignored their complaints.

Letter from William Harris to the *Sunday Times*, 14 November 1926:

Ever since the whites settled in Western Australia the Aborigines have not lived in a more cruel or lawless state than they are living today. Since the inauguration of responsible government their condition have gone from bad to worse, and have now become intolerable. For hundreds of years, in song and story, it has been Britain's boast that under her flag was found justice and fair dealing for all. But in dealing with the Aborigines it has been reserved for Western Australia to overturn British law and justice … there is no law for Aborigines in this state. What law or justice can there be for people who are robbed and shot down, or run into miserable compounds? What part or parcel have they in the land in which they have a right to live?

Regarding massacres, heaps of human bones mixed with cartridge shells in different parts of the state appear to me evidence of the fact of their having been shot down. Most people hearing of the dispersion of natives think that a few shots were fired over their heads to scatter them. This dispersion takes a different form altogether.

The educated Aborigines … are about to form a protective union. As British subjects they claim and mean to have the protection of the same laws that govern the white man, not to be persecuted by the Aborigines Department and its officials.

At Laverton we had the spectacle of natives in that district decoyed into the police station on the pretence of being served with food. The doors were closed on them, they were kept under lock and key until the train was ready to start, then taken under armed escort and locked in the train for Mogumber [Moore River].

apologise to the Stolen Generations, those who were removed from their families and those of us affected by those removals.

As the day of the apology approached, friends and colleagues flew to Canberra from all over the country. There was a sense of disbelief but also a sense of grace as the preceding days were spent finding people places to stay and running them around town, and in debates surrounding the impact, legally, socially, politically and psychologically, of this action.

Mr Speaker, I move that today we honour the Indigenous peoples of this land, the oldest continuing cultures in human history. The time has now come for the nation to turn a new page. We apologise for the laws and policies of successive parliaments and governments that have inflicted profound grief, suffering and loss on these our fellow Australians.

Prime Minister Kevin Rudd

On the day, I sat on the ground with friends from as far afield as Nyikina Country in the Kimberley, Gurindji Country in the Northern Territory and Noongar Country in Perth. We were corralled halfway between the old Parliament House and the new Parliament House, symbolically sandwiched between the past and the future. Slowly, people gathered. A gentle rain fell for most of the morning, and a particularly sweet and gentle drizzle fell from the sky as the Prime Minister took centre stage to commit an act of resistance to the last two centuries of child removals:

There comes a time in the history of nations when their peoples must become fully reconciled to their past if they are to go forward with confidence to embrace their future. Our nation, Australia, has reached such a time. That is why the parliament is today here assembled: to deal with this unfinished business of the nation, to remove a great stain from the nation's soul and, in a true spirit of reconciliation, to open a new chapter in the history of this great land, Australia ... For the pain, suffering and hurt of these Stolen Generations, their descendants and for their families left behind, we say sorry. To the mothers and the fathers, the brothers and the sisters, for the breaking up of families and communities, we say sorry. And for the indignity and degradation thus inflicted on a proud people and a proud culture, we say sorry.[55]

As Prime Minister Rudd spoke, I could feel the relief in the crowd and I could feel the power of his action. It was a simple and intangible apology, a leap into a potential future beyond blood of the kind that was wrought into existence in the racist ideologies of past governments. It does not mean that future governments will not choose the ignorant path, or that individuals within the country still don't harbour such views. The apology was a seemingly intangible, yet powerful act of responsibility against the tide of past injustices.

CONTINUED RESISTANCE

It is deathly quiet in Fitzroy Crossing, but not because of sorry business. Children no longer light fires and sleep by the river to escape the humbug. They are at home. The Fitzroy Top Ten of alcohol-fuelled violence and menace no longer resonates throughout the town. Old people, who had been unable to get a good night's sleep and were constantly hassled for money on pension day, are rested and hopeful for the first time in years. This is not to say this will last or that, as you read these words, children are not already having to light those same signal fires. Thankfully, if and when they do, there are people on the ground willing to take up that responsibility.

The women of Fitzroy Crossing, through the Marninwarn-tikura Fitzroy Women's Resource Centre, aided by such key agencies as the Kimberley Aboriginal Law and Culture Centre, successfully lobbied the State Government to impose a ban on take-away alcohol in the town's two hotels. It is not seen as a solution to everyone's problems, but it is a reprieve, a breather, so that the real social reconstruction by which people can achieve their potential is developed.[56]

This ban, like the apology, is beyond blood, race and social engineering. June Oscar is a Bunuba woman who speaks her language, chairs the Kimberley Aboriginal Language Resource Centre and is CEO of the Marninwarntikura Fitzroy Women's Resource Centre in Fitzroy. It has been reported that June has received threats of violence from those who once profited before the ban and from those who are being forced to review their behaviour. June is not someone to take action lightly or to break under pressure. In her view, this action by Bunuba women and men is being made in the spirit of Jandamarra, breaking through what has seemed to be an intractable issue with action and choosing to live with the consequences.[57]

Within the communities of the Fitzroy Valley, people have taken responsibility in building outstations, schools, stations, organisations to support language and culture, homes and health clinics, and in taking care of country. The alcohol ban transformed Fitzroy Crossing within a matter of months. The chronic issues that were created through past policies and contemporary substance abuse will take more than this, but leading by example has provided the possibility of change, a reprieve from which there will be a forward movement beyond blood history towards individual and collective responsibility.

But, sitting on my backside in Canberra amid the reprieve of an act of grace, I could not help but think about the next steps towards tangible change, such as the work done by workers at the Kimberley Aboriginal Law and Culture Centre, a lifeblood of Fitzroy Crossing and the Fitzroy Valley. The Law and Culture Centre has consistently received between 30 and 40 per cent less funding than it has requested in the past seven years. It is being expected to operate on a budget that is $22 000 less than it received ten years ago. The apology is welcome, but something is clearly not connecting here, between those who have the ability to act yet few resources and those with the resources but no idea of how to be of any real use. If we are to sincerely 'deal with this unfinished business of the nation', as the Prime Minister has envisaged, let's support those who are already dealing with it, and stop talking about it.

Ngariarty
SPEAKING STRONG

6
THE SCHOOLS OF HUMAN EXPERIENCE
Wayne Atkinson

The Yorta Yorta belong to traditional lands that have been occupied by their ancestors since time immemorial.[1] Their traditional lands and waters span the Victorian and New South Wales border in what is now known as the Central Murray and Goulburn Valley region. The lands cover both sides of the Murray River in an oval shape and are replenished by a network of rivers, lakes, lagoons and wetlands characteristic of this part of Australia.

In Yorta Yorta history it is said that in the long-distant past the land and all of its natural and cultural splendour, including the Murray River, called Dhungulla in the Yorta Yorta language, came into being through the creative deeds of the great spirit ancestor Biami. The image and the story of Biami, which is painted on the wall of the Dharnya Cultural Centre in the Barmah Forest, reads:

> Biami created the river by sending his woman down from the high country with her yam stick to journey across the flat and waterless plain. Biami then sent his giant snake along to watch over her. She walked for many weary miles, drawing a track in the sand with her stick, and behind her came the giant snake following in and out and all about, making the curves of the river bed with his body. Then Biami spoke in a voice of thunder, from up high. Lightning flashed and rain fell, and water came flowing down the track made by the woman and the snake. After many moons she came to the sea, and went to sleep in a cave, while her dogs ran off and kicked up the sand hills about the river mouth.[2]

Many of the beliefs of the river and its significance to the Yorta Yorta have been passed down over the years by Yorta Yorta elders in such stories as that of the 'great flood', which is said to have nearly covered the tops of the old river red gums some 30 000 years ago and changed the course of Dhungulla. Yorta Yorta elder Colin Walker speaks of his relationship with the river and what it means to him:

> I think it is like a human body. The Murray River is the spine, and the Barmah Forest and Moira Lakes are the kidneys on both sides. That is how the old people used to look at it. They would say, 'This is our life.' It is a living thing. We are the land, and we are mother earth. We fit in like that. It is important that I teach the young children the respect for the forest, the trees, the water, the streams, the lagoons, the water ways, as it is a part of us, and we are a part of them.[3]

Another story of the waterways and the changes witnessed by the Yorta Yorta over time is told by Uncle Dan Atkinson, who took me to the place where the more recent course of the Murray cut through the sand ridge on which the old Maloga Mission was established. Pointing to the place where the elders decided to release the water by cutting a track through the sandy ridge with their digging sticks, he told me that this was the place where 'they decided to let her go'.[4]

This land belonged to our forefathers 150 years ago but today we are pushed further and further into the background—we have decided to make ourselves heard!

Jack Patten

Given the significance of water in Yorta Yorta tradition, it is true to say that the rivers and their surrounds are the spiritual and economic lifeblood of the Yorta Yorta nation. The extensive middens and mounds (campsites) along the banks of the rivers and lagoons, as well as the elaborate fish-trap systems constructed across the entrances of the river offshoots, are the tangible evidence of Yorta Yorta reliance on water resources for their everyday needs. Yorta Yorta people's oral knowledge of where their ancestors camped, fished and collected food indicates that just about everything happened in and around the watercourses. That the relationship between land, water and aspects of life is of one worldly creation in Yorta Yorta philosophy is crucial to understanding Yorta existence and their connections with country.

Putting the Yorta Yorta back in time and place provides a foundation for following the story of their love for country and their tenacious struggle to hold on to what they believe has always been theirs by inherent right.

This is the story, told from the Yorta Yorta world view, of my people's heroic struggle from its beginnings in the Scholars Hut at the Maloga Mission to the present struggle for land justice and racial equality within the settler state. For it was by candlelight in what has become immortalised as the Scholars Hut that the seeds of Yorta Yorta political awareness and activism were cultivated. This became the catalyst for the rise of the Indigenous political movement in Australia—a revolutionary point in Indigenous thinking that led to the 1967 referendum and beyond. Against this background I dedicate this chapter to the spirit of my great-grandfather TS James, my great-uncle William Cooper and the ongoing struggle of the Yorta Yorta Nation.

The authorities may close the school to them but they cannot close the schools of human experience.
Sir Doug Nicholls[5]

In 1874 the first generation of Yorta Yorta were gathered by Daniel Matthews at the old Maloga Mission. Matthews, a fervent Christian who had done well for himself and his ship-chandler business in Echuca during the heyday of the Murray River trade, was appalled at the Yorta Yorta's conditions, which he saw around him. In a letter to the editor of the *Age*, he wrote: 'Sir, are we doing too much for these Blacks? As a community have not the people of this colony ... benefited by the land taken from this uncivilized race? On the Murray and Goulburn Rivers there are hundreds of these poor wretches worse than uncared for ... Large tracts of land should be set apart for them and they should be encouraged in everything that would raise them above their present state.'[6] Matthews was particularly disturbed by the way the young women were being physically abused by squatters and their workers.[7]

After trying to persuade the government to do something about it
and not getting any results, he channelled his wealth into his own
private mission.

The site of the mission, as told to Matthews by Yorta Yorta
elders, was an important meeting place for local and surrounding
groups for as long as anyone could remember.[8] Its location
became more strategic as time went on. Being located on the
border of New South Wales and Victoria, the Murray River was
never considered a political boundary by the Yorta Yorta. In
geographic and political terms, Maloga and the later reserve
Cummeragunja were located on the New South Wales side of
the river. They were some 800 kilometres from Sydney but only
240 kilometres from the seat of the Victorian Government. The
river became a significant political boundary for both administrations, each passing the buck of responsibility for the Yorta
Yorta. In the 1860s the Victorian Aborigines Protection Board
played the boundary card by requesting the New South Wales
Government take responsibility for Indigenous people. It refused,
providing no proper assistance until its equivalent administration
was established in 1883.

Their experience of border politics could be the reason the
Yorta Yorta became so astute in dealing with the multiple layers
of political processes. They were also good swimmers and used
the political boundary as protection against their children being
taken away, as we will see. Their location on the Murray River
became a means by which they sought greater freedom from the
tyranny of reserve management in the 1930s.

Maloga's beginnings were grand, but unfortunately its
history was short-lived. It was basically a private venture set
up on the jointly owned land of Daniel and his brother William

Matthews. Being located on private land and outside the control of the New South Wales Protection Board's administration was perhaps the main reason for its demise in 1888.

However, while Maloga existed, it was in the Scholars Hut, away from the vagaries of mission life, that the foundations of Yorta Yorta political consciousness were laid. At that time the reality of what was happening in the Scholars Hut and its eventual influence on the broader Indigenous political scene had yet to be fully realised. One of its many graduates who would carry high the flag for Indigenous justice was the young William Cooper.

ORIGINS OF YORTA YORTA POLITICAL CONSCIOUSNESS

Born in Yorta Yorta lands in 1862, William Cooper was the son of Granny Kitty, a matriarch of her family group, whom she brought to Maloga. William Cooper was her eldest son on the Cooper line, and his hunger for knowledge and his ability to adapt to the white man's education system is revealed in Daniel Matthew's diary entries for August 1874. Matthews notes with particular attention that the 'boy Billy Cooper shows great aptitude for learning. He has acquired a knowledge of the Alphabet, capital and smaller letters ... in three days and then taught [his brother] Bobby in capitals only in one day.'[9]

Daniel Matthews had the foresight to seek out a decent education for the people under his care—or as decent as was permissible given that the standard allowed to be taught to Aboriginal people in New South Wales at the time was equal to that of third grade or an eight-year-old white kid. On a visit to Melbourne to drum up support for his privately funded mission, Matthews met Thomas Shadrach James, a distinguished scholar of Sri Lankan background, who came to Australia via Mauritius in the early 1870s and studied at Melbourne University. Grandpa

James, as he affectionately became known, was an exceptional scholar in medicine, history, politics and linguistics as well as a qualified teacher in education. He was also knowledgeable in dispensing medicines, and dentistry, and was often called upon to administer dental treatment. Grandpa brought these skills with him to Maloga and to Cummeragunja, where he became an admired leader, mentor and headmaster of the school.

Grandpa James encouraged his students to be confident in their own abilities. He taught them to be proud of their Yorta Yorta identity and to recognise the empowerment that comes from being able to articulate their grievances through the power of the voice and the spear of the pen. Being influenced by a passion for human dignity and respect for one's fellow people, regardless of race or creed, Grandpa was a strong believer in the political strategy of passive resistance. It was a process that required patience, leadership and collective people power. It was largely Grandpa James' style of teaching and William's desire to gain justice for his people that combined to lay the foundation stones of what arguably became the genesis of Yorta Yorta political thinking.

Against this background it is worth reflecting on the concept of the Scholars Hut and the quality of education that Grandpa's pupils were receiving, including the instructive nature of his teaching. This is brought home by the many non-Indigenous students whom Grandpa taught at Maloga and later at the Cummeragunja reserve, including Matthews' eldest son, John, who went on to enjoy a privileged education in Melbourne, Adelaide, London and Canada. On returning to Cummeragunja many years later with a sense of gratitude he paid great 'tribute' to Grandpa, whom he said 'laid the truest and finest foundation of his education' and was a 'teacher unsurpassed anywhere'.

In comparing the quality of education being taught at Maloga and in mainstream schools, Maloga was equal to or above that of the average school, which John Kerr Matthews attributes to 'the character and ability of Mr James'.[10]

Indeed the image of the Scholars Hut, a candle burning into the night, and the intellectual stimulus that TS James was imparting to his students, is a powerful metaphor. It is something that has had a profound effect on my generation's desires to carry on where Grandpa left off and achieve in higher education.

Thomas Shadrach James eventually married William Cooper's sister Ada and dedicated the rest of his life to Yorta Yorta education and to their political struggle. He remained headmaster until his retirement in 1922, after some fifty years of outstanding service. Indeed it was his knowledge and his style of teaching that inspired the next generation of Yorta Yorta political activists, including Sir Doug Nicholls, Bill Onus, Shadrach James (his son by Ada), Marj Tucker, Geraldine Briggs, Eddy Atkinson and many others. Names like these are synonymous with the achievements that were nurtured at Maloga and Cummeragunja, before and after the turn of the twentieth century.

One also needs to recognise that, while these leaders have etched their names into the history books, their achievements are indelibly linked to the support and the solidarity of the community they came from and whom they represented. They were also moulded by the unimaginable circumstances Indigenous people faced at that time in Australia.

Reflecting on Grandpa James' retirement many years later, one of his students said: 'He was the cog in the wheel, and when he left it left a big gap to fill because he set such a high standard to follow.'[11] After Maloga, Grandpa and his family moved to

Melbourne for a while, where he continued to mentor and advise his former students, who by this time had set up the first Aboriginal organisation in Australia, the Australian Aborigines League, in Melbourne in 1933. He is buried with his wife, Ada, in the Cummeragunja cemetery.

THE RESERVE SYSTEM

Aboriginal reserves in New South Wales were administered by the New South Wales Aborigines Protection Board (1883–1942). They were managed through the infamous legislative regime of the protection era, which dominated and controlled Aboriginal life throughout Australia. The Aborigines Protection Acts gave formidable powers to state-managed boards and reserve managers. By the 1930s these powers were used to segregate and control the everyday lives and movements of residents both on and off the reserve.[12] The policy and practice of segregation and control, however, had much deeper roots.

Aboriginal reserves, or 'concentration camps' as they were called by William Cooper, were a patchwork of lands established across the length and breadth of Australia.[13] Reserves have a complex history and are remembered with mixed emotions by Indigenous people. They have served both as havens and as places of control. The level of human dignity afforded to residents, or inmates as they were sometimes called, shifted according to public sympathy and the personalities of the 'mission managers' as they came and went. One of the reserves' main functions was to relocate the traditional owners from the lands so that their lands could be appropriated by settlers. Indeed it is argued that reserves went hand in hand with dispossession and the legal fiction that Australia was an unoccupied land open to be taken without recognition of its prior owners.

By the late 1920s most reserves were intent on trying to 'civilise' their Aboriginal residents in part by eradicating their traditional culture. Their origins, however, were planted in British colonial policy and practice, and by the time this system reached Australia in the late eighteenth century, trialled as it had been in other former British colonies, it was a well-oiled tool of dispossession, domination and control.

At least two centuries before Australia was colonised, the reserve system was used to relocate traditional Irish groups under the Cromwellian colonisation of Ireland, which was sanctioned by the Act of Settlement (1652). 'To Hell or to Connaught' was a scheme designed to remove the Irish forcibly from their ancestral lands and to relocate them west of the Shannon River in the western province of Ireland, where the British tried to keep them under their control. (The Irish response to British overlordship and control is beyond the scope of this chapter.)[14]

The practice of segregating American Indians and placing them on reserves underwrote the history of British colonisation in North America. After gaining control over most of North America in 1760, Britain proclaimed reserved lands for Canadian Indians. Power to regulate and control Indian life and movement was sanctioned under the Indian Act (1876), which empowered the Canadian Government to control land dealings and to oblige Indians to renounce title to land in return for reserved lands. This was to be the pattern for the next century. Indigenous people were isolated from mainstream society and reduced to the status of being wards of the state.[15]

Following the Canadian experience, the United States introduced its system of land control and the allocation of reserve lands for American Indians. The reserve system was sanctioned under the infamous Indian Removal Act (1830),[16] which ordered the relocation of American Indian tribes living east of the Mississippi River in the United States to lands further west. The Act established a policy of exchanging federal lands west of the Mississippi for other lands occupied by Indian tribes in the eastern portion of the United States.[17]

There are major differences between Australia and the recognition of prior occupation and indigenous rights in other former British colonies, but the practice of the reserve system itself was driven by a similar colonial mindset. Despite this mindset, however, other ironies arose from the indigenous response to the reserve system and the policies of segregation and control. Paradoxically, the reserves became important enclaves of indigenous political resistance and survival.[18] Reserves established within traditional lands, as demonstrated in the Yorta Yorta native title case many years later, became the means by which the indigenous political struggle took its shape and form.

THE PRESSURE BUILDS

Aspirations for the return of traditional lands have always been at the forefront of Yorta Yorta thinking. In 1881, forty-two residents of Maloga presented a petition for land to the New South Wales Governor, which highlighted the plight of the Yorta Yorta and pointed out to the Governor in most sincere terms that:

> All the land within our tribal boundaries has been taken
> possession of by the Government and white settlers; our hunting
> grounds are used for sheep pasturage and the game reduced
> and many exterminated, rendering our means of subsistence
> extremely precarious, and often reducing our wives and children
> to beggary. We, the men of several tribes are desirous of honestly
> maintaining our young and infirm who are in many cases the

subjects of extreme want and semi-starvation and we believe we could, in a few years support ourselves by our own industry, were a sufficient area of land granted to us to cultivate and raise stock. We more confidently ask this favor of a grant of land as our fellow natives in other colonies have proved capable of supporting themselves, where suitable land has been reserved for them. We hopefully appeal to your excellency, as we recognise you, the Protector specially appointed by Her Gracious Majesty the Queen 'to promote religion and education amongst the Aboriginal natives of the colony' and to protect us in our persons and in the free enjoyment of our possessions, and to take such measures as may be necessary for our advancement in civilisations. And your petitioners, as in duty bound will ever pray.

Maloga Mission,

Murray River NSW.

July 1881.[19]

In response to this petition 1800 acres of land was located for Aboriginal use upstream from Maloga, which became Cummeragunja (or, as it was also known, Cummera), the new government reserve. Further grants of land were made to bring Cummera up to its total of 2965 acres in 1900.[20] Keep in mind, however, that this derisory amount, set aside for a Cummera population of about 400–500 people at its height, was the average-size block that a European farmer was granted to support a single family.

The 1881 Maloga petition was used more than a hundred years later by Justice Olney in the Yorta Yorta native title case to deny the Yorta Yorta their native title claim. The judge distorted the genuine pleas for land explicit in the petition to support his view that the government and white settlers had dispossessed the Yorta Yorta of the claimed lands by the turn of the twentieth century. The petition was then used to justify the judge's conclusions: that, by this time in Yorta Yorta history, counter to the body of knowledge put before him, the 'tide of history' had washed away Yorta Yorta connections with their ancestral lands. That the Maloga petition was used to the opposite ends of its original intentions is still a bitterly contested issue.[21]

We were always told by our parents, 'If you see a black car coming into Cummeragunja, run and hide'... the kids were scared stiff because they were taking the kids away at that time, and a lot of those kids never, ever came back to Cummera.

Alf Turner, Yorta Yorta nation

In addition to the original Cummera land grant, and in response to other petitions for land by Yorta Yorta people, including that of William Cooper and his brother Jack, an additional twenty 40-acre blocks were allocated to individual farmers in 1896. As Cooper wrote to JM Chanter MLA: 'I most respectfully beg to state that I shall feel deeply obliged if you will be good enough to use your influence toward securing a piece of land for me. I am anxious to get a home and make provisions for my wife. I do trust you will be successful in securing this small portion of a vast territory which is ours by divine right ...'[22]

The farm blocks were allocated individually to farmers who wanted to 'support and to build homes for their families'.[23] The farm blocks venture, however, was short lived, and they were taken back in 1907, only a decade later. This was a bitter blow to those who attempted to adapt to individual farming enterprises as white settlers were allowed to freely enjoy. The irony of the farm blocks, considering the brave efforts of the individual farmers of the time, is that they were rewarded by being forced back into a cooperative effort on the Cummera lands.

Forcing the Yorta Yorta farmers into cooperative effort, rather than encouraging them to engage in individual economic pursuits, is a mindset that is arguably still around today. Some Yorta Yorta individuals who have attempted to exercise their own initiative by purchasing land on the open market for cultural and economic purposes have struck similar barriers from funding agencies.[24]

The stories of land loss, land disputation and lands being granted then whittled away has stayed at the front of the Yorta Yorta consciousness. As Priscilla McKray, daughter of TS James and Ada Cooper, says, 'To this day we think about that! The way they treated them very badly and took their farm blocks back without telling them why. They worked their blocks and the Board came along and took them back just like that. They never gave any warning or reason for it, and they were very upset about it when they took them back.'[25]

Being cut off from their traditional lands and living under such an oppressive regime created much tension and antagonism between the management and the residents of Cummera. Perhaps the most significant of these was the taking of the young girls, who were sent to Cootamundra to be trained as domestic servants. Disturbing stories of the 'black car' coming from over the hill to take the children away continue to resonate in the folk memory of Yorta Yorta people today.

Sir Doug Nicholls, who was the first child born on Cummera, reflects on the legacy of that experience. He saw his sister Hilda and other girls forcibly taken by the police. Sir Doug said he was very bitter because it was instilled in them by their parents: '... then when we saw the police coming and the welfare officers taking our kiddies ... this created more bitterness. We lived in fear ... and I seen it when I was a schoolboy and how they used to get under the schoolhouse waiting to see who was coming in fear that we might be taken next.'[26]

After police raided his school and took some girls away, Thomas Shadrach James wrote an impassioned letter, which was ignored:

> I beg to report that after an enrolment of fifty-nine our
> attendance today is eight, and even this number cannot be
> maintained in the circumstances that the police have arrested
> and carried off three girls from here, the people panic stricken
> have fled with their children and are camped on the Victorian
> side of the river. My opinion about the matter is that the people
> strongly resent the summary measure that the Board has adopted
> through the police for removing the girls to Cootamundra.[27]

Similar harrowing stories of other girls who were taken are told by Yorta Yorta elders. Aunty Margaret Nelson was among those who were taken. Her expected arrival home from Cootamundra brought further anguish when family members were shocked to learn that only her bags were dispatched at the Echuca railway station, where she was expected to arrive. The painful story is that she died at Cootamundra of a broken heart. Melancholic-type illnesses were a common symptom of the forced removal policies.[28]

Life on the reserve was dominated by subjugation and control. The management had sole authority over the lives and movements of people. Although it is hard to imagine, if you were black in New South Wales at that time a long list of insults were your lot. You couldn't vote; you weren't allowed in hospitals, cafés or pubs; you would wait until last to be served in a shop; your kids couldn't go to the school in town; you needed the mission manager's permission to move on and off the reserve; you could be sent out as a servant or labourer at the discretion of the board; your wages were controlled; your house would be inspected for cleanliness; and, worst of all, your children could be taken without a word of warning.

WILLIAM COOPER MOVES TO MELBOURNE, 1930s

After Cooper left Cummera, he worked as a shearer and labourer in the bush for many years, where he became involved in the union movement. Eventually, in his seventies, Cooper returned to Cummera but was unable to receive a pension if he remained there, so he moved to Melbourne in 1933 to take up the plight of his people. Cooper rented a series of run-down houses in suburban Footscray with no electricity or gas and became part of a larger black urban scene drawn together from communities across the state. He became the centre of a core group of Cummera people who had moved to Melbourne, among them his niece Marg Tucker, who recalled sitting around the fireplace, 'the candles flickering on the mantelpiece'.[29] Other key supporters were his nephew Shadrach James and Pastor Doug Nicholls, who at the time was a champion sportsperson and football star with Fitzroy.

Cooper's first fundamental political act, at the age of seventy-one, was the organisation of the famous 'petition to the King' for which he gained the signatures of more than 2000 people. The petition highlighted the appalling conditions of Aboriginal people as a result of land loss and marginalisation. It also highlighted the denial of civil and political rights and called on the Australian Government for Aboriginal representation in parliament, which became a focus for Cooper.

TO THE KING'S MOST EXCELLENT MAJESTY, IN COUNCIL THE
HUMBLE PETITION of the undersigned Aboriginal inhabitants of
the Continent of Australia respectfully sheweth:—

THAT WHEREAS it was not only a moral duty, but a strict
injunction, included in the commission issued to those who came
to people Australia, that the original inhabitants and their heirs
and successors should be adequately cared for;

AND WHEREAS the terms of the commission have not been
adhered to in that—

(a) Our lands have been expropriated by Your Majesty's
     Governments, and

(b) Legal status is denied to us by Your Majesty's
     Governments;

AND WHEREAS all petitions made on our behalf to Your
Majesty's Governments have failed.

YOUR PETITIONERS humbly pray that Your Majesty will
intervene on our behalf, and, through the instrument of Your
Majesty's Governments in the Commonwealth of Australia—will
prevent the extinction of the Aboriginal race and give better
conditions for all, granting us the power to propose a member
of parliament, of our own blood or a white man known to have
studied our needs and to be in sympathy with our race, to
represent us in the Federal Parliament.[30]

Cooper's petition was a major undertaking in those times—
particularly given the poor communication infrastructure, the
lack of funds to support its distribution and the resistance from
managers of missions who controlled access to places where
signatures could be sought. Some protection boards such as the
one in Queensland refused outright for Murris in their state to be
allowed to sign the petition at all.[31] These obstacles did not deter

Cooper. 'My first step was to write to the Aboriginal Protection Boards in the five states, replys received as follows Queensland refuses, South Australia gives permission, Victoria very stubborn ... it is the duty of every man and woman of Aboriginal Blood in them over the age of 20 to signe [*sic*] the petition, and I hope my people will not fail to signe, and help all they can that we may get improvement.'[32]

William Cooper's daughter Sally describes some of the frustrations and disappointments she shared with her father. Collecting the 2000 signatures, 'back in those days', she told me, 'was mostly done by foot'. 'He walked everywhere,' she said, and 'when he found out that the petition never left Australia he was a very disappointed man'—shedding a tear of affection for her father whom she dearly loved.[33]

The sad irony is that the King never received the petition. The Federal Government argued that, as the appointment of an Aborigine to parliament was currently a constitutional impossibility, it was useless to forward it to the King.

William's irrepressible desire for justice was strong, however, and he bounced back. To give his people a voice, Cooper was instrumental in forming a political organisation called the Australian Aborigines League. Membership was exclusively open to those with 'some degree of Aboriginal blood',[34] and its 'ultimate object' was 'the conservation of special features of Aboriginal culture and the removal of all disabilities, political, social or economic, now or in the future borne by Aboriginals and to secure their uplift'. Cooper became its secretary, and his extraordinary letters began in earnest and arrived on the desks of newspaper editors, premiers and the then prime minister, Joseph Lyons: 'We do plead for one controlling authority, the Commonwealth and request that all Aboriginal interests be absolutely federalised.

Australian Aboriginal Progressive Association

The Australian Aboriginal Progressive Association (AAPA) was the first formalised Black political organisation in Australia. It operated in New South Wales from 1924 to 1928 and was the basis of later organsations that continued on into the 1930s. Inspired by the Black American movement led by Marcus Garvey's Universal Negro Improvement Association, which had hundreds of chapters across the world at its height, the AAPA's President, Fred Maynard, was deeply influenced by these international models and meeting the African American boxer, Jack Johnson, who visited Australia. Maynard was inspired to form the AAPA. Its target was the Protection Act and the Aborigines Protection Board, which governed Aboriginal life. Fred Maynard addressed Jack Lang, the NSW Premier, in the following letter in 1927:

> I wish to make it perfectly clear on behalf of our people, that we accept no conditions of inferiority as compared with European people. Two distinct civilisations are represented by the respective races … That the European people by the arts of war destroyed our more ancient civilisation is freely admitted, and that by their vices and diseases our people have been decimated is also patent. But neither of these facts are evidence of superiority. Quite contrary is the case … We are therefore striving to obtain full recognition of our citizen rights on terms of equality with all other people in our land. The request made by this association for sufficient land for each eligible family is justifiably based. The Australian people are the original owners of this land and have a prior right over all the other people in this respect. Our request to supervise our own affairs is no innovation. The Catholic people in our country possess the right to control their own schools and homes, and take pride in the fact that they possess this privilege. The Chinese, Greeks, Jews and Lutherans are similarly favoured and our people are entitled to precisely the same conditions.

Dr John Maynard (historian and Fred Maynard's grandson) describes the letter as 'one of the most eloquent and powerful statements ever written by an Aboriginal activist'. He goes on to describe that 'the AAPA

➤

demands encompassed the entire spectrum of Aboriginal bitterness, focusing on both land rights and civil rights. The massive loss of reserve land and the way of life it offered were the two catalysts which ignited the AAPA into existence … From the ashes of what many believed have perished, have risen the buds of an Aboriginal movement that continues to this day.'

Extracts from John Maynard, 'Fred Maynard and the Australian Aboriginal Progressive Association (AAPA): One God, One Aim, One Destiny', Aboriginal History, *vol. 21, 1997.*

This will enable a continuous policy of uplift. We request that parliamentary representation be considered.'[35]

Cooper didn't stop at letters. In trying to draw public attention to the plight of his people, he saw a clever political opportunity to use the celebrations of the 150th Australia Day anniversary on 26 January 1938.

THE DAY OF MOURNING

The Australian Aborigines' Progressive Association of New South Wales has called on all aborigines in the advanced stages of civilisation and culture to observe a DAY OF MOURNING concurrently with the white man's DAY OF REJOICING to celebrate the 150th year of the coming of the white man to Australia. The aborigines, by this means, hope to call the attention to the present deplorable condition of all aborigines, of whatever stage of culture, after 150 years of British rule. It is expected that such action will create such sympathy on the part of the whites that full justice and recompense will follow.[36]

In developing this strategy Cooper was assisted by William Ferguson, Jack Patten and Pearle Gibbs, who worked in solidarity

A way to equality

Bain Atwood: What Cooper tries to emphasise again and again is that Aboriginal people have the same capacity as white Australians ... and he keeps on saying to government, 'Give us the opportunity. Our people are capable of being doctors and teachers and leaders and so on and so forth. Give us the opportunity, give us the resources, educate us and we will show you that we are as capable as you are.'

Heather Goodall: The Protection Board changed to become the Aborigines Welfare Board; and what the Welfare Board tried to do was to continue the concentration to be able to educate Aboriginal adults; to assimilate them but first to control them and educate them. The attempt was to force adult Aboriginal people to conform to particular sorts of employment and household and living arrangements: saving money, having particular jobs, not travelling, not associating with other Aboriginal people.

Richard Broome: The Liberal Party reintroduced the assimilation policy, I think for the very important view that Aboriginal people had to become citizens. They should have equal rights. That this was important for Australia's reputation in the world, but along with it was this view that they become like everyone else. So it was a double-edged sword. Here they were being offered what they'd been fighting for, but the cost was high. You had to become like everyone else, forget your Aboriginality ... and just become Australian.

with Cooper in the 1930s. They were instrumental in setting up the Aborigines Progressive Association (APA), one of the first Aboriginal organisations to be established in Sydney in 1937, and a sister organisation of 'the League' in Melbourne.

These organisations paved the way for Indigenous rights, and were responsible for raising the political awareness of mainstream society. They rejected the oppressive policies of protection and assimilation, and demanded full citizenship rights. Social justice and racial equality were a central part of their policy objectives, and the issue of land rights and compensation were at the front of their demands.

The Day of Mourning gained wide public and media attention. It used the 150th celebrations to expose the appalling condition of the original Australians and to focus on human rights issues. The message to the Australian public was loud and clear: Kooris[37] had nothing to celebrate about the arrival of Captain Cook.

The Aboriginal now has no status, no rights, no land ... He has no country and nothing to fight for but the privilege of defending the land which was taken from him by the white race without compensation or even kindness.
William Cooper

The Day of Mourning wrote itself into Australian history as a significant Aboriginal protest against the celebration of imposed British sovereignty. Newspapers reported on the protest, and it put the issues of Indigenous rights in the minds of the broader public, thereby laying a basis in the broader community for equal rights for Aboriginal people.[38] The Day of Mourning protest was revisited fifty years later, on 26 January 1988, when up to 50 000 people rallied in support of Koori protests against the Bicentenary Celebrations in Sydney—otherwise known as the 'March for Justice'.

THE CUMMERA WALK-OFF

Around the time of the Day of Mourning protest and the public attention that reserves were receiving from their exposure by APA members, the plight of Indigenous Australians began to hit home. Jack Patten, who was born on Cummera in 1904, visited

reserves and spoke out about 'the frightful conditions in which
the native Aborigines of this continent live'.[39] Yorta Yorta elder
Geraldine Briggs reflects on Jack Patten's visit to Cummera and
the events that followed:

> When Jack Patten came ... he continued to talk and tell everyone
> what their rights were. At that time there was a petition going
> around which we were trying to get people to sign for better
> conditions. Many signed it but those who were employed by the
> Board to work on the reserve wouldn't sign, because they would
> then jeopardise their jobs. That's the way the Board used to keep
> people divided because they knew if all the people united they
> could stand up against the Board and for their rights. Jack was
> eventually caught up with by the police and charged under a very
> old law which was 'inciting Aborigines'.[40]

The law of incitement, or sedition, as it is now known, was a
harsh provision of the Protection laws that were designed to
keep people under the board's control and to deny their voices.
Jack Patten's visit certainly got things moving at Cummera, but
unfortunately he and his brother George were arrested by the
Moama police and held in custody until they could get bail.[41]

The constant frustration of Aboriginal initiative and the
continued interference by the board pushed the Cummera residents to the point of an uprising. With the unrest created by
the board's shady land dealings, together with the frustration
of the conditions that people had to live under and the violent
management tactics of the manager, Cummera people decided
to take direct political action. They wanted to break free from the
shackles of oppression under the Protection regime and to enjoy
the same citizenship rights as white people, including the right to
own and to control land that was theirs by birthright.

We, representing the Aborigines of Australia, hereby make
protest against the callous treatment of our people by the white man
in the past 150 years, and we appeal to the Australian nation
to make new laws for the education and care of Aborigines, and
for a new policy which will raise our people to FULL CITIZEN STATUS
and EQUALITY WITHIN THE COMMUNITY.
Jack Patten

In February 1939 a mass strike of Aboriginal people, called the Cummeragunja walk-off, took place. By this time, conditions on the reserve were so bad that they prompted Cooper to ask in a letter to the New South Wales Premier, 'We are not an enemy people, and we are not in Nazi concentration camps. Why should we be treated as if we were?'[42] Cooper's letter listed the grievances of the Cummeragunja residents, including land, inadequate rations, housing, education and ill-treatment by the manager.[43] Finally, residents formed a petition to have the manager of Cummera, McQuiggan, dismissed and an inquiry carried out into the conditions on the reserve.[44] Not only did the Protection Board not reply but also it sent the petition straight back to McQuiggan, who used it to intimidate the signatories. Cooper was furious and wrote to the Premier:

> On November 28th I forwarded a letter, copy herewith, to the
> Chairman of the Board for the Protection of Aborigines, covering
> a petition of the natives of Cummeragunga for the removal of
> Mr and Mrs McQuiggan from the charge of the aboriginal station.
> To this communication I did not receive a reply but it was received
> for the names of the petitioners were posted at the Station, inviting
> those who wished to remove their names to do so. I submit that
> this is not in accordance with British tradition and would not

be done for a fully white community and in itself constitutes a further grievance. The conditions which were so objectionable became more aggravated until the victimization experienced forced a number of the people to leave New South Wales for Victoria, where they are living under very hard conditions.[45]

The walk-off attracted widespread support, especially in Melbourne, where a solidarity campaign led by Cooper's Australian Aborigines League drew other religious and political groups and trade unions together in efforts to collect food and blankets for the strikers. Public support for the walk-off was so high in Melbourne that the Victorian Government was forced to accede to demands to provide unemployment relief for the strikers.[46]

150 years of oppression. 80 000 Aborigines deliberately kept from uplift and refused one representative in Parliament. We want the right to take our place beside the white race in full equality.

William Cooper

Lasting nine months, the strike also demonstrated the persistence, resolve and organisational prowess of the Yorta Yorta amid the hardest conditions. Although by the time the strike was called off the Protection Board had not acted on its demands, the fruits of the Yorta Yorta struggle became more apparent in 1940, when McQuiggan was eventually fired, and the loathed Protection Board was reconstituted into an Aborigines Welfare Board.[47]

CUMMERA AFTER THE STRIKE

The walk-off played a significant role in changing policy direction from one of protection to one of assimilation. The new policy was aimed at assimilating Aborigines into mainstream society, and in the transition process they were to be assisted in housing, education and employment. In reality, however, little if any support was forthcoming, and those people who moved from Cummera ended up on the fringes of local towns camping on the riverbanks and rubbish dumps.[48]

All Aborigines and part Aborigines are expected to eventually attain the same manner of living as other Australians ... enjoying the same responsibility, deserving the same customs and influenced by the same beliefs, hopes and loyalties as other Australians.
Government

Following the Cummera strike Cooper continued to campaign for Aboriginal rights, including the return of Cummera lands that had been leased to European farmers. After a long, protracted struggle to achieve justice for his people he eventually returned from Melbourne and died in Mooroopna in 1941. He was laid to rest in his ancestral lands at Cummera.

The ultimate object of our League shall be the conservation of special features of the Aboriginals' culture and the removal of all hardships: political, social or economic.
William Cooper

Some families moved back and held on to Cummera, and many followed work in the seasonal and labouring industries around the Goulburn Valley region. The main movement, however, was to the fringes of local townships like Shepparton and Mooroopna, where people regrouped at a place called the Flat, which is where I was born. The address of my parents in my birth certificate is 'River Bank Mooroopna'. 'The Flat' was located

on the bend of the Goulburn River near Mooroopna, and Dash's
Paddock was an alternative campsite located on higher ground,
where people would retreat when the river rose. The story of the
Flat and Dash's Paddock is depicted in the Archie Roach song
'Move It On':

> Oh I was born in Mooroopna,
> Down by that river bend,
> Yeah I was born in Mooroopna,
> We lived by the river bend,
> Then the Queen come and visited us,
> Had to move it on again.
> Move across to Dash's Paddock,
> When the river it did rise,
> Moved across to Dash's Paddock,
> When the river it did rise,
> At the edge of the rubbish tip
> Amongst the rubbish and the flies
> Then the Queen come and visit back in 1956,
> Yeah the Queen come and visit back in 1956,
> And they moved us on to Rumbalara,
> Move us off the rubbish tip.[49]

The conditions under which Indigenous people were forced
to live in the fringe camps of Mooroopna at the time are exposed
in the McLean Royal Commission of 1957, which found that
Aboriginal people on the fringes of white society were living
in extreme poverty.[50] To overcome the crisis, McLean recommended the establishment of an Aborigines Welfare Board with
an emphasis on rehousing people from the fringes and improving educational and employment opportunities. Following the
McLean Commission and the visit by the Queen in 1956, which

exposed the state and local governments' lack of regard for the impoverished conditions of the fringe camps, the people were eventually rehoused on land at Rumbalara (meaning 'end of the rainbow'). Rumbalara is now the home of the Rumbalara Aboriginal Cooperative, which is one of the major service delivery organisations in Victoria.

The thing about combat situations is a bullet doesn't know what colour you are, and if you're wearing a uniform, the enemy just wants to kill you. And if someone's going to save your life, you're not going to give a shit whether they're black, white or brindle. I think that war can sometimes eradicate colour, it can eradicate heritage and you can just become a man. You hear stories of Aboriginal men going back to their communities and being rejected by society as our people were at the time. Every Anzac Day their mates pick them up and take them for a couple of beers. And that was the only day of the year they were allowed in the RSL or in the pubs. Place yourself in their shoes to try and imagine what it was like at one moment to be a contributor to your country and feel that you had earned a place and then you come home and you are treated like scum.
Richard Frankland, Gunditjamara nation

With the passing of William Cooper, other Cummera leaders took up the struggle; prominent among them was Pastor Doug Nicholls. Nicholls worked closely with William Cooper and was the treasurer of the Australian Aborigines League. Photographs of Cooper and Nicholls taken at the time indicate their close working relationship: Pastor Doug Nicholls was never far away from William Cooper's side. Nicholls carried on the pioneering work of Cooper and was a strong advocate for the right of Indigenous people to maintain their own cultural identity

Australian natives are not a primitive people but a people living in primitive conditions. They are entitled to a better deal than they are receiving from white people... If given the opportunity they could 'fly high' but they have been denied their rights by being kept a race apart.

Sir Doug Nicholls

and to speak for themselves as a distinct cultural group. Speaking against the idea of assimilation, Nicholls said, 'Let us enter your society on our terms, living side by side with you but remaining at all times a race of people with our own identity.'[51]

Pastor Doug Nicholls picked up the message stick and went on to become an outstanding advocate for his people in the post–World War II period. He headed up the Aborigines Advancement League, which grew out of Cooper's Australian Aborigines League. The League is still regarded as the mother of other community-based organisations that sprang up in Melbourne during the heyday of the self-determination policy. Nicholls played a significant role in establishing the Federal Council for the Advancement of Aborigines and Torres Strait Islanders (FCAATSI), the first national Indigenous organisation, which was instrumental in achieving changes to those sections of the Constitution that discriminated against Indigenous Australians before the 1967 referendum.

'NOT ONE IOTA'

The struggle for justice and the return of Cummera lands continued. The board's response, however, was that the persistence of separate Aboriginal communities was inconsistent with the policy of assimilation and adhered to its plans for revocations and the dispersal of residents. In 1959 Cummera residents and supporters petitioned for the return of the land that was still reserved and were finally successful in gaining 200 acres after the lease had expired.[52]

In 1960 around seventy people were living on the 200 acres of the Cummera reserve. A delegation of leaders and supporters from the Victorian Aborigines Advancement League asked the New South Wales Government for the return of this land. Some of the original lands were returned to Cummera residents in 1966. After years of complaints and negotiations with the board, the descendants of the pioneer farmers finally won permission to begin farming Cummera again.

You knew your place. You always know your place, when you live outback in those little towns. Even though you've got a lot of good white people around, that are good to Aboriginal people, you still know your place. And I think it's still like that today.
June Barker, Yorta Yorta/Ngemba nations

However, the agreement signed in 1966 made them merely 'tenants at will', and the board could cancel their tenure on a month's notice and retain all fixed properties and assets. In 1970 the New South Wales Ministry of Aboriginal Affairs granted a loan to the fifth-generation descendants of the pioneers to develop their farming on the remaining land.[53]

The Aborigines Advancement League made claims for the Barmah/Moira Forest in 1975 and again in 1983, both of which were unsuccessful. In 1994, following the Mabo decision, which acknowledged ownership of the land before white settlement, the Yorta Yorta native title claim began in earnest. After eight years of working through the courts, in 2002 the claim was rejected, twisting the interpretation of the original 1881 Yorta

Yorta petition to justify its position. With the case lost, the land struggle has retreated from the legal realm back to the political process initiated by William Cooper and the founding leaders of Maloga and Cummera. In many ways it seems that the struggle has come full circle. The Yorta Yorta native title claim, which was one of the first to be lodged following the success of Mabo, is the most recent setback in the long, arduous process of achieving land justice through the imported legal system.

Now the assumption was that many of the arid inland areas of Australia were vacant. The maps they used to plan that [atomic] testing had the words 'vacant lands' written across the great western desert, Aboriginal people's country, and it really reflects the colonial ideas that Aboriginal people didn't exist. It was absolute terra nullius in practice.

Professor Heather Goodall, historian

Yet despite this, the Yorta Yorta have held on to their connections to their ancestral lands with incredible dignity, solidarity and persistence. This is perhaps best reflected in their eighteen separate attempts to claim land on the basis of their inherent rights. Disappointingly, however, in the words of Uncle William Cooper, 'not one iota' has been delivered on the basis of the right to own and to control lands that the Yorta Yorta have occupied since time immemorial: 'How much compensation have we had? How much of our land has been paid for? Not one iota! Again, we state that we are the original owners of the country. We have been ejected and despoiled of our god-given right and our inheritance has been forcibly taken from us.'[54]

The reserve lands set aside for Yorta Yorta use were integral in maintaining an ongoing occupation of the ancestral land by its traditional and rightful owners. Cummera still provides this vital link. It was never disbanded and has steadily increased to a population of more than 300.

Looking back at the foundation leaders and the events that shaped the spirit of the Yorta Yorta nation, one can reflect on the continuity between past and present political actions. Collective organisation, mobilisation and protest by the way of the spear of the pen and the power of the voice remain the tools of political engagement. As I write this the struggle continues.

Kara ged
HOMELAND

7
THE DAWN IS AT HAND
Marcia Langton and Noel Loos

In several cases in Queensland, Indigenous men and women cut the Gordion knot of hateful laws that denied them their humanity. In doing so, they followed their brothers and sisters elsewhere who had blazed the trail. Edward Koiki Mabo, the man who, with his co-claimants, destroyed *terra nullius*, the legal basis on which Australia was colonised, was one of them. He was born in 1936 on Mer, or Murray Island, one of the smallest and most remote islands in Torres Strait. Early in his life he realised that he had to master the ways of the whites to develop his full potential in the land they dominated but never to lose his Islander customs and language. His flaring imagination, intellect and courage finally enabled him to persist through the ten years of the Meriam High Court challenge that acknowledged the native title that Aboriginal and Torres Strait Islander people had to their land 'since time immemorial'. He died of cancer on 21 January 1992, four months before the High Court decision swept away the concept of *terra nullius*. This is now referred to as the *Mabo* decision, or sometimes simply *Mabo*.

Eddie Koiki Mabo and his co-claimants stood on the shoulders of courageous men who refused to be denied their rights. These earlier leaders included Milirrpum and other Yolngu clan leaders who, in 1965, unsuccessfully petitioned parliament in Canberra with a plea to recognise their land ownership and desist from a lease and project approval arrangement for a bauxite mine. They had then asserted their ancient rights to their land in the Supreme Court of the Australian Capital Territory.

The findings in this case supported the supremacy of imperial powers who obtained colonies around the world, which were either conquered or ceded. Australia was considered in the latter category because Aboriginal property systems—seen to belong to the society of an inferior race—were incapable of recognition. The *Mabo* arguments successfully challenged this antediluvian view. To understand what motivated these men— Milirrpum and Mabo—and those who rallied behind them, and the persistence of formal racial separation, particularly in Queensland, where the *Mabo* case was tested, we must look at the history of Aboriginal and Torres Strait Islander aspirations for freedom and land rights.

Koiki (as he preferred to be known) grew up on Mer, or Murray Island, in his own Melanesian Australian culture with his own language, Meriam, closely related to those of the Kiwai region in New Guinea. His second language was Brokan, a kriol understood throughout Torres Strait. English was his third language and, like other Islanders at the time, he had a very limited grasp of it. Koiki believed his ancestors had colonised the Murray

Islands from the north-east and could recount a genealogy that went back seventeen generations. Traditionally, the Meriam were agriculturalists who grew luxuriant gardens of taro, yams, bananas, coconuts and fruit trees in their rich volcanic soil. Their identity, status and economic and social life derived from the plots of land they inherited within villages. But there was also the excitement and satisfaction of the sea; they would set out on expeditions in their 20-metre-long, dugout outrigger canoes to catch turtle or travel to other islands. They worked the rock-walled fish traps, caught crayfish or used their scoops to catch sardines from silver-flashing schools near the shore.

But the society in which Koiki Mabo grew up was no longer free and independent. From 1871 it had been a London Missionary Society mission but as, increasingly, the Torres Strait Islands had become part of the pearlshell, bêche-de-mer and trochus shell fisheries, the Queensland Government had extended its border in 1872 and 1879 to control the industry. Throughout the twentieth century, the Queensland Government had segregated the Islanders from contact with mainland Australia under the policy of protection while fostering the development of a cash economy based on the fisheries. The Islanders could sell only to the government and were paid much less than whites for their trochus and pearlshell. The crew's wages were also meagre in comparison with wages paid on boats owned by white businessmen.

After the 1936 Torres Strait Island–wide maritime strike, the government used a form of soft control through each island's council, which was effective but very different from their admin-istration of Aboriginal reserves. A teacher-administrator on each island and a Protector based at Thursday Island complemented this form of Queensland control. One enlightened teacher, Bob Miles, recognised Koiki's potential, fostered his grasp of English and encouraged him to master white culture. In 1985 Koiki reflected on his early life: 'My lifetime on Murray, I think, was the best time of my life I ever spent, growing up on Murray and having an opportunity to learn both the white man way of life from my schoolteacher Robert Miles, and my traditional heritage as well.'[1]

This childhood idyll came to an end when Koiki reached adolescence and fell foul of the puritanical values the Islanders had accepted. At fifteen he was found guilty of drunkenness and a youthful 'misdemeanour' with a Meriam girl and banished from Mer for twelve months. On Thursday Island the then Protector of the Torres Strait Islands, Pat Killoran, prevented him from going south and set him to work on local trochus luggers. Koiki realised how powerless Islanders were before the white colonialist administration and its agents, the Islander councils. He continued working on trochus luggers for a number of years and visited mainland ports like Cairns and Halifax, soon discovering that the Islanders were being exploited as cheap labour. At this time, in the late 1950s, the pearlshell and trochus industries were collapsing because of competition from newly developed plastics. Islanders were being allowed to travel to the mainland to find work in such low-status labouring jobs as cane-cutting and fettling on the railways. Mabo's mother, Maiga, urged him to find work on the mainland where the Islanders could at least get equal pay in these demanding jobs, pay that seemed lavish compared with their previous experience.

In 1959 the 23-year-old Mabo had a job working on the railways at Hughenden in western Queensland when he married Ernestine Bonita Nehow. When in town, they had to sleep at the railway station, even with little children, as the publicans refused them accommodation. Later, Mabo was able to joke that the whites were presumably worried their blackness would rub off on the white sheets: 'They wouldn't accept black money, or probably they thought we'd leave our skin on their sheets.'[2]

This experience was common. Aboriginal and Torres Islander people living in Queensland in the 1960s were entitled to feel outrage at their situation. While in the south, in the cities of Melbourne, Sydney and Canberra, enlightened politicians and campaigners for equal rights were overturning the old system of separatist exclusion of Aboriginal people, in Queensland, the state intensified its draconian racialist grip on their lives.

LIFE 'UNDER THE ACT'

All Aborigines and Torres Strait Islanders living in Queensland were wards of the state under the Aborigines Act and the Torres Strait Islanders Act, legislation that originated in 1897 during the final colonial push for control of all land in the State of Queensland and the removal or 'pacification' of its Indigenous inhabitants. The creation in 1898 of the office of the Protector of Aborigines, a special administrative agency, under the terms of the original Act, the *Aboriginals Protection and Restriction of the Sale of Opium Act 1897*, was aimed at the absolute control of Aboriginal peoples in Queensland, which was achieved in large part by the appointment of police as agents of the colonial state with the task of removing Aborigines from areas where colonists were taking up blocks of land to graze their stock. If female, old and infirm, or young and weak, the Aboriginal detainees were confined in the administered settlements of the reserves; and if male and fit, they were usually contracted as unfree— and unpaid—labourers to the new settlers.[3] In Queensland, the

widespread removal of Aboriginal people from their traditional
territories and detention in Aboriginal reserve settlements was
authorised by this legislation. Historian Rosalind Kidd, in her
thorough account of the administration of Aboriginal people
in Queensland,[4] established that the legislation set up a regime
that

> contrived various social categories and defined Aborigines who
> fell within those parameters as 'Aboriginal' and therefore wards
> of state ... and entrenched as policy a range of areas around the
> state reserved for 'the use and benefit' of Aboriginal people;
> it introduced procedures to relocate Aboriginal individuals and
> groups to such reserves; it delegated a network of 'protectors'
> to act for, and in the interests of, Aboriginal individuals in their
> dealings with other races and initiated a web of regulations to
> encompass all activities.[5]

At the time of the 1897 Aborigines Act, a few large reserves
existed on Cape York Peninsula at Yarrabah in North Queensland,
and several smaller ones operated in southern Queensland, such
as at Cherbourg, near Kingaroy, and around Brisbane; others
operating in the 1870s had already been sacrificed to colonial
expansion. The reserves became restricted areas under the
Act, accessible only by permit. The administrative machinery
of this regime depended on a 'network of protectors' who, as
Kidd explains, invoked relocation provisions to incarcerate
thousands of Aboriginal people. The protectors were capable
of extraordinarily arbitrary decisions, yet they dutifully wrote
in their Removals Registers an ever-growing number of reasons
for their verdicts on the fate of each person they selected for
removal:

... being born of Aboriginal parents; of mixed parentage and
under the age of sixteen or associating with "full-blood"
Aborigines; being a female of mixed parentage; refusing to work
where directed; failing to "support" one's family; being defined
as a neglected child; being described as promiscuous; using
alcohol or opium (a legal drug until 1905), to name a few. Any
of these categories was grounds for removal from family and
country and confinement on the reserves.[6]

The Act's provisions enabling these assignments were
unequivocal. Section 9 stated: 'It shall be lawful for the Minister
to cause every aboriginal within any District, to be removed to,
and kept within the limits of, any reserve, in such manner, and
subject to such conditions, as may be prescribed.' The state
regime was aimed at separating, controlling and exploiting the
thousands of remaining Aboriginal and Torres Strait Islander
people, with the result that, both in the communities in the controlled reserves and throughout the rural areas where they were
forced into labour, Queensland's Indigenous people suffered starvation, illness and debilitating discrimination measures designed
to ensure that they could not escape the system administered by
the Department of Native Affairs. Hundreds of 'troublemakers'
who resisted were sent to Palm Island, or Great Palm Island,[7] an
Aboriginal reserve off the coast near Townsville, controlled by
the department and used as a penal settlement.

For the tens of thousands incarcerated on the mainland,
mostly Aboriginal reserves, life changed little until the late
1960s. Their lives were administered by superintendents, and
they could not leave unless they had formal documentation
which required that they report to police at their destination. If

they were employed at all, they were paid 'training' wages, which were often garnisheed or confiscated by the state, and sometimes by local police. Dormitories were maintained for the incarceration of children, and 'troublemakers' were separated from their families and removed to remote reserves as punishment. The poverty on the reserves was dire. Residents of the reserves were denied the right to vote, to marry without the permission of the superintendent, to travel and, in most cases, to attend school beyond elementary school. Some Aborigines and Islanders, if they had left the reserves, could obtain an exemption from the status of controlled ward by proving their commitment to 'live like the white man', the infamous goal of the assimilation policies that had been adopted by all states and territories after 1937. But most could not achieve this goal, being prevented at every turn by discrimination and race hate. To rent a house was sometimes possible, but to buy a home was impossible. To get a job was sometimes possible, but to be paid equal wages was not. Some Aboriginal people 'passed' as people of other ethnicities and lived a pretence, claiming to be Maori or Hawai'ian. Even in the suburbs of Brisbane, the regime had agents who would report on the people exempted from some of the conditions of the Acts, and in such circumstances, if too many relatives came to visit or the garden was untidy, a window broken or music played too loud, a report would be made to Pat Killoran, who was promoted to director of the Department of Native Affairs (later the Department of Aboriginal and Islander Affairs) throughout the entire State of Queensland. They would be promptly arrested and returned to a reserve chosen by Killoran. Some families managed to evade the scrutiny of departmental agents, but they were a wily minority. They were encouraged by the inspirational words of the poet Oodgeroo Noonuccal (Kath Walker):

Dark brothers, first Australian race,
Soon you will take your rightful place
In the brotherhood long waited for,
Fringe-dwellers no more.

Sore, sore the tears you shed
When hope seemed folly and justice dead.
Was the long night weary? Look up, dark band,
The dawn is at hand.[8]

THE RESISTANCE

Even in these claustrophobic and dangerous conditions, some brave people raised their objections to the inequity and cruelty of the administration of Aboriginal affairs. They were organised, sometimes, under the banner of the Federal Council for the Advancement of Aborigines and Torres Strait Islanders (FCAATSI). The council developed from a meeting in Adelaide in February 1958 to form a national approach to improving the situation of Aborigines and Torres Strait Islanders. Their goals included repeal of discriminatory legislation, amendment to the Commonwealth Constitution, improved housing, equal pay for equal work, facilities to be provided for education, and retention of all reserves with communal or individual ownership to be transferred to the Aboriginal and Islander residents. The organisation brought together unions, religious groups, communists, students, artists and activists united by their commitment to a 'fair go' for Aborigines and Torres Strait Islanders.

The president, Joe McGinness, had come from the Northern Territory where his keen sense of justice had been honed. Joe McGinness was president of FCAATSI from 1961 until 1974, and again from 1975 until 1978. He joined the Waterside

Workers' Federation while working on the wharves on Thursday Island and moved to racially divided Cairns in 1951, where his involvement with the union expanded after he was elected to its executive committee. Here, while working on the wharves, his determination to overcome the blatant racial discrimination and abuse won many supporters among Aborigines, Islanders and those who supported their aspirations for equality and rights. In 1958 the Cairns Aboriginal and Torres Strait Islander Advancement League was established with Gladys O'Shane and Joe McGinness as the inaugural president and secretary respectively. The Cairns Trades and Labour Council, the Union of Australian Women and the Waterside Workers' Federation, provided both moral and financial support to the League.[9]

Koiki's understanding of white racism was shaped by listening to radio broadcasts of Joe McGinness and the poet Oodgeroo Noonuccal, another staunch FCAATSI leader. As with McGinness, Koiki increasingly found himself influenced by the working-class movement and became a union representative for his gang on the Townsville–Mount Isa rail reconstruction project. After Koiki's marriage, he had continued working in the west to save money for a deposit on a house in Townsville. He returned to Townsville to a job as deckhand with the Harbour Board. During the seven years he worked for the Harbour Board, he became more involved with Townsville's union movement. Many of the leaders were communists, which, in one way, was fortunate as the Communist Party had committed itself to Aboriginal advance-ment in 1931 and reaffirmed its commitment in 1943, decades before the ALP or the conservative parties did so. However, in the Queensland of the 1960s, it was not long before Mabo was tarred by association as a 'commo'. He believed that this was the cause of persecution he was receiving from the Harbour Board administration when he was moved to an unattractive job where he was paid less. In 1967 he resigned and became a gardener at James Cook University: 'Everybody would look at me as a red commo. The Advancement League was regarded as a Communist organisation ... the Vietnam War was on at the time, too— someone called me a Viet Cong ... it was only six months after that they transferred me from the job that I had to a sledge hammer gang on the wharf. Yes, hard slugging and less money.'[10]

While with the Harbour Board, Mabo had begun participating actively in black organisations, becoming the first secretary of Townsville's small Aboriginal Advancement League. They invited Joe McGinness to speak, and Koiki and his friend Dick Hoolihan went on to become the Torres Strait Islander and Aboriginal representatives on the Townsville Trades and Labour Council. This was to become an important link between Mabo's involvement in black activism and his working-class involvement.

By 1967 FCAATSI members, including Koiki, were campaigning across the country for a 'Yes' vote in a referendum to remove two racist clauses from the Australian Constitution. This was the most successful of the FCAATSI campaigns, and it led to an overwhelmingly positive outcome: the inclusion of Aboriginal and Islander peoples in the census, and the right of the Federal Government to legislate for Aborigines and Torres Strait Islander peoples.[11]

Far less successful during this same period was the tireless work of supporters in the south to end the racially discriminatory practices of the Queensland Government. They painstakingly documented the abuse of Aborigines and Islanders living in

Queensland in a series of documents and pamphlets, aiming to bring the Queensland Government regime to the attention of Australians and perhaps, they hoped, to win support from the Commonwealth Government in Canberra.

Eventually, there was change, but it was not brought about by the goodwill of governments. Men like Joe McGinness and, later, Eddie Koiki Mabo stood up to the might of the State of Queensland and the Commonwealth and demanded change. Their objections were persuasive, and thousands of people became convinced that the racism of the State of Queensland was unacceptable. There were church meetings, street marches and petitions, leading up to the 1967 constitutional referendum.

Following the overwhelming success of the 1967 referendum, Mabo suggested to supporters on the Trades and Labour Council that there should be a conference in Townsville to involve North Queensland's white and black communities in exploring the future of race relations in Australia, and in Townsville in particular. From Mabo's proposal came the 1967 Inter-Racial Seminar, 'We the Australians: What is to Follow the Referendum?' It involved 300 black and white participants meeting in Townsville as equals, a first in Townsville for such a large formal conference. The organising committee had brought together, with black activists and the trade unions, supporters from the churches and James Cook University, a committed coalition, some of whom remained confidantes and friends for the rest of Mabo's life. Yet Mabo was still most active in Townsville's black community, in the Aboriginal Advancement League and other black organisations as they emerged in Townsville, and in the rich cultural life of the Torres Strait Islanders, which was most obvious not only in their dances, singing and Islander hymns but also increasingly in social and political issues of a uniquely Torres Strait Islander focus.

MILIRRPUM V. NABALCO: THE BEGINNINGS OF NATIVE TITLE

In the Northern Territory, where hard-won rights were recognised much earlier than in Queensland, it was the granting of mining leases over Aboriginal reserves that instigated Aboriginal action, including litigation.

For the leaders of the north-east Arnhem Land clans of the Northern Territory, men like Milirrpum, Liyapadiny, and Mawalan of the Rirratjingu clan, Mungarrawuy of the Gumatj clan, Gawirrin of the Dhalwangu clan, and many others, the realisation that the Crown had ultimate ownership of their land, and the news that more than 300 square kilometres of their land would soon be leased by the Commonwealth Government to a bauxite mining company, Nabalco Pty Ltd, was shocking and distressing. In 1963 they gathered the clan leaders together at Yirrkala, where the Methodists had established a mission in 1935, and prepared petitions to parliament on pieces of bark. After affixing the petitions, typed on paper, to the two bark pieces, they painted their sacred clan designs in framing borders around the petitions to protest the excision of their land and the decision to allow mining without their consent.[12] The petitioners sought the recognition of rights to their traditional lands on Gove Peninsula in Arnhem Land and the establishment of a House of Representatives committee, accompanied by competent interpreters, to hear the views of the people of Yirrkala before permitting the excision of their land.

With their painted designs of the ancestral narratives of the creation of the Yolngu clans, languages and land and sea estates, and text in both English and Gumatj languages, the two bark petitions were remarkably different from all previous petitions to parliament with its rules of procedure and forms relating to petitions. They were the first traditional documents recognised by the Commonwealth Parliament through this instrument proclaiming those rights in traditional form. They were presented to the House of Representatives, and a parliamentary committee of inquiry was established. In 1963 it reported to parliament, acknowledging the rights of the Yolngu set out in the petitions and that compensation for loss of livelihood be paid, that sacred sites be protected and that an ongoing parliamentary committee monitor the mining project. These recommendations were ignored.

In 1968, after their petitions to parliament failed to gain recognition of their rights to land, the Yolngu took their case to the Supreme Court in Canberra, to assert their continuing ownership of traditional lands by challenging the validity of the Commonwealth Government's grant of mining leases over their territory in what has come to be known as the Gove Land Rights case. Edward Woodward (later Justice Woodward) was retained as legal counsel by the Yolngu plaintiffs. Eminent anthropologists WEH Stanner and RM Berndt presented expert evidence in the first case litigated by Aboriginal claimants for the recognition of their native title rights. Their evidence laid the groundwork for the definition of 'traditional Aboriginal owners'.[13]

In the result, Richard Blackburn, the judge, held that native title was incapable of recognition at common law. The plaintiffs 'asserted on behalf of the native clans they represented that those clans and no others had in their several ways occupied the areas from time immemorial as of right'. Justice Blackburn found that, indeed, 'If ever a system could be called "a government of laws, and not of men", it is that shown in the evidence before me'.[14] Blackburn found, however, that this system of laws was not one that the court could recognise. While acknowledging that the Aboriginal clans had a distinguishable system of law that involved a relationship to land, he did not recognise this relationship as being proprietary in nature.[15] He upheld the decisions of previous courts whereby the Crown was the source of all title to land, maintaining the status of Australia under the doctrine sometimes called *terra nullius*.[16] The decision was made despite the fact that many other common law jurisdictions, particularly Canada and the United States, had in various ways recognised the existence of indigenous rights and interests in land.[17]

Disappointment in the decision was felt by Indigenous people across the country, who had hoped the case would establish the principles for land rights and set a precedent for all. A further betrayal was experienced when the Commonwealth Government did not act in the interests of the Yolngu, although the referendum had given them the power to do so. Indigenous people resolved to take their battle for land rights to the streets; the most prominent protest being on the lawns of Parliament House in Canberra with the establishment of the 'Tent Embassy' in 1972.

THE ROAD TO NATIVE TITLE

This was the state of the law when Koiki similarly discovered that the Crown owned all rights in his land. It occurred at James Cook University where, as well as being the gardener, Koiki lectured students in race relations and education. One of the most important insights he gained at the university, and one that was to have Australia-wide significance, came about by accident. Mabo was having lunch with Noel Loos and Henry Reynolds in Reynolds' study. He began describing his land holdings on Murray Island. Like all Islanders at the time, he believed traditional land ownership and inheritance still applied because the Queensland Government had allowed Islanders to believe it. Loos and Reynolds exchanged glances, then explained to him that all of the outer Torres Strait Islands were Crown land. Loos was even able to show him that they were designated on an old map of Queensland as 'Aboriginal Reserve'. Initially shocked, Mabo responded with great determination: no one would take his land away from him! Subsequent events indicated that this was not mere bravado.

Mabo's long absence from Mer often made him out of step with the conservative council and its Meriam supporters. They had to work with the Queensland Government, from whom their authority—and even their land and way of life—was derived or supported in a world that was changing around them. He was a known non-Christian at a time when Torres Strait Islanders were probably the people with the strongest Christian affiliation in Australia. In the Islands, the Queensland Government's appraisal of Mabo as an urban activist with communist affiliations, a troublemaker, was apparently accepted. He had been prevented from visiting his Island home on a number of occasions on procedural grounds, such as an alleged lack of a berth on the government cargo boat. His hostility to the conservative Bjelke-Petersen government blazed forth in 1973 over the 'border issue', the redefinition of the border between Australia and Papua New Guinea. He was subsequently denied entry by the councils of Yorke and Murray when he sought permission to visit to record oral history. In 1974, when his father, Benny Mabo, was seriously ill, he was granted permission to visit only if he did not involve himself in 'political affairs'. Benny Mabo died on 11 February 1975 before Mabo could make the journey. His own people were making him pay a very high price for the political activism that would lead to the High Court.[18]

Meanwhile in the Northern Territory, in 1973 Nabalco started its mining and processing venture on a 250-million-tonne bauxite deposit, one of the world's largest, despite the objections of Rirratjingu leaders.[19] The failure of the plaintiffs' case and the growing protest movement inspired the newly elected Labor Prime Minister EG Whitlam to take action to redress the injustice of the Australian common law. The Commonwealth Government introduced the Aboriginal Land Rights (Northern Territory) Bill into Parliament in 1975. Whitlam explained how it came about:

> When Parliament resumed for the Budget in August I
> immediately raised for discussion the Government's delay and
> confusion in discharging the mandate given at the referendum
> to promote health, training, employment and land rights for
> Aborigines. I quoted the first international instrument which
> had direct relevance to the conditions of Australia's Aborigines,
> ILO Convention No.107–Indigenous and Tribal Populations
> 1957 ... 'The right of ownership, collective and individual, of
> the members of the populations concerned over the lands which
> these populations traditionally occupy shall be recognised.'
> ... On 12 December 1972, a week after taking office, I
> announced that Justice Woodward, who had been counsel for
> the people of Yirrkala in their unsuccessful case against Nabalco

before the Supreme Court of the Northern Territory, would hold a royal commission to inquire into and report upon arrangements for granting titles to land for Aboriginal groups and procedures for examining Aboriginal claims to land in the Northern Territory.[20]

After attending large meetings of elders convened in the Northern Territory, Woodward proposed procedures for claiming land and conditions of tenure: Aboriginal land should be granted as inalienable freehold title and that title should be held communally. He envisaged the transfer to Aboriginal ownership of reserves that were Crown land and hearings of claims by an Aboriginal Land Commissioner. He also recommended that smaller areas on pastoral leases and town areas could also be claimed on the basis of need. In 1976 the *Aboriginal Land Rights (Northern Territory) Act 1976* (Cwlth) was enacted by federal parliament; it provided the first statutory recognition of Aboriginal rights to land. The response of the Federal Government in this case was the legislative breakthrough that finally changed the Australian tradition of excluding and abusing its Indigenous people by denying their existence and connection to their traditional lands. A claims process was established that aimed to resolve with certainty the traditional Aboriginal owners of an area in question who 'have common spiritual affiliations to a site on the land, being affiliations that place the group under a primary spiritual responsibility for that site and for that land; and are entitled by Aboriginal tradition to forage as of right over that land'.[21] In Queensland, Indigenous people had no such rights and, to make matters worse, were forced to litigate in several cases to find remedies, usually unsuccessfully, for the blatantly racist acts of the State Government.

APARTHEID QUEENSLAND STYLE

The extraordinary regime of control persisted in Queensland until the 1980s, long after similar systems of controlling Aboriginal populations had been dismantled in other jurisdictions.

Until 1984, almost a century after the introduction of the 1897 Aborigines Act, the intent of this system of removing and controlling the state's Aboriginal population in administered reserve settlements continued, under the terms of 'the Act', as it was known.[22] Two exceptions were made in 1978 by Premier Bjelke-Petersen's government: Aurukun and Mornington Island were the subject of an extraordinary takeover executed under the terms of a new Queensland statute, the *Local Government (Aboriginal Lands) Act 1978* (Qld).[23] The statute was designed to allow a bauxite mining project at Weipa to proceed without the inconvenience of any Aboriginal rights in land.

In the 1950s the mining company Comalco discovered the world's richest deposits of bauxite in western Cape York. Then, in 1957, the Queensland Parliament passed the *Commonwealth Aluminium Corporation Pty Ltd Agreement Act 1957* (Qld; the Comalco Act) and the government issued mining leases to the company. Nearly 8000 square kilometres were excised from the mission reserve. Further exploration established that the ore body extended from north of Weipa, where the Presbyterian mission Mapoon, established in 1891, was located to the south of the Emberley River, where another Presbyterian mission, Aurukun, lay.

Both missions were operated as closed communities under the supervision of missionaries. The Queensland Government, motivated by Comalco's enthusiasm to proceed with this lucrative project, decided to remove the residents forcibly from the Mapoon mission, and the Queensland police were tasked with the operation. Many residents refused to go. On the morning of 15 November 1963 at Mapoon, they woke to find a contingent of police burning their houses and church, and shooting their dogs. The people were rounded up by the police and relocated to the Northern Peninsula, to an area at the tip of Cape York named New Mapoon by the Queensland Government. One of the residents removed in this raid was Rachel Peter, who described the events:

> We're the ones that were moved out by police, by gunpoint, [on] that boat they sent for us ... sneaked in on us in the night ... they came from Thursday Island. We were really sad, but we just had to go because they told us we were going for questioning. At the Bamaga wharf they told us there were seven houses waiting for us to walk in and light the stoves. And when we arrived in Bamaga there were no homes. We were just standing out in the streets like a mob of cattle with nowhere to go.[24]

> This is what they do, but the world doesn't know. People don't know how we were treated. They destroyed the homes, burnt them down, you know. And I seen all the burning down of the homes, the church ... it was destroying our culture, our lives.[25]

Further to the south, at Weipa, Comalco was given mining leases over 587 802 hectares of Aboriginal reserve land. Later, Comalco set aside a mere 125 hectares of it for Aboriginal use.

The Aurukun people challenged the Queensland Government's right to give control of their lands to a mining company, and eventually won the active support of the Fraser government. In a series of cases that eventually led to the Queensland Government's appealing to the Privy Council (which was then the highest court of appeal), the Queensland Government retained control over the Aboriginal land under dispute.

The residents of Aurukun were outraged by the Privy Council decision and by the Queensland Government's sacking of the missionaries. In 1978 senior council members of both Aurukun and Mornington Island travelled to Canberra with missionary John Adams to seek the assistance of the Commonwealth Government. Eventually, their concerns were raised in parliament in a 'matter of public importance' debate. The Fraser government passed an Act to assert control over the reserve, which began a legislative battle for power between Malcolm Fraser and Joh Bjelke-Petersen.

The *Peinkinna* case and several that followed, all brought by Wik people to prevent the loss of their rights by government decree, are still celebrated at Aurukun, where the school publishes a calendar that, along with cultural and seasonal information, recalls the leaders who defended their rights and land.[26] The litigious bent of several generations of Aboriginal leaders from western Cape York inspired others to pursue their rights through the courts as well as bringing the parlous state of affairs for Indigenous people in Queensland to the attention of successive Commonwealth governments, which held the constitutional power to override the excessive measures of the state. Premier Bjelke-Petersen would not acquiesce, however.

KOOWARTA V. BJELKE-PETERSEN

Queensland state governments from the early 1970s to the 1990s used environmental conservation legislation and instruments to prevent Aboriginal groups from acquiring and using land.[27] The most notorious of such actions was that taken against the late John Koowarta of the Winychanam group of Cape York.

He sometimes lived at Aurukun and at settlements further inland following his attempted purchase, with the assistance of the Aboriginal Land Fund Commission, of the Archer River Pastoral Holding, located on his traditional territory in central Cape York. In February 1976 Koowarta and the Aboriginal Land Commission, established by the Federal Government to purchase land for Aboriginal people, entered into a written contract with the lessees for the purchase of the lease and cattle and horses on the lease on behalf of Koowarta. The transfer of the lease was subject to the approval of the Queensland Minister for Lands, and on 23 March 1976 the commission sought the minister's consent to the transfer of the lease to the commission, which was refused. According to Collings, Queensland Government policy explicitly opposed 'proposals to acquire large areas of additional freehold land or leasehold land for development by Aborigines or Aboriginal groups in isolation'.[28] The government gazetted a number of national parks over the pastoral properties that Aboriginal peoples had expressed interest in buying, to prevent their legally purchasing the land.

On or about 8 December 1976 the Minister for Lands stated the reason for refusing to grant approval for Koowarta:

> The question of the proposed acquisition of Archer River
> Pastoral Holding comes within the ambit of declared
> Government policy expressed in a Cabinet decision of
> September 1972, which stated:—'The Queensland Government
> does not view favourably proposals to acquire large areas
> of additional freehold or leasehold land for development by
> Aborigines or Aboriginal groups in isolation.' ...Cabinet said
> in June 1976—'(1) That Cabinet's policy regarding Aboriginal
> reserve lands, as approved in Decision No. 17541 of 4 September

1972 remains unchanged ... no consent be given to the transfer of
Archer River Pastoral Holding No. 4785 to the Aboriginal Land
Fund Commission.[29]

Koowarta's appeal to the High Court was successful. It was
alleged that the Queensland Government had breached the
Act by refusing to grant a lease to the Aboriginal Land Fund
Commission.

However, Koowarta and the Winychanam group were never
able to acquire title to their beloved country. The Queensland
Government had gazetted the lease area as a national park,
which made the land unavailable for purchase. Although he was
unable to acquire land because of the racist intransigence of
Bjelke-Petersen's government, Koowarta nevertheless scored a
key victory in opposing racial discrimination. The High Court
decision in *Koowarta v. Bjelke-Petersen* upheld the provisions of
the Racial Discrimination Act and confirmed the Commonwealth
Government's role in Aboriginal land rights legislation.[30] The
Koowarta case is the first example of the Commonwealth using
the external affairs power as the basis for legislation to limit the
actions of state governments.

MABO V. QUEENSLAND

Eddie Koiki Mabo was watching these events closely. In 1981
Erik Olbrei, president of James Cook University Students'
Union and the Townsville Treaty Committee (of which Mabo was
co-chairman), organised a conference called 'Land Rights and
the Future of Australian Race Relations'. Mabo delivered an
address, 'Land Rights in the Torres Strait', which clearly spelled
out his understanding of land ownership and land inheritance on
Murray Island:

In the Torres Strait, land ownership is the same throughout ...
This system existed as long as we could remember ... The land was
inherited always by the male descendants ... during his lifetime,
he would make sure that his family and friends knew his wish as
to which one of his sons would be heir to his land. He would also
insist that the heir to his land must not deprive the rest of his sons
or daughters of the use of his land ... None of the land will ever be
sold for cash.[31]

Barbara Hocking, then a Melbourne barrister, delivered a
paper in which she detailed the international and Australian legal
history that would support an Indigenous group's challenge in
the High Court for land rights. She described many of the major
issues such a test case would face but insisted that it would have a
positive impact even if the legal challenge failed. 'In my opinion,
such a claim, whether or not it was successful, might very well act
as a catalyst for action at the political level.'[32]

After all the papers had been delivered, the Aboriginal
people and the Torres Strait Islanders met separately to discuss
the issues confronting them. The Murray Islanders returned
determined to take up Hocking's challenge to seek native title in
the High Court. Eddie Koiki Mabo became the leading litigant.[33]
This case would, in effect, become the appeal to Blackburn's
decision in *Milirrpum v. Nabalco*.

Murray Islanders of Mabo's generation still had enormous
respect for their culture hero, Malo, an *agud* or god, who was
traditionally represented by the octopus, each of its eight ten-
tacles corresponding to a Meriam clan and the central body to
the strength and unity of the Meriam people. Malo is especially
associated with the district and village of Las, which is in the

territory of the Piadram clan, where Koiki Mabo grew up as the adopted son of Benny and Maiga Mabo. The inheritance and ownership laws sanctified by Malo were etched into the minds of the Meriam and rolled easily off the tongue whenever a dispute or discussion of land ownership arose:

> *Malo tag mauki mauki*
> (Malo keeps his hands to himself;
> he does not touch what is not his.
> *Teter mauki mauki.*
> (He does not permit his feet
> to carry him towards another's property.)

The inheritance of individuals living in villages was very different from the association of Aboriginal people with their clan land. It was hoped that this would make it more obvious in the minds of white Australians. It was deeply felt that the view Indigenous Australians had no ownership of land was an obscene travesty of truth and justice, a consequence of colonial conquest and the doctrine that might is right.

Mabo's ten-year involvement with the lawyers associated with the High Court challenge and the Murray Islanders who were claimants or witnesses led to his developing a sophisticated understanding of the legal process and its broader significance that impressed those who discussed it with him. He was certainly not overawed and seemed always confident of success. Mabo had met opposition and even hostility from white and black Australians on several occasions but always eventually took it in his stride. However, it was the issue closest to his heart and the one to which he had devoted so many years of his life that gave him the most savage and public slap in the face.

In his 1990 report to the High Court of Australia on the factual basis of the claims made by Mabo and the other two surviving claimants, the Rev. David Passi and James Rice, Justice Moynihan of Queensland's Supreme Court declared him an unreliable witness and totally rejected all Mabo's claims to inherit land on Murray Island. He believed that Mabo's land claims were invalid and that his explanation of Meriam inheritance custom was self-seeking. Yet, of Mabo's thirty-six claims to land ownership, seventeen were wholly uncontested by his relatives, thirteen partly contested and a border change requested, and only six wholly contested. Disputes over land ownership and inheritance were common on Murray Island and in all Melanesian communities. Clearly those relatives contesting Mabo's claims did not do so for the reasons Moynihan advanced. Most importantly, Moynihan did not accept that Mabo was the adopted son of Benny and Maiga Mabo and therefore could not inherit their land. Yet, by their acceptance of most of his claims and their challenges to others, the Islanders were clearly accepting him as Benny Mabo's heir.

During 1991 Mabo was diagnosed with a cancer in his spine, which spread to his lungs and throat. In January 1992 he was advised to go to Brisbane, probably for two weeks, for radium treatment. An entry Mabo made in his diary in the last weeks of his life brings together his long commitment to the struggle for justice and the recognition of native title to land and his love for his wife.

> I thought about the struggles I have been through over the past
> years since 1963 to 1991 or to the beginning of 1992, while the
> rest of Black Australia awaits with me for the High Court
> decision to be brought down at any time. Or would it be in

time for me to receive it and make further decisions on the
outcome of that decision—for further actions if this decision is
not favourable?

If I am not around I want my children to work closely with
my lawyers and other advisers to plan future actions. Working
with other plaintiffs is also important. I also thought about how
my wife, the most important person in my life, has stuck to me
over many hardships and hurdles in life but somehow we made
it, perhaps better than others. To me my wife has been the most
adorable person, a friend closest in my life, a most wonderful
lover, and we loved every minute of our lives together.[34]

A week later in Brisbane, on 21 January 1992, he died. His last
words to Bonita were 'Land claim'. On 1 February Mabo was buried
in Townsville in one of the largest funerals seen in that city.

The High Court declared in June 1992 that the Meriam
people were holders of native title, overturned the concept of
terra nullius and, in considering the possibilities, left open the
possibility that native title might apply elsewhere if Aborigines
could demonstrate their connection with the original people
before annexation and had maintained a continuity of tradition
in relation to their land.

It was the *Mabo* case that brought matters to a head, this
time in the federal arena where the representatives of state governments and industry bodies for mining, exploration, agricul-
ture and pastoralism lobbied hard with substantial media clout
for a land management system that favoured their interests. The
reaction of the vested interests ranged against the Indigenous
inheritors of native title was hysterical and vindictive. While
the Murray Islanders celebrated, pastoralists and miners
expressed more and more wild theories and fears for the future

of the Australian land tenure system and whether Aborigines
would demand compensation. Without certainty for their titles,
investment would dry up, they asserted. Tim Fischer of the
National Party called the High Court Judges 'pissants'. Although
the Prime Minister, Paul Keating, reassured them that there was
and could be no legal challenge to freehold or leasehold title, the
campaign of fear continued until the end of 1993, when the Senate
passed legislation affirming the common law as discovered by the
High Court.

At Redfern Park in Sydney on 10 December 1992 Keating
delivered one of the most famous speeches in Australian history at the launch of Australia's celebration of the 1993 United
Nations International Year of the World's Indigenous People.
He traversed the terrible history of Australia's treatment of
Aboriginal people, the need for reconciliation, the Aboriginal
deaths in custody and the then very recent High Court decision
recognising Aboriginal native title that had survived the British
declaration of sovereignty. His view was unequivocal: 'By doing
away with the bizarre conceit that this continent had no owners
prior to the settlement of Europeans, *Mabo* establishes a
fundamental truth and lays the basis for justice. It will be much
easier to work from that basis than has ever been the case in the
past.' He appealed to his fellow Australians to imagine justice for
indigenous people:

> Imagine if ours was the oldest culture in the world and we
> were told that it was worthless. Imagine if we had resisted this
> settlement, suffered and died in the defence of our land, and then
> were told in history books that we had given up without a fight.
> Imagine if non-Aboriginal Australians had served their country
> in peace and war and were then ignored in history books. Imagine

if our feats on sporting fields had inspired admiration and patriotism and yet did nothing to diminish prejudice. Imagine if our spiritual life was denied and ridiculed.

Imagine if we had suffered the injustice and then were blamed for it.

It seems to me that if we can imagine the injustice then we can imagine its opposite. And we can have justice.

His support for the High Court's *Mabo* judgment was a beacon for Aboriginal leaders who hoped that it might deliver justice at last. Keating had called state premiers and industry representative bodies to Canberra to resolve the mounting national furore that pitted the farmers and miners against Indigenous people in a vicious debate based on fear and bald lies about the supposed threat to the land tenure system that native title represented. Aboriginal leaders—including Noel Pearson, who headed the Cape York Land Council, Mick Dodson, who had campaigned at the UN in Geneva and New York for recognition of Indigenous rights, David Ross from the Central Land Council and Peter Yu from the Kimberley Land Council, the late Charles Perkins, former head of the federal Department of Aboriginal Affairs, among many others—convened in Canberra to fight back.

On 30 June 1993 the Wik people lodged a native title claim over their territories, excluding the mining leases, in the Federal Court of Australia. Their longheld grievance against the Queensland Government would soon become another *cause célèbre* in the long struggle for the recognition of Aboriginal rights. The case was more complex than any before it. The claim covered 35 000 square kilometres of land, including an unused 100-year bauxite mining lease granted in 1958 and held by

Comalco, ten pastoral leases, a 50-year lease to local Aborigines and a deed of grant in trust, and two national parks located on western Cape York Peninsula.

With 155 Wik applicants, the claim represented a thousand people. The High Court's judgment in the *Wik* case, handed down in December 1996, found in favour of their arguments and established the principle of co-existence, which, in tandem with the growing and powerful movement for reconciliation with Aboriginal people, fundamentally changed the relationship between settler and Indigenous Australia. For the Wik people, the adage that justice delayed is justice denied was more than apt. The toll on their society was heavy and the measure of justice that was finally accorded them hard won. Almost half a century had passed since the mining leases had been granted over their land, and all the great leaders of that time who had resisted were long gone.

Six months earlier, on 3 June 1995, Mabo's tombstone was unveiled in a magnificent Torres Strait Islander ceremony that was open to the public. Annita Keating, the Prime Minister's wife, had represented the Prime Minister. The unveiling had been preceded by a celebration of Mabo's achievements in the city mall, followed that night by a huge feast and Islander dancing.

That night the grave was desecrated. Eight swastikas were spray-painted in red on the black tombstone and the word 'Abo' twice. The bronze image of Mabo's smiling face fixed into the marble with long bolts had been removed and has never been recovered. Bonita Mabo immediately decided that she would have him reburied on Murray Island where his grave would be safe, cared for and respected. In September, Mabo's body was transferred with traditional ceremony from the Murray Island airport to Las, where his body lay in state for three days. He was buried with his ancestors on a hill in his village at Las facing the sea.

The following day the tombstone, with a new bronze image of Mabo, was again ritually unveiled to 'this great man'. That night there was a feast to celebrate again the tombstone unveiling, 'the end of sorry'. The focus was a Malo dance that reached back past the intrusion of the colonists to the time when Malo's law prevailed, sanctified land ownership and unified the eight Meriam clans. Out of the dark at Las that night the great *agud*, Malo, walked with stately dignity into the light of the celebrations, his huge turtle-shell head intimidating the Meriam with its awful dignity.

Whenever Mabo spoke of Malo he had always done so with the greatest respect, perhaps even faith.[35] What is certain is that Koiki Mabo would have wished for no other burial site than one on Las overlooking the sea. His turbulent life had ended in extraordinary triumph, and he had at last returned home.

The struggle of Eddie Koiki Mabo is only the most dramatic and successful example of Indigenous Australians' fighting to reverse the consequences of colonial conquest and dispossession that had defined them in white law as an inferior caste unfit to own and occupy land in British and, later, Australian law. Mabo had the support of other Meriam people and the precedents of the historic battles of Northern Territory and Queensland Aboriginal people to preserve their relationship with the land that they had occupied 'since time immemorial'. The legal basis of *terra nullius*, on which Australia had been colonised by the British, had been overturned. More developments of great significance in the history of the First Australians followed Mabo's final return home. This is part of the nation's narrative that future historians will tell.

EPILOGUE

Marcia Langton

As we come to the end of our telling of the nation's story and the part played by the First Australians, we want to reflect on the great changes described in these chapters. After two centuries and a few more years, the world that Arthur Phillip, David Collins, Watkin Tench and others in the First Fleet encountered no longer exists. As we look at the shores of Sydney Harbour today, we might think about the struggle of the nation during these past two centuries and more with the presumption expressed in the words of Watkin Tench as the first settlement was cleared at Port Jackson: 'in order to take possession of his new territory, and bring about an intercourse between its old and new masters'. A few shards of evidence of the lives of Bennelong, Pemulwuy and the men and women of the clans of Sydney Harbour can be found here and there: the point where Bennelong's house was built, the Tank Stream now enclosed in urban infrastructure, or the remains of the settlement in an archaeological pit under the glass floor of the Sydney Museum. The hope that they held out for accommodation was destroyed by a lack of imagination and compassion, the propensity for violence and greed, and a loss of faith. Yet there are descendants today who hold on to the vision of their forebears. With Mabo's great achievement—the rejection of the doctrine of *terra nullius*, which held that Australia was an empty land, and the recognition of native title—these descendants have an honourable place in modern Australian society. We should ask why it took so long, but inevitably the answer lies in history.

In 1770, while Captain James Cook was steering up the east coast of New Holland, Benjamin Franklin was writing a pro-slavery tract in reply to anti-slavery campaigner Granville Sharp, one of many correspondences that firmed the resolve of the American rebels to preserve the traditions of slavery on which their wealth and way of life so depended. Cook would not have countenanced that Port Jackson would prove to be his most useful chart entry along the east coast of Australia, providing, in due course, a place for the English convicts who could no longer be sent to the American colonies after the War of Independence.

The British tradition of not allowing its own citizens to be slaves, as distinct from selling their labour, was a value highly regarded by Arthur Phillip in establishing the colony of New South Wales. He wrote stridently in one of his memoranda: 'The laws of this Country will of Course be introduced in South Wales [*sic*], and there is one that I would wish to take place from the moment His Majesty's Forces takes Possession of the Country—That there can be no Slavery in a Free Land—& consequently no Slaves.'[1]

We might find some inspiration in Phillip's words, but we should leave the last word to history itself. As we see in each of these chapters, that potential was glimpsed by rare men and women throughout Australian history. Their efforts to transform the raw colonial relationships into viable communities with different and yet common interests were so often dashed by petty politics and human failings, a problem that Arthur Phillip himself so presciently described: 'it is perhaps the fate of this theory, in common with many others of a very pleasing nature, to be more attractive in contemplation than efficacious in real practice.'[2]

Yet something of the vision of the men and women whose narratives run through our history has remained a part of Australian society. They are present in the pages of the records, and their imprint on our cities and landscapes can be understood when we know their stories. Whereas William Suttor wryly cited the annals of Roman history in his remark at the end of the wars with the Wiradjuri—'A solitude called peace'—history helps us to hear the voices of the First Australians in each place they inhabited.

NOTES

Prologue

1 Ryan, L, *The Aboriginal Tasmanians*, University of Queensland Press, Brisbane, 1981, p. 67.

2 Durack, M, *Kings in Grass Castles*, Corgi Books, Sydney, 1986.

3 Pedersen, Howard, transcript, *First Australians* documentary series, episode 5, 2007.

4 *Age*, 26 May 1866.

5 See the online catalogue description of the FCAATSI archive held at the Australian Institute of Aboriginal and Torres Strait Islander Studies: www1.aiatsis.gov.au/finding_aids/MS3759.htm.

1. 'They made a solitude and called it peace'

1 Meaning 'the people' in the Sydney language. See Val Attenbrow, *Sydney's Aboriginal Past*, UNSW Press, Sydney, 2002, for further information on the use of the word *eora*.

2 Watkin Tench, *Sydney's First Four Years*, Library of Australian History in association with the Royal Australian Historical Society, Sydney, 1979 [1789, 1793], p. 35.

3 ibid., p. 53.

4 ibid., p. 54.

5 George Bouchier Worgan, *Journal of a First Fleet Surgeon*, Library Council of New South Wales/Library of Australian History, Sydney, 1978, p. 7.

6 Tench, *Sydney's First Four Years*, p. 38.

7   David Collins, *An Account of the English Colony in New South Wales*, AH & AW Reed/Royal Australian Historical Society, Sydney, 1975 [1798], p. 4.

8   Worgan, *Journal of a First Fleet Surgeon*, p. 33.

9   Arthur Bowes Smyth, Wednesday, 6 February 1788, *Journal of A Bowes-Smith, Surgeon in the* Lady Penrhyn, *1787–1789*, Trustees of the State Public Library, New South Wales, Sydney, 1979.

10 ibid.

11 Tench, *Sydney's First Four Years*, p. 39.

12 ibid., p. 142.

13 ibid., p. 141.

14 Collins, *An Account of the English Colony*, p. 496.

15 ibid.

16 ibid.

17 ibid.

18 Noel Butlin, *Our Original Aggression*, George Allen & Unwin, Sydney, 1983, pp. 21-2.

19 Tench, *Sydney's First Four Years*, p. 150.

20 ibid., p. 147.

21 ibid., p. 158.

22 ibid., p. 160.

23 William Bradley, *A Voyage to New South Wales: The Journal of Lieutenant William Bradley RN of HMS* Sirius, *1786–1792*, Ure Smith/Public Library of New South Wales, Sydney, 1969, p. 183.

24 John Hunter, *An Historical Journal of Events at Sydney and at Sea, 1787–1792*, ed. John Bach, Angus & Robertson/Royal Australian Historical Society, Sydney, 1968 [1793].

25 Bradley, *A Voyage to New South Wales*, p. 183.

26 Newton Fowell to his father, Batavia, 31 July 1790, quoted in Nance Irvine (ed.), *The* Sirius *Letters*, Fairfax Library, Sydney, 1988, p. 115.

27 Tench, *Sydney's First Four Years*, p. 159.

28 ibid., p. 179.

29 Philip Gidley King, *Journal of Philip Gidley King: Lieutenant, RN, 1787–1790*, 9 April 1790, Australian Documents Library, Sydney, 1980, pp. 394–5.

30 For further discussion see Keith Vincent Smith, *Bennelong: The Coming in of the Eora: Sydney Cove 1788–92*, Kangaroo Press, Sydney, 2001.

31 Tench, *Sydney's First Four Years*, p. 167.

32 ibid.

33 Hunter, *An Historical Journal of Events at Sydney*, p. 308.

34 Tench, *Sydney's First Four Years*, p. 188.

35 ibid., p. 200.

36 Hunter, *An Historical Journal of Events at Sydney*, p. 144.

37 Phillip in Hunter, *An Historical Journal of Events at Sydney*, p. 136.

38 Elizabeth Macarthur to Bridget Kingdon, 7 March 1791, *Historic Records of New South Wales* (HRNSW), vol. 11, p. 502.

39 Collins, *An Account of the English Colony in New South Wales*, p. 122.

40 ibid., p. 464.

41 Tench, *Sydney's First Four Years*, p. 222.

42 ibid., p. 206.

43 G Bond, *A Brief Account of the Colony of Port Jackson in New South Wales, Its Native Inhabitants, Productions, &c &c*, London, 5th edn, 1809, p. 5.

44 *Oracle and Public Advertiser*, 19 April 1794.

45 John Hunter to John King, London, 123 Mount Street, Berkeley Square, 5 August 1794, CO202/Pt II, Public Record Office, London, pp. 77–8.

46 Baron Charles von Hügel, *New Holland Journal November 1833–October 1834*, trans. & ed. Dymphna Clark, Melbourne University Press/State Library of New South Wales, Melbourne, 1994, p. 347.

47 John Hunter to John King, 25–26 January 1795, CO201/12, p. 3, Public Record Office, London; HRNSW, vol. 3, p. 745.

48 Jacqueline Bonnemains & Pascal Hauguel (eds), 'Sejour de Milius au Port Jackson 25 avril–22 juillet 1802', *Recit de voyage aux Terres Australes par Pierre Bernard Milius, second sur le 'Naturaliste' dans l'expedition Baudin (1800–1804)*, Sociéte Havrais d'Etudes diverse Muséum d'Histoire Naturelle du Havre, Le Havre, 2000 (trans. Jeremy Steele & Keith Vincent Smith, 2004), p. 49.

49 *Sydney Gazette*, 9 January 1813.

50 JW Price, *The Minerva Journal of John Washington Price, A Voyage from Cork, Ireland, to Sydney, New South Wales, 1793–1800*, trans., ed. & intr. by Pamela Jane Fulton, Miegunyah Press, Carlton, 2000, p. 174.

51 Collins, *An Account of the English Colony in New South Wales*, p. 348.

52 ibid.

53 ibid.

54 ibid.

55 Reverend Thomas Fyshe Palmer to Dr John Disney, Sydney, 3 June 1796, MSS 948, p. 18, Mitchell Library, State Library of NSW, Sydney.

56 Price, *Minerva Journal*.

57 Philip Gidley King, Government and General Orders, 17 November 1801, *Historical Records of Australia* (HRA), series 1, vol. 3, p. 466.

58 Philip Gidley King to Sir Joseph Banks, 5 June 1805, HRA, vol. 5, p. 654.

59 *Sydney Gazette*, 19 May 1805.

60 *Sydney Gazette*, 9 June 1805.

61 *Sydney Gazette*, July 1805.

62 *Sydney Gazette*, 11 August 1805.

63 Richard Atkins to Governor PG King, 8 July 1805, HRNSW, vol. 5, p. 654.

64 John Easty, *Memorandum of the Transactions of a Voyage from England to Botany Bay, 1787–1793: A First Fleet Journal*, Angus & Robertson/Public Library of New South Wales, Sydney, 1965.

65 PG King to Lord Castlereagh, 27 July 1806, HRA, vol. 5, p. 753.

66 PG King to Lord Hobart, 20 December 1804, HRNSW, vol. 5, p. 513.

67 *Sydney Gazette*, 7 January 1810.

68 Rose Marie de Freycinet, quoted in Marnie Bassett, *Realms and Islands: The World Voyage of Rose de Freycinet in the Corvette* Uranie *1817–1820*, Oxford University Press, London, 1962, p. 184.

69 Lachlan Macquarie to Lord Bathurst, HRA, vol. 8, p. 467.

70 Macquarie to Bathurst, 18 March 1816, HRA, series 1, vol. 9, p. 54.

71 Charles Throsby to D'Arcy Wentworth (in Sydney), Wentworth Papers, 5 April 1816, A752/CY699, Mitchell Library, Sydney, pp. 183-6.

72 Lachlan Macquarie, *Governor's Diary and Memorandum Book Commencing on and from Wednesday the 10th Day of April 1816 at Sydney, in N. S. Wales*, Lachlan and Elizabeth Macquarie Archive, www.lib.mq.edu.au/lema/1816/1816april.html.

73 Captain James Wallis, Journal, 17 April 1816, Colonial Secretary in Letters, 4/1735, Reel 2161:52–60, State Records New South Wales, Sydney.

74 Lachlan Macquarie to Lord Bathurst, 4 April 1817, HRA, series 1, vol. 9, p. 342.

75 Lachlan Macquarie, 10 May 1815, *Journal of Tours of Towns in New South Wales and Van Diemen's Land, 1810–22*.

76 Theo Barker, *A History of Bathurst*, vol. 1, Crawford House Press, Bathurst, NSW, 1992, p. 63.

77 Macquarie, 10 May 1815, *Journal of Tours*.

78 ibid.

79 Barker, *A History of Bathurst*, p. 64.

80 JM Bennett, 'Bigge, John Thomas (1780–1843)', *Australian Dictionary of Biography* (ADB), vol. 1, Melbourne University Press, Carlton, 1966, pp. 99–100.

81 Lachlan Macquarie, Thursday, 20 December 1821, 'Journal of a Tour of Inspection to Bathurst in Decr. 1821', MS A785, Mitchell Library, State Library of NSW, Sydney.

82 JD Heydon, 'Brisbane, Sir Thomas Makdougall (1773–1860)', ADB, vol. 1, pp. 151–5.

83 ibid.

84 'Colo' (George Suttor), *The Australian*, 25 August and 14 October 1826.

85 Peter Read, *A Hundred Years War: The Wiradjuri People and the State*, Australian National University Press, Canberra, 1988, pp. 5, 8.

86 WH Suttor, *Australian Stories Retold*, Bathurst, 1887.

87 ibid.

88 *Sydney Gazette*, 10 June 1824.

89 LE Threlkeld, *Australian Reminiscences and Papers*, Niel Gunson (ed.), vol. 1, Institute of Aboriginal Affairs, Canberra, 1974, p. 49.

90 *Sydney Gazette*, 10 June 1824.

91 William Lawson Jnr, February 1824.

92 *Sydney Gazette*, 5 August 1824.

93 Suttor, *Australian Stories Retold*.

94 *Sydney Gazette*, 21 October 1824.

95 *Sydney Gazette*, 30 December 1824.

96 Governor Brisbane, to Colonial Office.

97 Suttor, *Australian Stories Retold*.

2. 'What business have you here?'

1 Tim Murray and Christine Williamson, 'Archaeology and history', in Robert Manne (ed.), *Whitewash: On Keith Windschuttle's Fabrication of Aboriginal History*, Black Inc., Melbourne, 2003, pp. 319-20. Roslynn D Haynes, *Tasmanian Visions: Landscapes in Writing, Art and Photography*, Polymath Press, Sandy Bay, Tas., 2006, p. 2.

2 Patsy Cameron, 'Aboriginal life pre-invasion', in Alison Alexander (ed.), *The Companion to Tasmanian History*, Centre for Tasmanian Historical Studies, University of Tasmania, Hobart, 2005, pp. 3-6.

3 Colin Dyer, *The French Explorers and the Aboriginal Australians 1772-1839*, University of Queensland Press, Brisbane, 2005, p. 3.

4 Frank Horner, *The French Reconnaissance: Baudin in Australia*, Melbourne University Press, Carlton, 1987, pp. 271-3.

5 NJB Plomley (ed.), *Friendly Mission: The Tasmanian Journals of George Augustus Robinson 1829-1834*, Tasmanian Historical Research Association, Hobart, 1966, p. 375.

6 *Van Diemen's Land: Copies of All Correspondence between Lieutenant Governor Arthur and His Majesty's Secretary of State for the Colonies on the Subject of the Military Operations Lately Carried on against the Aboriginal Inhabitants of Van Diemen's Land, Hobart*, Tasmanian Historical Research Association, 1971, p. 259.

7 See James Boyce, *Van Diemen's Land*, Black Inc., Melbourne, 2008, pp. 63-126.

8 Plomley, *Friendly Mission*, pp. 552-3.

9 Archives Office of Tasmania CSO 1/36, CSO 1/359/7578.

10 Peter Chapman (ed.), *Historical Records of Australia*, series 3, vol. 7, Canberra, AGPS, 1997, pp. 625-30.

11 Batman to Anstey, 7 September 1829, Archives Office of Tasmania CSO1/320/7578.

12 *Van Diemen's Land: Copies of All Correspondence*, pp. 63-4.

13 Peter Chapman (ed.), *The Diaries and Letters of GTWB Boyes*, vol. 1, 1820-32, Oxford University Press, Melbourne, 1985, pp. 378-80.

14 For a more detailed (and fully referenced) account of government policy to the Aborigines in all three phases of Robinson's work than can be given here, see Boyce, *Van Diemen's Land*, pp. 261-313.

15 Alison Alexander, 'Truganini', in Alexander (ed.), *The Companion to Tasmanian History*, p. 370.

16 Henry Reynolds, *Fate of a Free People*, Penguin Books, Melbourne, 1995, p. 142.

17 Plomley, *Friendly Mission*, p. 280.

18 Archives Office of Tasmania, Executive Council Minutes, 23 February 1831, in *Van Diemen's Land: Copies of All Correspondence*, pp. 80-3.

19 Plomley, *Friendly Mission*, p. 394.

20 ibid., p. 398.

21 Boyce, *Van Diemen's Land*, pp. 295-313.

22 NJB Plomley, *Weep in Silence: A History of the Flinders Island Aboriginal Settlement*, Blubber Head Press, Hobart, 1987, p. 608.

23 Reynolds, *Fate of a Free People*, pp. 7-16.

24 Greg Lehman, 'Matriarchs of survival', in Alexander (ed.), *The Companion to Tasmanian History*, pp. 229-30.

25 Rebe Taylor, *Unearthed: The Aboriginal Tasmanians of Kangaroo Island*, Wakefield Press, Adelaide, 2002.

26 James Boyce, *God's Own Country? The Anglican Church and Tasmanian Aborigines*, Anglicare Tasmania, Hobart, 2001, pp. 49-76.

27 ibid., p. 66.

28 ibid., p. 81.

29 Plomley, *Friendly Mission*, p. 88.

3. How it starts

1   Reverend Mackie, Evidence, *Report of the Board Appointed to Enquire into, and Report Upon, the Present Condition and Management of the Coranderrk Aboriginal Station, together with Minutes*, VPP 1882, Public Record Office of Victoria (hereafter PROV), p. 92.

2 William Thomas to Redmond Barry, 21 October 1861, Mitchell Library (ML), State Library of NSW, Sydney.

3 Alistair Campbell, *John Batman and the Aborigines*, Kibble Books, Malmesbury, Vic., 1987, pp. 101–5.

4 Thomas to Barry, 21 October 1861.

5 AIATSIS, *First Australians*, DVD, directed by Rachel Perkins; interview rushes Joy Murphy, Blackfella Films, Sydney, 2008.

6 Thomas, Journal, 29 February 1849, ML, State Library of NSW, Sydney.

7 Diane Barwick, *Rebellion at Coranderrk*, Aboriginal History Inc., Canberra, 1998, p. 64.

8 William Hull, evidence to Select Committee, 1858, p. 12, cited in Barwick, *Rebellion at Coranderrk*, p. 64.

9 AIATSIS, *First Australians*.

10 Thomas to Barry, 21 October 1861.

11 Green to Board of Protection of Aborigines, cited in Barwick, *Rebellion at Coranderrk*, p. 67.

12 *Post*, Melbourne, 18 June 1863.

13 Queen's Secretary, 17 November 1863, cited in Barwick, *Rebellion at Coranderrk*, p. 67.

14 Source attributed to Green, cited in Lou Lane, *History*, Kardinia Prehistory Society, 2001, p. 105.

15 Barwick, *Rebellion at Coranderrk*, p. 96.

16 ibid., pp. 109–10.

17 ibid., p. 296.

18 BPA's Secretary's letter book, 16–24 April 1883, PROV. See also Barwick, *Rebellion at Coranderrk*, p. 271.

19 Barwick, *Rebellion at Coranderrk*, p. 96.

20 AIATSIS, *First Australians*.

21 Barwick, *Rebellion at Coranderrk*, p. 19.

22 *Report of the Board Appointed to Enquire into, and Report Upon, the Present Condition and Management of the Coranderrk Aboriginal Station, together with Minutes.*

23 AIATSIS, *First Australians.*

24 Anne Bon correspondence, PROV.

25 *Age*, 16 December 1886. See also Barwick, *Rebellion at Coranderrk*, p. 300.

26 Quoted in Barwick, *Rebellion at Coranderrk*, p. 299.

27 *Argus*, 23 June 1923.

4. The sea met the desert, and the desert met the sea

1 The spelling varies between Arunta, used by early ethnographers; Aranda, used by early missionaries and still used in the western territories; and Arrernte, a more recent spelling, which has been used for consistency in this chapter.

2 *Observer*, Adelaide, 16 September 1905, p. 47. Also RG Kimber, unpublished research.

3 Day, 'Central Australia', p. 11. Gibbers are stones polished smooth by wind-blown sand.

4 CPP, vol. 11, 1920–21, p. 28.

5 Tietkens, *Journal of the Central Australian Exploring Expedition, 1889*, pp. 63–4.

6 WHT, 'Black Tracker'.

7 Gillen, *Gillen's Diary*, p. 18, and 'Notes on Some Manners and Customs of the Aborigines of the McDonnell Ranges', pp. 177–9.

8 Henson, *A Straight-out Man*, p. 11. See also Vallee, *God, Guns and Government*, p. 145.

9 Schwarz, quoted in translation in *Register*, Adelaide, 10 January 1890, p. 6.

10 See Nettlebeck and Foster's *In the Name of the Law*, and Vallee's *God, Guns and Government on the Central Australian Frontier* for recent accounts of the Barrow Creek attacks and reprisals, as well as government, police, missionary and other people's responses between the 1870s and 1890.

11 Schwarz, quoted in *Register*, Adelaide, 10 January 1890, p. 6.

12 ibid.

13 In *Northern Territory Times*, 9 January 1890.

14 Nettlebeck and Foster, *In the Name of the Law*, pp. 82–91.

15 Quoted in Vallee, *God, Guns and Government*, p. 279.

16 ibid.

17 *Port Augusta Dispatch*, 24 July 1891.

18 Vallee, *God, Guns and Government*, p. 295.

19 Willshire, *The Land of the Dawning*.

20 Willshire, *The Aborigines of Central Australia*, p. 15.

21 Grant, *Camel Train and Aeroplane*, p. 117.

22 Kimber, 'Genocide or Not?', pp. 58–60.

23 Baume, *Tragedy Track*, p. 90. Also pers. comm. senior Warlpiri men. See also Napaljari and Cataldi, *Warlpiri Dreamings and Histories*, pp. 105–17, for a mythological account with strong similarities.

24 Chewings, *Back in the Stone Age*, pp. 16–17.

25 Kimber, 'Erlikilyika', pp. 92–3; Morphy, *Aboriginal Art*, pp. 263–5.

26 Spencer, *Report on the Work of the Horn Scientific Expedition to Central Australia*, p. 85.

27 ibid., p. 87.

28 ibid., p. 50.

29 Stirling, 'Anthropology'.

30 Gregory, *The Dead Heart of Australia*, pp. 210-21; Hercus, 'How we danced the Mudlunga', pp. 4-31; Kimber, 'Mulunga Old Mulunga', pp. 175-91; Roth, *The Queensland Aborigines*, pp. 120-5; Spencer and Gillen, *The Arunta*, vol. 2, pp. 560-1.

31 Spencer and Gillen, *The Native Tribes of Central Australia*. See also, in particular, Spencer and Gillen, *The Arunta*, vol. 1, fig. 2, facing p. 12, which gives all ceremonial leaders' names.

32 Mulvaney, *Encounters in Place*, pp. 131-40; Winnecke, *Journal of the Horn Scientific Expedition, 1894*, p. 42.

33 C Strehlow, letter to 'The Chairman Royal Commission on Aborigines'.

34 See Henson, *A Straight-out Man*, for an appreciation of the life and work of Moses; Kimber, 'Strehlow, Carl Freidrich Theodor', pp. 282-4, for Carl Strehlow; Strehlow, *Journey to Horseshoe Bend*, for his father Carl.

35 Murif, *From Ocean to Ocean*, p. 43.

36 ibid., pp. 55-6.

37 Gillen, *Gillen's Diary*, p. 7; Holmes, *Australia's Open North*, pp. 162-4; Vamplew, *Australians*, p. 68.

38 Gregory, *The Dead Heart of Australia*; Hercus and Sutton, *This is What Happened*; Jones, 'Ngapamanha', pp. 157-73; TGH Strehlow, 'Geography and the Totemic Landscape in Central Australia', pp. 92-140.

39 Carnegie, *Spinifex and Sand*, pp. 346, 395; EC Cowle, in Mulvaney, Petch and Morphy, *From the Frontier*, pp. 104, 146.

40 Blackwell and Lockwood, *Alice on the Line*.

41 Gillen, *Gillen's Diary*, p. 47.

42 *Observer*, Adelaide, 21 December 1901, p. 32.

43 *Register*, Adelaide, 12 February 1901.

44 Gillen, *Gillen's Diary*, p. 15.

45 Finlayson, *The Red Centre*; Gregory, *The Dead Heart of Australia*.

46 Murray, 'Record of Prospecting Operations', p. 24.

47 Chewings, *Back in the Stone Age*, p. 9.

48 Gillen, *Gillen's Diary*, pp. 163–4.

49 Henson, *A Straight-out Man*.

50 ibid., pp. 14, 32, 108, 118. Also RG Kimber, unpublished research.

51 Gillen, *Gillen's Diary*, pp. 17–22.

52 ibid., p. 29.

5. Blood history

1 Community Development Employment Scheme Payments, along with Unemployment Benefits, Old Age Pension and Supporting Mothers Pensions, are the main source of income in Fitzroy Crossing. There are two pay weeks, Big Pay, which constitutes the main slate of payments, and Little Pay, which is made up of Child Endowment and other Family Benefit Payments. Indigenous incomes from CDEP and non-employment incomes represent 61 per cent of all income in the Fitzroy Valley, as related by J Taylor, *Indigenous People in the West Kimberley Labour Market*, Centre for Aboriginal Economic Policy Research, ANU, Working Paper No. 35, 2006, pp. 34–8.

2 The campaign for equal Aboriginal award wages in the pastoral industry began in 1965. The legislation was passed in 1966, but the pastoral industry was not required to comply until 1968. 'Timeline of Indigenous Rights',

http://indigenousrights.net.au/timeline.asp?startyear=
1960 (viewed 30 June 2008). See also Mary-Ann Jebb, *Blood,
Sweat and Welfare: A History of White Bosses and Aboriginal
Pastoral Workers*, UWA Press, Perth, 2002.

3   Alistair Hope, *Inquest into the deaths of—Edward John Riley,
Rachael Henry, Chad Atkins, Teddy Beharral, Maitland
Brown, Jonathon Dick, Lloyd Dawson, Benjie Dickens,
Ivan Barry Gepp, Owen Gordon, Jonathan Hale, Ernest
James, Laurel Joshua Middleton, William Robert Miller,
Gordon Oscar, Celeste Antoinette Shaw, Shawn Surprise,
Davina Kaye Edwards, Nathalia Maree Cox, Desley Sampi,
Llewellyn Sampi, Troy James O'Sullivan, Zedrick Yamera*,
Ref 37/07, Western Australia Coroner's Office, February
2008.

4   R Hill, K Golson, PA Lowe, MK Mann, S Hayes & JE
Blackwood (eds), *Kimberley Appropriate Economies
Roundtable Forum Proceedings*, convened 11–13 October
2005, Fitzroy Crossing, WA, by the Kimberley Land
Council, Environs Kimberley and Australian Conservation
Foundation, Australian Conservation Foundation, Cairns,
2006.

5   I attended hearings for this inquest in Broome in October
2007. The proceedings were also followed in the press, in
particular the *West Australian* newspaper, throughout 2007
and 2008.

6   The term 'Killing Times' has been used by Kimberley
Aboriginal people to describe the period of colonisation
between 1881 and approximately 1905 when numerous
countrymen were killed and the perpetrators of these crimes,
mostly non-Indigenous but also Indigenous, were rarely
brought to justice. See: Stephen Kinnane, *Shadow Lines*,

Fremantle Arts Centre Press, Fremantle, WA, 2003; Andrew Gill, 'Aborigines, settlers and police in the Kimberleys, 1887–1905', *Studies in Western Australian History*, vol. 1, June 1977, pp. 1–28; Henry Reynolds, *Why Weren't We Told? A Personal Search for the Truth about Our History*, Penguin Books, Melbourne, 1999; and J Sullivan and B Shaw, *Banggaiyerri: The Story of Jack Sullivan*, AIAS Press, Canberra, 1983.

7   The Department of Environment and Conservation (WA) estimates that approximately 30 000 visitors traverse this road in the dry season alone (pers. comm., 24 June 2008).

8   C Clement, 'Monotony, manhunts and malice: Eastern Kimberley law enforcement, 1896–1908', *Early Days: Journal and Proceedings of the Royal West Australian Historical Society*, vol. 10, 1986, and C Clement, 'Pre-settlement intrusion into the East Kimberley', East Kimberley Working Paper No. 24, East Kimberley Impact Assessment Project.

9   M Durack, *Kings in Grass Castles*, Corgi Books, Sydney, 1986.

10 S Lindqvist, *Exterminate All the Brutes*, Granta Books, London, 1998.

11 'Kartiya' is a Kimberley term used to describe non-Indigenous people, specifically, Europeans.

12 Dillon Andrews, transcript, *First Australians*, Episode 5, 2007.

13 The Skin system is central to Aboriginal Law in the Kimberley, and the consequences of breaking it can be severe. See Howard Pedersen and Banjo Woorunmurra, *Jandamarra and the Bunuba Resistance*, Magabala Books, Broome, WA, 1995, p. 77.

14 Andrews, transcript.

15 Howard Pedersen, transcript, *First Australians*, Episode 5, 2007.

16 Andrews, transcript.

17 Pedersen, transcript.

18 Andrews, transcript.

19 Pedersen, transcript.

20 ibid.

21 Andrews, transcript.

22 Pedersen, transcript.

23 Andrews, transcript.

24 Pedersen, transcript.

25 ibid.

26 Andrews, transcript.

27 *Aborigines Act 1905*, Act No. 14 of 1905, Western Australian Parliament, 23 December 1905, WA.

28 Anna Haebich, *For Their Own Good: Aborigines and Government in the Southwest of Western Australia, 1900–1940*, UWA Press, Perth, WA, 1988.

29 Anna Haebich, transcript, *First Australians*, Episode 5, 2007.

30 Stephen Kinnane, 'Skin', in *Shadow Lines*, p. 34.

31 Haebich, *For Their Own Good*.

32 Anna Haebich, *Broken Circles*, Fremantle Arts Centre Press, Fremantle, WA, 2001.

33 Kinnane, *Shadow Lines*.

34 Haebich, transcript.

35 Marcia Langton, transcript, *First Australians*, Episode 5, 2007.

36 This episode is detailed in Kinnane, *Shadow Lines*, p. 186, and Haebich, *For Their Own Good*, pp. 194-9.

37 Haebich, transcript.

38 Details of Noongar beliefs associated with moodjar trees and the Moore River Native Settlement Cemetery are documented in the Department of Indigenous Affairs' Aborigines Department File Cemetery 1916-64, 149/48.

39 Sam Dinah, transcript, *First Australians*, Episode 5, 2007.

40 Doris Pilkington, transcript, *First Australians*, Episode 5, 2007.

41 Haebich, transcript.

42 Mary Bennett's advocacy of Indigenous rights and her role in the 1934 Mosely Royal Commission has been comprehensively documented in Haebich, *For Their Own Good*, pp. 322-30, and Peter Biskup, *Not Slaves Not Citizens*, University of Queensland Press, Brisbane, 1973, pp. 94-5. Bennett's criticisms of Neville and the department are also detailed in Pat Jacobs, *Mr Neville: A Biography*, Fremantle Arts Centre Press, Fremantle, WA, 1990, pp. 200-1. Steve Kinnane has documented the debate between Bennett and Neville from an Indigenous community perspective in *Shadow Lines* (pp. 250-3) while also utilising primary sources such as the Department of Indigenous Affairs' Aborigines Department file, Royal Commission into the Treatment of Aborigines, 1934 (333/1933).

43 Haebich, transcript.

44 Haebich, *For Their Own Good*; Jacobs, *Mr Neville*.

45 Haebich, transcript.

46 Kinnane, *Shadow Lines*.

47 Haebich, transcript.

48 ibid.

49 ibid.

50 Una Ashwyn (Augustine), interview, Oral History 1992, in Stephen Kinnane and Lauren Marsh, Card Fever Research

Project, 1988, 1991-93, 1995-96 (16 hr 30 min), restricted material, AIATSIS Library, Canberra.

51 Kinnane, *Shadow Lines*.

52 I realise this could be taken as an oxymoron but, sadly, a government can enforce a state of neglect. It takes energy and focus, but it can be done, and has been done in this country with regard to Indigenous issues for centuries.

53 Haebich, transcript.

54 ibid.

55 Kevin Rudd, 'Apology to Australia's Indigenous Peoples', www.pm.gov.au/media/Speech/2008/speech_0073.cfm (viewed 7 July 2008).

56 L Henderson-Yates, S Wagner, H Parker & D Yates, *Fitzroy Valley Liquor Restriction Report: An Evaluation of the Effects of a Six-month Restriction on Take-away Alcohol Relating to Measurable Health and Social Benefits and Community Perceptions and Behaviours*, University of Notre Dame Australia, Drug and Alcohol Office Western Australia, March 2008, pp. 15-16.

57 Barrgana Lecture Series, University of Notre Dame Australia, Broome, 24 July 2008.

6. The schools of human experience

1 The people who identify as Yorta Yorta–Bangerang are the descendants of the original ancestors who occupied the traditional lands, the majority of whom identify as Yorta Yorta. In light of the collective nature of the relationship between the Yorta Yorta–Bangerang, and for the purpose of this discussion, I use the term Yorta Yorta.

2 Dharnya Centre mural, Dharnya Cultural Centre, Barmah Forest, Victoria.

3 Wayne Atkinson, 'Not one iota: the Yorta Yorta struggle for land justice', PhD, LaTrobe University, Melbourne, 2000, pp. 154-5.

4 ibid., p. 34.

5 Sir Doug Nicholls, *First Australians*, directed by Beck Cole, research materials, AIATSIS, Canberra, 2008.

6 *Age*, 26 May 1866.

7 Nancy Cato, *Mister Maloga: Daniel Matthews and His Mission, Murray River, 1864–1902*, University of Queensland Press, Brisbane, 1976, p. 47.

8 ibid., p. 28.

9 ibid., p. 51.

10 *Riverine Herald*, 16 August 1946.

11 WR Atkinson, 'A picture from the other side: an oral history of the relationship between Cummeragunja and Coranderrk reserves' (manuscript), Australian Institute of Aboriginal and Torres Strait Islander Studies (AIATSIS), Canberra, 1981, p. 79.

12 Human Rights and Equal Opportunity Commission, *Bringing Them Home: Report of the National Inquiry into the Separation of Aboriginal and Torres Strait Islander Children from Their Families*, 1997, p. 34; available at www.hreoc. gov.au.

13 Heather Goodall, *From Invasion to Embassy: Land in Aboriginal Politics in NSW from 1770 to 1972*, Allen & Unwin, Sydney, 1996, p. 252.

14 See PB Ellis, *To Hell or Connaught: The Cromwellian Colonisation of Ireland, 1652–1660*, Blackstaff Press, Belfast, 2000; and WR Atkinson, 'Tracking the origins of Indigenous reserves through the lenses of Cummeragunja:

the Irish connection', paper presented at the 5th Annual Conference on Settler Colonialism, National University of Ireland, Galway, 2007, pp. 3–8.

15   Mabo Papers, 1994, National Library of Australia, pp. 70–81.

16   4 Stat. 41, 1 May 28, 1830.

17   William Christie MacLeod, *The American Indian Frontier*, 1928, pp. 26-7; *Crime of Crimes*, SBS, 2003.

18   Christie MacLeod, *The American Indian Frontier*, pp. 26-7; J Chesterman and B Galligan, *Citizens Without Rights: Aborigines and Australian Citizenship*, Cambridge University Press, Melbourne, 1997, pp. 16–30.

19   Cato, *Mister Maloga*, p. 23.

20   DE Barwick, 'Coranderrk and Cummeragunja: pioneers and policy', in TS Epstein & DH Penny (eds), *Opportunity and Response: Case Studies in Economic Development*, Hurst, London, 1972, p. 50.

21   *Yorta Yorta Community v. State of Victoria & Ors* [1998] FC VG 6001-95.

22   William Cooper to JM Chanter MLA, 11 November 1887.

23   Daniel Matthews, diary entries for 19 July 1887.

24   Barwick, 'Coranderrk and Cummeragunja: pioneers and policy', p. 24; see also experiences of Yorta Yorta Nations Inc in recent attempts to buy the Maloga property, 2008.

25   Priscilla McKray, in Atkinson, 'A picture from the other side', p. 79.

26   ABC footage of Pastor Douglas Nicholls returning home to Cummeragunja, 'Mission voices', www.abc.net.au (viewed 29 June 2008).

27   Interview with Brett Vickers, *Late Night Live*, ABC Radio, 7 February 2008.

28 HREOC, *Bringing Them Home*; Oral History Recording, Banjulaka Museum, Melbourne, 2005; Yorta Yorta Elder George Nelson, pers. comm., Echuca, 2001.

29 Bain Attwood and Andrew Markus, *Thinking Black: William Cooper and Australian Aborigines' League*, AIATSIS, Canberra, 2004, p. 4.

30 *Herald*, Melbourne, 15 September 1933.

31 Murri is a term used broadly to describe Queensland Aborigines.

32 Cooper to Revd Gribble, 26 October 1933.

33 Interview with Aunty Sally Russell (née Cooper) at Footscray Elderly Care Centre, Koori Oral History Program, 1990.

34 William Cooper, Secretary, AAL, to the Hon. Minister of the Interior, 22 February 1936.

35 William Cooper to Joseph Lyons, Prime Minister, 23 July 1936.

36 Cato, *Mister Maloga*, p. 97.

37 A term used by some south-eastern Indigenous communities to identify Indigenous people.

38 A Markus (ed.), *Blood from a Stone: William Cooper and the Australian Aborigines League*, Monash University Publications in History, Melbourne, 1988, pp. 80–1.

39 Horner, *Vote Ferguson for Aboriginal Freedom*, Australian and New Zealand Book Co., Sydney, 1974, p. 64.

40 Geraldine Briggs, in Atkinson, 'A picture from the other side', p. 129.

41 Horner, *Vote Ferguson for Aboriginal Freedom*, pp. 76–7.

42 Markus, *Blood from a Stone*, p. 107.

43 ibid.

44 Goodall, *Invasion to Embassy*, pp. 249–50.

45 William Cooper Hon. Sec., AAL, to Mr Stevens, the Hon. the Premier of New South Wales, 20 February 1939.

46 Goodall, *Invasion to Embassy*, p. 250.

47 Barwick, 'Coranderrk and Cummeragunja: pioneers and policy', p. 191.

48 K McConnochie, D Hollingsworth & J Pettman, *Race and Racism in Australia*, Social Science Press, Wentworth Falls, NSW, 1988, pp. 37–8.

49 Archie Roach, *Sensual Being* (album), 2002.

50 Charles McLean, 'Report on the operation of the Aborigines Act 1828 and the regulations and orders made thereunder', in *Victorian Parliamentary Papers 1956–58*, Legislative Assembly, vol. 2, paper no. 18, 1957, pp. 6–7.

51 Sir Doug Nicholls, in N Peterson & M Langton, *Aborigines, Land and Land Rights*, AIATSIS, Canberra, 1983, p. 253.

52 Barwick, 'Coranderrk and Cummeragunja: pioneers and policy', p. 64.

53 ibid.

54 Cooper in Atkinson, 'Not one iota: the Yorta Yorta struggle for land justice'.

7. The dawn is at hand

1 Noel Loos and Koiki Mabo, *Edward Koiki Mabo: His Life and Struggle for Land Rights*, University of Queensland Press, Brisbane, 1996, p. 29.

2 ibid., p. 127.

3 Rosalind Kidd, *The Way We Civilise: Aboriginal Affairs— The Untold Story*, University of Queensland Press, Brisbane, 1997; and 'Deficits of the past or deceits of the present? defining Aboriginal disadvantagement', in *Southern Review*,

vol. 31, no. 1, 1998, pp. 11–17. Archibald Meston, *Report on the Aboriginals of Queensland*, Queensland Government, Brisbane, 1896.

4   Kidd, 'Deficits of the Past or Deceits of the Present?', p. 1; see also Kidd, *The Way We Civilise*, and *Black Lives, Government Lies*.

5   Kidd, 'Deficits of the Past or Deceits of the Present?', p. 1.

6   ibid.

7   Great Palm Island was gazetted as a 'reserve for the use of the Aboriginal people of the State' on 20 June 1914. All but two of the remaining islands of the Palm Islands Group were added to the reserve in later years. Palm Island was intended to be used for the resettlement of Aborigines brought from remote parts of Queensland. The state's Chief Protector of Aboriginals intended, under the provisions of the *Aboriginals Protection and Restriction of the Sale of Opium Act 1897* (Qld), to use Palm Island to intern people who had been removed from the northern regions of Queensland. It remains a restricted area under government regulation. The Manbarra people are the traditional owners, many of whom live on the island among the descendants of Aboriginal people incarcerated on the island when it served as a penal settlement. These latter call themselves the Bwegcolman people.

8   Oodgeroo Nunuccal, 'The Dawn is at Hand', in *The Dawn is at Hand*, Jacaranda Press, Brisbane, 1966.

9   See the entry on the Cairns Aboriginal and Torres Strait Islander Advancement League at http://indigenousrights. net.au/organisation.asp?oID=5.

10 Loos and Mabo, *Edward Koiki Mabo*, pp. 106, 111.

11 See the online catalogue description of the FCAATSI archive held at the Australian Institute of Aboriginal and Torres Strait Islander Studies at www1.aiatsis.gov.au/finding_aids/MS3759.htm.

12 The text and historical explanation of these petitions are available at: www.foundingdocs.gov.au/item.asp?dID=104.

13 In the *Aboriginal Land Rights (Northern Territory) Act 1976* (Cwlth) (hereafter ALRA). For an explanation of some of these events, see former Prime Minister EG Whitlam's lecture, 'Dragging the chain 1897–1997: the second Vincent Lingiari memorial lecture, Northern Territory University, 29 August 1997', at www.austlii.edu.au/au/special/rsjproject/rsjlibrary/car/lingiari/2whitlam.html; see also http://whitlam.alp.org.au/lingiari.html.

14 J Blackburn, 1971, FLR Vol. 17, 10: 267.

15 ibid., 273–4.

16 For a detailed explanation of the evolution of this concept, see Merete Borch, 'Rethinking the origins of *terra nullius*', in *Australian Historical Studies*, vol. 32, no. 117, 2001, pp. 222–39.

17 See, for instance, *Johnson v. McIntosh* (1823) 21 US 54; *Worcester v. Georgia* (1832) 31 US 515; *Mitchell v. United States* (1935) 34 US 711; *Calder v. Attorney-General (British Columbia)* (1973) 34 DLR (3d) 145; Re Southern Rhodesia [1919] AC 211; *Amodu Tijani v. Secretary, Southern Nigeria* [1921] 2 AC 399 at 407.

18 Loos and Mabo, *Edward Koiki Mabo*, pp. 14–15.

19 Mining is expected to continue until the middle of the twenty-first century. The Nabalco operations, including the mining and processing project at Nhulunbuy, were later purchased

by the Canadian multinational company Alcan. Both Nabalco and Alcan refused to negotiate an agreement with the Yolngu about the mining project.

20 Whitlam, 'Dragging the chain 1897–1997'.

21 ALRA s50(1)(a).

22 Frank Brennan provides an important reference to information about the progress towards this Act. He cites Gordon S Reid's 'History of philanthropic movements towards protection of Aboriginals in Queensland in the nineteenth century' (PhD thesis, Australian National University, Canberra, 1988). The Revd Duncan McNab, a Catholic missionary and a member of the Aborigines Commission, applied on 24 July 1876 on behalf of Aborigines for selection of homestead blocks of land in the Logan district under the *Crown Lands Alienation Act 1868*. They were refused because deposits for the first year's rent and survey fees had not been sent. McNab explained that they (i.e. Charles Diper Ghipara, William Watiman Nilapi and James Diper) had not sent the money as they 'conceive and maintain that because they and their ancestors, from time immemorial, have occupied and possessed those lands and their appurtenances for their use and benefit, especially of residence, hunting, fishing, and of otherwise providing for the necessaries of life' (*Land Rights Queensland Style: The Struggle for Aboriginal Self-management*, University of Queensland Press, Brisbane, 1992, p. 29).

23 Commissioner Wyvill's interpretation was as follows: 'The State Government sought to avert threatened Commonwealth Government intervention with the enactment of the *Local Government (Aboriginal Lands) Act 1978*,

which established Aurukun and Mornington Island as local government authorities. In April 1978, the Commonwealth and Queensland governments reached agreement that the Aurukun community would be operated according to "self-management under Queensland law" with a shire council being elected by the Aurukun people and a lease over the old reserve area being granted to the council.' (Australian Government, Royal Commission into Aboriginal Deaths in Custody, 'Report of the Inquiry into the Death of the Young Man Who Died at Aurukun on 11 April 1987 by Commissioner LF Wyvill, 1 June 1990', at www.austlii.edu.au/cgi-bin/sinodisp/au/other/IndigLRes/rciadic/individual/aurukun/4.html?query=Aurukun%20and%20Mornington%20Island).

24 As cited by Neva Collings in 'The Wik: a history of their 400 year struggle', *Indigenous Law Bulletin*, www.austlii.edu.au/au/journals/ILB/1997/29.html#fn18.

25 Rachel Peter in *Mapoon Story*, Book 3 (ed. J Roberts & D McLean), International Development Action, Melbourne, 1976, p. 10.

26 The calendar is published by Western Cape College. A copy can be viewed at www.westerncapecollege.eq.edu.au/aurukun_cultural_calendar_2007.pdf.

27 Bruce Rigsby, 'Aboriginal people, land rights, and wilderness on Cape York Peninsula', in *Proceedings of the Royal Society of Queensland*, Brisbane, 92, pp. 1-10, 1996; and 'Aboriginal people, land tenure and national parks', in *Proceedings of the Royal Society of Queensland*, 106 (Pt 2), pp. 11-15; K Guy, 'Development and conservation in Queensland: environmental racism?', in Perspectives

on Indigenous People's Management of Environment Resources: Ecopolitics IX Conference Papers and Resolutions, Northern Land Council, Darwin, 1996, pp. 108-12.

28 PJ Hanks, *Australian Constitutional Law: Materials and Commentary*, 4th edn, Butterworths, Sydney, 1990, p. 6, cited by Collings, 'The Wik', n. 27.

29 ALFC, *Koowarta v. Bjelke-Petersen* (1982) 153 CLR 168, 1982, paragraph 2.

30 Brennan, *Land Rights Queensland Style*.

31 Eddie Koiki Mabo, 'Land rights in the Torres Strait', in Erik Olbrei (ed.), *Black Australians: The Prospects for Change*, James Cook University of North Queensland Students' Union, Townsville, 1982, pp. 143, 144, 146.

32 Barbara Hocking, 'Is might right? An argument for the recognition of traditional Aboriginal title to land in the Australian courts', in Olbrei, *Black Australians*, p. 207.

33 'Conference Resolutions' in Olbrei, *Black Australians*, p. 247, Resolution 20. See also Resolutions 21-24 for the radicalisation of mainland Torres Strait Islander demands.

34 Eddie Koiki Mabo, Diary, 1992, 31 December 1991, one of the introductory pages to 1992 Diary, Mabo Papers.

35 Eddie Koiki Mabo, conversation with Loos.

Epilogue

1 Arthur Phillip, undated memorandum, CO (Colonial Office) 201/2, Document No. 70, p. 5. Public Record Office, London (also in HRNSW, vol. 1, pt 2:50-4.

2 ibid.

ACKNOWLEDGEMENTS

First Australians began with a request from Professor Gordon Briscoe to the then head of SBS Television, Nigel Milan, to 'give back history' to Aboriginal and Torres Strait Islander people. From this request a major television series, online experience and this book have evolved. We acknowledge Professor Briscoe for his conviction that Indigenous people must learn and interpret their own history.

We are grateful to SBS for inviting Blackfella Films to take up this vision. We thank SBS for their substantial commitment to the project over six years, and in particular those who have assisted us, including Nigel Milan, Glenys Rowe, Shaun Brown, Matt Campbell, Ned Lander and Denise Eriksen.

We would like to acknowledge the very generous support of the following people who gave their time to assist us in researching pictorial (for the original edition), genealogical and historical information, including Keith Vincent Smith, Jeremy Steele, Sandra Smith, Genevieve Grieves, Philip Batty, Professor Anna Haebich, Professor John Maynard and Bonita Mabo.

We are sincerely appreciative of the extraordinary team of dedicated publishers at Melbourne University Publishing who sustained their belief in the book. We thank CEO and Publisher Louise Adler, who made an enthusiastic commitment in the early stages, and her team who realised the project: Elisa Berg, Publisher, editors Cathryn Game, Helen Koehne and Felicity Edge, and the very dedicated and patient Tracy O'Shaughnessy, Publisher.

The book drew on collections that include restricted material. We sought the help of the following people and organisations, for which we are especially grateful: Brian Connelly and David Ross of the Central Land Council; Daryl Pearce, Brian Stirling, and Benedict Stevens of Lhere Artepe; Herman Malbunka; and RG Kimber for his advice and support.

The team at Blackfella Films gave freely of their time on top of their substantial commitment to completing the television series. They include Rhea Stephenson and Jeff Parker. Thank you for your long hours to get the book across the line.

We also acknowledge the extraordinary research undertaken by Lea Gardam who compiled the pictorial materials for the original edition, which have been brought together for the first time to tell the sweeping story of Indigenous experience.

Finally, thank you to the authors who readily agreed to contribute within a short time frame. In particular, thank you to Professor Marcia Langton who graciously agreed to support the *First Australians* project as our senior advisor. Her support has been invaluable and our constant guide from the project's inception through the past six years. Thank you, Marcia.

Rachel Perkins and Darren Dale
Producers, *First Australians*

INDEX